Academy Hill

THE ANDOVER CAMPUS, 1778 TO THE PRESENT

Plan
of
REAL ESTATE
PHILLIPS ACADEMY
ANDOVER

1836

ESSAYS BY

Paul V. Turner, David Chase, Roger G. Reed,
Susan C. Faxon, Kimberly Alexander Shilland,
and Cynthia Zaitzevsky

Academy Hill

THE ANDOVER CAMPUS, 1778 TO THE PRESENT

Addison Gallery of American Art
PHILLIPS ACADEMY
ANDOVER, MASSACHUSETTS

Princeton Architectural Press
NEW YORK

The research for this publication has been supported by grants from The Montauk Foundation, J. Mark Rudkin, Fiona and Michael J. Scharf, and Anthony M. Schulte. The accompanying exhibition organized by the Addison Gallery of American Art was supported by the Sidney R. Knafel Fund.

Addison Gallery of American Art
Phillips Academy
Andover, Massachusetts 01810
978.749.4015

Princeton Architectural Press
37 East 7th Street
New York, NY 10003
212.995.9620

For a free catalog of other books published by Princeton Architectural Press, call toll free 1.800.722.6657 or visit www.papress.com

Editing: Jan Cigliano
Design: Anne L. Galperin
Maps: Jane Garvie

Frontispiece: Frederick A. Barton, *Plan of the Real Estate of Phillips Academy,* 1837, ink.
Photographs of historic images in the Phillips Academy Archive are by Frank W. Graham, except for the following: pp. 79, 104, 169 by Greg Heins, Boston.

Special thanks to Ann Alter, Eugenia Bell, Caroline Green, Beth Harrison, Mia Ihara, Clare Jacobson, Leslie Ann Kent, Mark Lamster, Anne Nitschke, Lottchen Shivers, Sara E. Stemen, Jennifer Thompson, and Deb Wood of Princeton Architectural Press—Kevin C. Lippert, publisher

Library of Congress Cataloguing-in-Publication Data
Addison Gallery of American Art
Academy hill : the Andover campus, 1778 to the present / essays by Paul V. Turner. . .
[et al.] ; Addison Gallery of American Art. — 1st ed.
        p. cm.
    Includes bibliographical references and index.
    ISBN 1-56898-236-4 (alk. paper)
        1. Phillips Academy—Buildings—History. I. Turner, Paul V.   II. Addison Gallery
of American Art

LD7501.A5 A32 2000
727'.2'097445—dc21   CIP
                                                      99-087158

Contents

The word campus, *more than any other term, sums up the unique physical character of the American college and university. When it was first used to describe the grounds of a college, probably at Princeton in the late eighteenth century,* campus *had simply its Latin meaning, a field, and described the green expansiveness already distinctive of American schools. But gradually the word assumed wider significance, until at most colleges it came to mean the entire property, including buildings, so that one could speak even of an "urban campus" that might possess nothing remotely resembling a field. In 1925, the German city planner Werner Hegemann, writing about America, defined* campus *for his countrymen as "a piece of land that is covered with the buildings of an American university." But beyond these purely physical meanings, the word has taken on other connotations, suggesting the pervasive spirit of a school, or its* genius loci, *as embodied in its architecture and grounds.* Campus *sums up the distinctive physical qualities of the American college, but also its integrity as a self-contained community and its architectural expression of education and social ideals. As early as the 1870s the term was so evocative that an observer of one American college could write, "There is no spell more powerful to recall the memories of college life than the word* Campus."

—— Paul Venable Turner,
Campus, An American Planning Tradition (MIT Press, 1984), 4.

Foreword

AT PHILLIPS ACADEMY, THE PAST HAS ALWAYS ANIMATED THE PRESENT and given hope to the future. The Phillips Academy constitution was drafted in the age and in the spirit of our nation's founding documents. Our constitution holds within it ideas so universal, so noble, so powerful that they live in all we do today. Its phrases are the text, the litany of the Andover way of life: *Finis Origine Pendet*—the end depends upon the beginning; Youth From Every Quarter; *Non Sibi*—not for self; the Great End and Real Business of Living.

The academy has passed many milestones, has mounted many great initiatives over the years, from the original working out of these ideas in the small carpenter's shop that stood in the shadow of the American Revolution, to the founding of the Andover Theological Seminary, Teachers' Seminary, and Abbot Academy, to the modernization of the school and physical plant under principal Cecil Bancroft, to the great era of building and campus reorganization in the 1920s and 1930s, to the important new physical growth and academic direction of the 1960s, to the merger with Abbot and the birth of coeducation twenty five years ago. Today, we build the future of the academy and its campus on the strong foundation of our past.

Understanding how generations of academy leaders, trustees, donors, architects, and builders brought this present campus into being helps us to understand its present power and sets the very highest standard for those who plan for the future of the campus. We at the academy are grateful to the authors of the essays that follow and to the Addison Gallery of American Art, that remarkable institution within Phillips Academy, for undertaking this important history of our campus.

BARBARA LANDIS CHASE
Head of School

Pendleton's Lithog'y, Andover Theological Seminary, 1830s, lithograph. Collection of the Addison Gallery of American Art, Phillips Academy [Addison Gallery, hereafter]

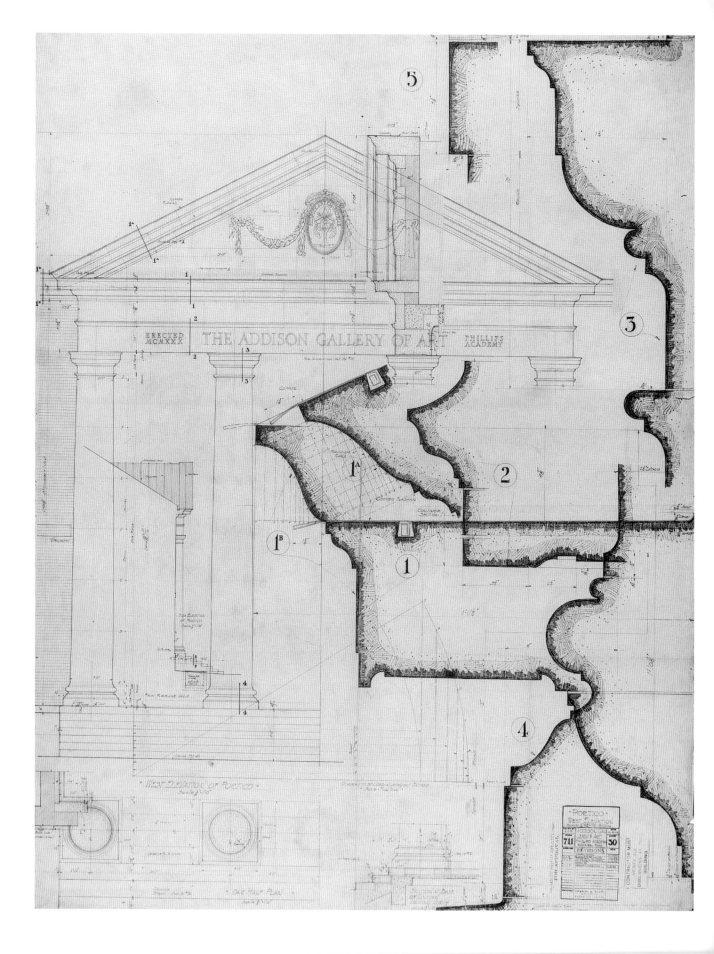

Acknowledgments

IN THE ART WORLD TODAY it is common to consider the way the modern museum provides a context for art. The art museum, a nineteenth-century innovation, provides a setting divorced from a particular religious, governmental, or domestic function for which artworks were historically made; the museum's sole purpose is to provide a place where visitors can muse and contemplate objects of beauty. It is a place where the works themselves—grouped together by theme, period, or geographical regions—largely create their own context.

As the Addison Gallery of American Art is a context for the art it contains, so the building itself is set in a context, a designed environment, that needs to be considered. The purpose of the Addison was effected by its location, the time it was built, the person who commissioned it, and the architect who designed it. The gallery's *raison d'être,* its mission devoted to American art, as well as the central role it has played in the life of students, were part of a larger design. This book and the exhibition it accompanies elucidate how the Addison and the structures past and present that have formed the Phillips Academy campus are integral parts of a fabric of social, stylistic, and philosophical interrelationships.

In this volume the authors consider the Phillips Academy campus, in its numerous incarnations, as a growing and changing environment that responds to practical needs, expresses aspirations and ideals, molds social behavior, and gives physical form to religious and educational doctrines. Although in its early years the campus' development was as much *laissez-faire* as planned, by the late nineteenth century evolving and successive master planning guided the campus. The campus today may be thought of as a large-scale museum, a controlled environment in which buildings and landscape were arranged, and sometimes rearranged, for the sake of aesthetics, to convey meaning, and to provide settings, both interior and exterior, that were conducive for the contemplation of ideas and the full development of the individual.

The Addison Gallery is grateful to the many individuals who have helped make this undertaking possible. Like the campus itself, it took the involvement of many intellectual and organizational forces over an extended period to bring the book and exhibition to fruition. These

Charles A. Platt, Portico and West Elevation, Addison Gallery of Art, 1929, drawing. The Drawings and Archives Department, Avery Architectural and Fine Arts Library, Columbia University in the City of New York [Avery Architectural & Fine Arts Library, hereafter]

individuals have helped us to realize that this study of Phillips Academy is not a narrow quest for self-identity but an endeavor that will be of interest to anyone who is broadly concerned with American history, education, and taste.

The staffs of the following archives have enthusiastically supported this project. They are the keepers of the materials that have revealed the history that unfolds in this publication, and have truly made the project come alive. Ruth Quattlebaum, archivist of the Phillips Academy Archive, has borne the brunt of our never-ending questions and requests. The academy's archive is filled with extraordinary material—records, letters, photographs—without which the project could not have proceeded. Phillips Academy's Oliver Wendell Holmes Library, Susan Ezell Noble, librarian, and the entire staff of the Holmes Library opened their resources to all the essayists, facilitating access, and graciously answering demands. Diana Yount, archivist at the Andover-Newton Theological Seminary, Trask Library, Newton, Massachusetts, has unlocked important secrets of the early history of both the Andover Theological Seminary and Phillips Academy.

The Drawings and Archives Department of the Avery Architectural & Fine Arts Library, Columbia University, New York, New York, maintains the invaluable architectural archive of Charles Adams Platt, whose involvement with Phillips Academy through the 1920s and 1930s transformed the campus. Janet Parks, curator, and Anne-Sophie Roure, assistant to the curator, have given every care to requests for materials and information. We are thankful to them for enabling us to use Platt's elegant drawings to grace this publication.

For the overview of the building campaigns that continued from the 1890s through the 1950s, as well as the specific study of the Olmsted Brothers' involvement in the Andover campus, the range and depth of material housed at the Frederick Law Olmsted National Historic Site, National Park Service, Brookline, Massachusetts, has proved invaluable. The staff, including Jill Trebbe, archivist, Joyce Connelly, and Michael Dorsch, have extended themselves to accommodate our many extraordinary requests.

This project has also received generous assistance from the following individuals and repositories: Andover Historical Society, Barbara Thibault, director; Cambridge Historical Commission (Massachusetts), Susan E. Maycock; Governor Dummer Academy, Byfield, Massachusetts, Mary Leary and Shirley French; David P. Handlin and Associates, David P. Handlin, architect; Haverhill Public Library (Massachusetts), Special Collections, Gregory Laing; Historic Deerfield (Massachusetts), Kenneth Hafertepe; Historical Society of Old Newbury (Massachusetts), Jay S. Williamson; Immigrant City Archives, Lawrence, Massachusetts, Ken Skulski; Lawrenceville School (New Jersey), Marilyn Love, archivist; Manuscript Division, Library of Congress, Washington, D. C.; Peabody Essex Museum, Phillips Library, Salem, Massachusetts, Will LaMoy; Arts and Artifacts Committee, Phillips Academy, Loring Strudwick, chair; Society for the Preservation of New England Antiquities, Archive, Boston, Lorna Condon.

Throughout the project, advice and support have been freely offered by the Phillips Academy Office of Physical Plant, Michael E. Williams, director of facilities; Neil McEleney, Administrative Systems, manager; and the Public Safety Department at Phillips Academy, Thomas Conlon, manager.

This publication has been enhanced by the fine work of photographers Greg Heins and Frank Graham. In addition, as Elson Artists-in-Residence at the Addison Gallery in 1998–99, photographers Michael Jacobson-Hardy and Mark Klett explored the campus, studied the academy's archive, interacted with students and faculty, and encouraged us to see the school anew through their photographs which will be presented in the exhibition that accompanies this publication.

It has been a great pleasure to work with the exceptional staff of Princeton Architectural Press, Kevin Lippert, publisher; Jan Cigliano, editor; Jane Garvie, map maker, Sara E. Stemen, art director; Anne Galperin, designer; and Walter Smalling Jr., photographer. Their excitement about the Andover campus and their willingness to expend extraordinary efforts on behalf of the publication have been immensely gratifying.

Those who have labored long and hard for this project deserve our special thanks. Project advisors, Keith N. Morgan, Susan Child, Michael E. Williams, and Barbara Timken have shared their considerable knowledge, offered suggestions, and provided encouragement throughout the two years of planning and execution of this project. The distinguished authors David Chase, Roger G. Reed, Kimberly Alexander Shilland, Paul V. Turner, and Cynthia Zaitzevsky each have captured the unique spirit of Phillips Academy in their essays. It is an honor to have their cogent intellectual contributions included in these pages.

Special thanks are due to Susan J. Montgomery, research associate. Her scholarly approach, her prodigious work, her careful eye, and her generous sense of humor have kept the project moving in the face of seemingly insurmountable deadlines. Previously, Karen Haas devoted a year to uncovering treasures that set the project on its way. Ellen Roberts, Boston University Graduate Intern, also provided invaluable administrative assistance. Research and scholarly assistance was gratefully received from Page Ayres Cowley, the late Margaret Henderson Floyd, Helen Lefkowitz Horowitz, Mr. and Mrs. Charles Platt, Carmel Rodriquez-Walter, and Charles H. Sawyer, former director of the Addison Gallery.

The prime mover in this project has been Susan Faxon, associate director and curator of the Addison. For years her passion for the subject has been consuming. She has brought all of her prodigious talents to bear on this book and exhibition. For her the campus is a living entity, an entity that is important to study and cherish. Her work represents the efforts of many—to assure that the historic architecture and landscape of the campus is appreciated and renewed in the future.

The Addison Gallery is immensely grateful to those who have financially supported the project, in particular, The Montauk Foundation, Sidney R. Knafel, class of 1948, J. Mark Rudkin, class of 1947, Fiona and Michael J. Scharf, class of 1960, and Anthony M. Schulte, class of 1947, who recognized the significance of this project from its inception. To all whose encouragement of the project and affection for the Phillips Academy campus have rallied our spirits, thank you.

ADAM D. WEINBERG
The Mary Stripp and R. Crosby Kemper Director
Addison Gallery of American Art

Introduction:

HISTORY AND CHANGE ON ACADEMY HILL

IN 1778 SAMUEL PHILLIPS JR. established an academy "for the purpose of instructing Youth, not only in English and Latin Grammar, Writing, Arithmetic, and those Sciences, wherein they are commonly taught; but more especially to learn them the GREAT END AND REAL BUSINESS OF LIVING." In a renovated carpenter shop on newly purchased land on what is now called Academy Hill, and with funding from his father and uncle, Samuel Phillips began his academic experiment to provide a classical education to "youth from every quarter." By 1808 Phillips Academy was joined on the hill by the Andover Theological Seminary, established to train Calvinist ministers. By the late 1820s two more institutions of learning were also sharing Academy Hill—Abbot Academy, established in 1828 by prominent Andover citizens and members of the Phillips Academy community to educate young women, and the Teachers' Seminary, founded in 1827 to train teachers for common schools. As memorialized in the 1996 *Campus Master Plan*, the four institutions created "a discrete precinct of higher learning amidst rural New England farmland."

Over time, the four institutions merged into one, the present campus now an amalgamation of these parts. The fact that Phillips Academy, in one form or another, has occupied the same site since its founding provides a rare opportunity to read the school's varied and rich history through physical examination of its extraordinary campus, layer by layer. The educational institutions that have shared the hill over the years have each contributed, enriched, and embellished it, and through them a nearly eternal focus on learning has seeped into the Andover ground. There is a palpable sense of place on the Andover campus, a compelling sense of history, an over-riding sense of the intersection of past, present, and future. Newness and tradition simultaneously; complexity and simplicity; Calvinism and independent thinking—the whole is a multiple of parts, of layering, of erasures and additions—what Paul V. Turner, in his introductory essay, calls the campus as palimpsest.

For more than two hundred years, Phillips Academy has struggled to reconcile the needs fostered by growth and change with reverence and protection of its architectural and landscape patrimony. From the start, the school has been proud to be one of the earliest schools incorporated in the state. Throughout the nineteenth century, the school honored "its ancient traditions," in the

Vista looking west from portico of Samuel Phillips Hall [Unless otherwise noted, all illustrations are from the Phillips Academy Archive]

words of trustee James Hardy Ropes in 1902. A writer in *The Phillips Bulletin* in the early twentieth century took pride in the connections between important figures of American history and the school. He went on to caution us,

> Traditions . . . cannot preserve an institution from decay, and any school which relies entirely on them for prestige has already lost its vitality; but, like healthy ancestry, they do in a large degree guarantee stability and offer promise of a fine future.

Over time the ways in which the school has manifested pride in its campus have changed. In July 1931, an editorial in *The Phillips Bulletin* observed, "It is the amazing function of Phillips Academy today to be both the preserver of the old and the originator of the new." In fact, the editor was extolling the virtues of the newly erected Cochran Chapel and expressing little regret over the demolition of the out-of-style Stone Chapel it replaced. In the context of the article, which referred to this fine Ruskinian Gothic building of 1875–76 as having "no unusual charm as an ecclesiastical edifice," preserving the old meant simply applying a colonial model to the new structure.

Today Phillips Academy is "both the preserver of the old and the originator of the new" in a literal sense. We take pride in our ability to acknowledge and accommodate change in a way that preserves and respects the fabric of the original buildings. It is in this duality that today's school balances its role as steward of its campus. It has been played out several times: in the rededication of the Abbot Academy campus to meet new needs; in the sensitive addition of a balcony in the Cochran Chapel; in the careful historic examination of Phelps House that served as the guide for refurbishing this extraordinary 1809–10 house; in the restoration of our earliest surviving structure, the 1804 Hardy House, while adding a new wing for the admissions office; and in the ongoing landscape planning for the campus that acknowledges its unique past and develops plans for future care. The *Campus Master Plan* of 1996 puts this duality clearly and emphatically before us:

> The Phillips Academy campus is widely acclaimed as one of the finest in America. It appears completed, a balanced composition of stately trees and well proportioned buildings in generous settings of lawn, open spaces, and woods. Yet this seemingly perfect campus is in a constant state of change. Landscapes and buildings age, new programs are introduced, old ones phased out. Through master planning, the Academy works to control this change so as to preserve and develop the campus and to further the mission of the school.

The campus mission statement, recited in the *Campus Master Plan*, defines our goals for the school's physical plant.

Phillips Academy will preserve, maintain and develop the buildings and landscapes which constitute its common heritage; both
to provide the best possible educational experience, work-place
and home for the members of its community and to hold the
campus in trust for future generations.

The commitment Phillips Academy expresses is not merely preservation for its own sake,
but rather advocacy for a unique place that has been entrusted to us. Through stewardship of our
past, we build for our future. There is an inextricable bond between what we do and where we do
it. Our past has always animated the present and given hope to the future. As James Hardy Ropes,
one of our early twentieth-century trustees, pointed out in 1926 in *The Phillips Bulletin*:

An institution is a living thing. It inhabits its buildings; it has
material surroundings and possessions but it is a living thing . . .
which resides in memories and traditions, in hopes and incen-
tives, and which has as its soul living men and their work and
love and effort, sacrifice, loyalty and aspiration.

SUSAN C. FAXON
Exhibition Curator
Addison Gallery of American Art

Paul V. Turner

The Campus as Palimpsest:

LAYERS OF HISTORY AT PHILLIPS ACADEMY

THE CAMPUS IS LARGELY AN AMERICAN INVENTION. Starting in the English colonies, the first American colleges developed a new type of environment, different from those of European institutions. American colleges—as well as academies and preparatory schools—have normally been self-contained communities, in which students live and play and study in a spacious setting more rural than urban in character. Moreover, the institution is not cloistered within an enclosed quadrangle, like the traditional English college, but outward-turning—a kind of utopian community open to the world.

Despite these common traits, American campuses have produced many variations, in response to changing educational values and architectural styles, as well as local conditions. And even an individual school can reveal several patterns, sometimes superimposed over one another, as a result of divergent principles at work in successive periods. The campus is then a living record of the forces that have shaped the institution.

Phillips Academy in Andover, Massachusetts (commonly called simply Andover) is one of the most remarkable cases of an institution whose buildings and grounds embody a complex history.[1] The Andover campus reveals not only successive generations' attitudes toward education, society, and architecture, but also the school's unusual history as the combination of four institutions—Phillips Academy, Andover Theological Seminary, the Teachers' Seminary, and Abbot Academy. Each was housed in certain buildings and spaces, which were shaped by the individual school's character. Moreover, many structures that once existed at Andover have been demolished, and other buildings have been moved from place to place—an odd practice that probably occurred more often here than at any other school.

The Andover campus is like a palimpsest—a manuscript that reveals a previous text that was erased and written over. At Andover the palimpsest is multiple and irregular, with successive writings, partial erasures, transpositions, and revisions. It is thus a rich document that takes effort to decipher and understand. In reconstructing this artifact, this study focuses on the layers that have been altered or partly destroyed and are difficult to perceive. The goal is to illuminate the processes of growth, destruction, and change that have produced the campus, not merely to describe it as it exists today.

The Elm Arch from Salem Street, 1880s

THE ACADEMY AND THE TOWN

A study of Andover's campus suggests a basic question. Are the buildings and grounds of an academy such as Phillips significantly different from those of a college? The answer might seem to be no, since Phillips Academy today, with its impressive classroom buildings, dormitories, cultural resources, athletic facilities, and landscaped grounds, could easily be mistaken for a fine private college. Moreover, the planning of the Andover campus, for most of its history, has been influenced mainly by colleges rather than other academies, probably because of the school's unusual resources and ambitious goals.[2]

But the palimpsest reveals a more complex answer. In its early years, the Phillips Academy campus was different from that of colleges—more domestic in certain respects, and more integrated into its surrounding town. Although little of this original academy survives, it was the basis of later developments and has affected today's campus in significant ways. In 1778 when Phillips was founded, there were few colleges in the new nation, roughly one per state, yet these represented distinctive types of campus. Harvard boasted impressive academic buildings, dormitories, and a chapel, arranged around three-sided courtyards that opened to the town of Cambridge.[3] Yale at this time was constructing its row of five buildings facing the New Haven Green; and Princeton, Brown, and Dartmouth each had one massive, multipurpose structure that included classrooms, chapel, and dormitory rooms.[4] Despite these differences, the colleges presented imposing

Paul Revere, **A Westerly View of the Colledges in Cambridge New England**, 1767, engraving. Courtesy, Harvard University Archives

2

Governor Dummer Academy, Byfield, Massachusetts, c. 1830, watercolor. Private Collection

appearances that distinguished them from their surroundings and marked them as important institutions. In contrast, early American academies, grammar schools, Latin schools, and other public and private secondary schools were modest in character.[5] Their management and financing were often tenuous, they typically had only one master (sometimes with an assistant or two), and their enrollments were usually small, so that out-of-town students could be housed with the teacher or with neighbors. These schools tended to blend into their town or village environment.

Andover's principal founder, Samuel Phillips Jr., had attended Harvard in the late 1760s, having prepared at Governor Dummer Academy in South Byfield, Massachusetts. The grounds of Dummer Academy were the estate provided by the founder, with a two-room building for the classes, and the "Mansion House" where the schoolmaster and most of the students lived.[6]

Samuel Phillips Jr., with his father, Samuel, and uncle, John Phillips, founded Phillips Academy with more foresight and commitment than most previous academies.[7] (Three years later John Phillips would found Phillips Exeter Academy in Exeter, New Hampshire, with the same care and consideration.) Andover was established with an endowment; and its governing organization was carefully established with a state-incorporated board of trustees. It began with more than 100 acres of land, on a sparsely populated hill in Andover's South Parish.[8] Moreover, the founders were motivated by a fervent ideology, a strict Calvinism that gave them a special mission: to preserve the Puritan heritage of New England in the face of the liberal winds blowing through American society at the time of the Revolution. The writings of Samuel Phillips fulminated against the "depraved Nature" of man and "the present degeneracy" of society.[9]

Despite the sizable resources of this new institution, its buildings were of modest scale and unpretentious character, typical of academies of the period.[10] The land acquired for the school by its founders was in several parcels, on both sides of Main Street.[11] The first building used by the academy, a former carpentry shop on Main Street at the intersection of what is now Phillips Street, was a schoolroom for recitations.[12] Also on academy property, farther down Phillips Street, was the former Abbot house, used at first as the home for Samuel Phillips and his family, then for the school's first preceptor, Eliphalet Pearson.

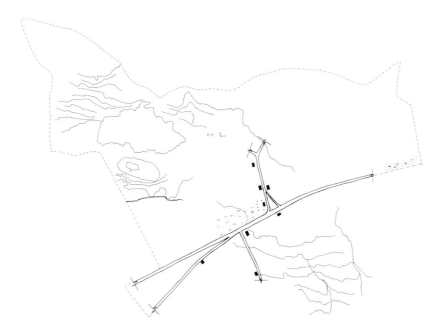

Academy Hill, 1805. Map by Jane Garvie

In 1785, new accommodations for the academy were provided by the erection of a two-story building, containing three school rooms downstairs and a meeting hall above. But the new structure was relatively distant from the original schoolhouse, being on the opposite (east) side of Main Street, and farther to the south; this created two separate areas of built-upon campus.[13] And as more private houses were erected along Main Street, including the Mansion House built by Samuel Phillips for his family in 1782, the academy became integrated into a typical New England townscape.[14] This was especially true as the academy had no chapel and no dormitories. For the first forty years of its existence, students attended obligatory services in the local church, the South Parish Meeting House.[15] And for at least the first half-century, all students were housed and took their meals in private homes at the school and in the neighborhood—a practice also found at other early academies as well.[16]

In the academy's early years, much of the trustees' and preceptors' attention was devoted to problems of the students' room and board. The first class of thirty students was accommodated in twenty-nine homes. As enrollment increased and suitable arrangements became more difficult, compromises had to be made.[17] One student described his Andover life with "my schoolfellows, six or eight in number," in the home of the parish minister: "We slept in one large chamber, in which were three or four beds, two boys occupying each." A student who lodged in another home wrote that "four of us occupied a small chamber with a sanded floor. . . . Owing to the want of cleanliness in the place, the boys were seldom free from . . . diseases."[18]

Historians of Phillips have documented the problems resulting from students being housed in the town—"this practice, never satisfactory was a continual source of trouble."[19] When in 1808 the trustees created a new institution, the Andover Theological Seminary, they built proper collegiate dormitories for its students, one financed by Madame Phillips and her son, the other by William Bartlet of Newburyport. Unfortunately, Phillips Academy did not have a benefactor willing to meet its housing needs. Differences in campus development between these two institutions suggest different notions of what the academy and the theological seminary should be. The trustees evidently felt that a seminary of advanced students ought to have dormitories, whereas an academy for younger scholars ought to be plain and domestic in character. The modest physical nature of the early academy and its integration into town life perhaps reflected the founders' ideas about the appropriate education of boys—as well as their belief in the educational value of physical work for the academy students.[20]

None of Phillips Academy's academic buildings erected before 1818 survive today; only several houses used by the early preceptors or other academy officials still stand.[21] Today's campus nevertheless retains vestiges of this early period. One is its very location on both sides of Main Street—a fact that has complicated the physical planning of the school ever since, making it difficult to create a unified campus. Further evidence of the original academy is the presence of buildings that were originally private houses in which students roomed and boarded. These vestiges of the early, domestically-scaled academy are the faintest layer of the palimpsest—the basis on which the later history of the institution was superimposed.

THE SEMINARY ON THE HILL

When Andover Theological Seminary was founded in 1808 it was separate from Phillips Academy, yet shared Academy Hill and the same board of trustees.[22] The seminary was founded with the same inspiration as the academy: the preservation of Calvinist puritanism in the face of liberalism. But the threat was now more acute as Harvard was becoming dominated by Unitarianism. The response of the seminary founders was focused on training orthodox ministers. Sizable endowment funds were donated, substantial buildings were planned, and for much of the nineteenth century the seminary eclipsed the academy in resources, reputation, and the trustees' attentions.[23] One Andover writer later said that the seminary "was the favored child, while the Academy played the joyless part of Cinderella."[24] But since the seminary's campus was eventually acquired by the academy when the seminary became moribund and departed from Andover in 1908, the two institutions' physical histories are intertwined.

Over the period from 1808 to 1821 the academy and the seminary erected three substantial brick structures in a straight line east of Main Street.[25] "Seminary Row" consisted of Phillips Hall (now Foxcroft Hall), built in 1808–09; Bartlet Chapel (now Pearson Hall), built in 1817–18; and Bartlet Hall, built in 1820–21.[26] The three structures created a commanding group, with their

TOP: **Seminary Row: Foxcroft, Pearson and Bartlet Halls, 1860s** BOTTOM: **A.B. Doolittle, Old Brick Row, Yale College, 1807, engraving. Manuscripts and Archives, Yale University Library**

broad sides seen across the rising field from Main Street. For the rest of the nineteenth century Seminary Row was the most often portrayed view of the Andover institutions.

While the story is told of seminary founders traveling to the College of Rhode Island (now Brown University) to inspect the buildings,[27] the model for Seminary Row was more likely the "Brick Row" of five structures recently completed at Yale College.[28] Yale, in fact, became linked to the Andover schools at this time for theological reasons, as the bonds with liberal Harvard loosened.[29] In fact, in the mid nineteenth century Andover principal Samuel Taylor was said to hold the "oft-expressed view that a student who didn't plan to go to Yale was as good as damned."[30] So the Yale-like alignment of buildings on Andover Hill may have had ideological symbolism—a kind of fortress wall protecting the puritan tradition against infidelity.

In its first twenty years the theological seminary constructed, purchased, or was donated ten buildings for its use. In addition to the three Seminary Row structures, these included a wooden dining hall, built in 1809–10 to the east of the main buildings; Samaritan House, an infirmary erected in 1824; a stone building that was sometimes called the "Workshop," built in 1828 as a work and exercise space for the seminarians; and houses for seminary faculty members, including Park House, Phelps House, Pease House, Newman House, and Moses Stuart House.[31]

These seminary buildings reveal a grand spatial concept. They define a large quadrangle, with Seminary Row on the east side, Samaritan House and the Workshop to the north on Chapel

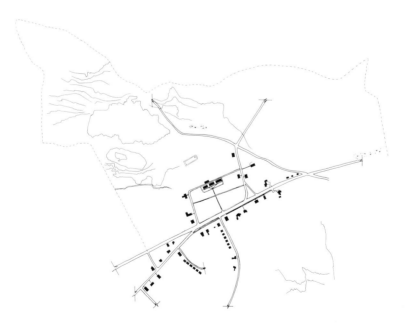

Academy Hill, 1836. Map by Jane Garvie

Bulfinch Hall, 1858–1864

Avenue, and the faculty houses to the west, along Main Street and facing Seminary Row. This immense space was intended to aggrandize Andover Theological Seminary, to give it a distinct identity.[32] It is reminiscent of New England commons, or of the large space between Nassau Hall and the main road at Princeton, to which the Latin word "campus" was first used in the late eighteenth century to describe an American college grounds.[33]

In contrast to this domination of the landscape by the theological seminary, the academy had only one academic building, the classroom structure erected in 1785.[34] This wooden building was located near the intersection of Main and Salem streets, close to where the Armillary Sphere now stands, on a site that was to become the location for the seminary's library in 1866.[35] This apparent overlapping of the academy and seminary grounds may explain why, when it burned in 1818, the academy building was not replaced with a structure on the same site. Instead, the wooden academy's replacement, Brick Academy—now known as Bulfinch Hall—went up to the south of Salem Street, clearly outside the boundaries of the seminary's quadrangular campus.

The design of Brick Academy, erected in 1818–19, went beyond parochial vernacular construction to reveal the hand of a professional architect—as did Pearson Hall, the central building of Seminary Row. Pearson Hall, erected in 1817–18, is known to have been designed by the prominent Boston architect Charles Bulfinch.[36] It has several features characteristic of his style, such as the Doric order framing the doors, the semi-circular windows above, and especially the manner in which the central portion of the main façade is emphasized by shallow projections, a simple horizontal band between the stories, and the roof balustrade.[37]

The Brick Academy's design has traditionally been ascribed to Bulfinch as well; it has been called Bulfinch Hall since 1937. Yet recently discovered documentation provides persuasive evidence that it was built to Asher Benjamin's design.[38] Both buildings signaled a new interest in architectural fashion at the academy and the theological seminary. This might appear to be inconsistent with the schools' ascetic Calvinism. However, the Federal style, while refined, was chaste enough not to appear dangerously fashionable.

THE TEACHERS' SEMINARY

In 1827 the board of trustees created a third institution, the Teachers' Seminary or "English School," whose purpose was to provide more practical training than the study of Latin and Greek.[39] This new school attracted many interested students, but the precise nature of its practical education was not well defined, its funding was precarious, and in 1842 it disbanded and merged with Phillips Academy. Despite its short life, the English School added a faint layer to the campus palimpsest.

In 1828–30, a stone classroom building was constructed on the northeast corner of Chapel and Main Streets.[40] It thus was positioned just to the north of the theological seminary's quadrangle, balancing Bulfinch Hall to the south. The building, later referred to as the Stone Academy, was a solid, two-story structure with a cupola.[41] Treasurer Samuel Farrar supervised construction of the Stone Academy as well as most of the buildings erected on the Andover campus during his long tenure, 1803–40.[42] Known for his strong sense of discipline and frugality, as well as the Calvinist orthodoxy shared by all the early administrators of the Andover schools, Farrar did not design buildings but he may have influenced the foursquare simplicity of the architecture of this period.

The most extreme case of architectural Puritanism were the two groups of "commons" buildings constructed about 1830, the Latin Commons and English Commons.[43] Intended to address the continuing need to house academy and teachers' seminary students, each Commons group was composed of identical wooden houses, aligned in a row: six in the Latin Commons for academy students, on the north side of Phillips Street; and six in the English Commons, for teachers' seminary students, on the north side of Old Campus Road near School Street. The concept was highly original: an alternate way of housing students, neither in private homes nor in dormitories, but in small three-story structures, each with six suites consisting of a study and two bedrooms—in which the students were to live and study with virtually no supervision. This might be seen as revealing either a disregard for the students' welfare (especially as these Commons were intended for the poorer, "charity" scholars), or an unusual faith in the students' responsibility and resourcefulness. But architecturally the scheme was extraordinary—perhaps unprecedented—in

Teachers' Seminary, 1863

English Commons, before 1892

RIGHT: "Andover Theological Seminary," HARPER'S NEW MONTHLY MAGAZINE, September 1877, wood engraving, left to right, Stone Chapel, Foxcroft Hall, Pearson Hall, Bartlet Hall, and Brechin Hall FAR RIGHT: Phillips Academy, 1892–1901, left to right, Phillips Hall, Graves Hall, Academy Hall, English Commons, and Draper Cottage

either academy or collegiate planning.[44] Moreover, the buildings' utter plainness and regularity epitomized not only practicality but also the Calvinist spirit of the entire Andover enterprise in its early years.

THE VICTORIAN CAMPUS

In educational matters and reputation, the conservative Andover Theological Seminary tended to dominate Phillips Academy in the mid nineteenth century.[45] Architecturally, however, the collective Andover campus—the grounds of the academy and the seminary—was given a new character during this period. The theological seminary maintained its dominance of the most prominent area, the vast quadrangle, and strengthened it with two additional buildings that framed Seminary Row: Brechin Hall, built in 1866 on the south side of the quadrangle, the first library building at either the seminary or the academy; and the Chapel (later called Stone Chapel), built in 1875–76 at the northeast corner of the space.[46] Brechin Hall was designed by Boston architect Charles A. Cummings, the Chapel by the partnership Cummings created in 1867 with Willard T. Sears.[47]

These two structures made a dramatic break with the earlier buildings at Andover. They were fine examples of the then popular Victorian Gothic or picturesque styles, which used medieval details, towers, irregular forms, and a variety of texture and color to evoke romantic associations and visual interest. In a similar spirit, a tall tower was added in 1875 to Pearson Hall, the center building of Seminary Row.[48] Also picturesque was the manner in which the Stone Chapel and Brechin Hall were sited, in an asymmetrical pattern in relation to Seminary Row and Main Street, in contrast to the regularity of the Seminary Row structures.

The academy, too, employed picturesque Victorian styles in the few buildings it constructed during this period: a new Academy Hall, erected in 1865–66; a small administration building (Phillips Hall), constructed in 1884–85; and a science building (Graves Hall), built in two stages in 1882–83 and 1891.[49] These buildings were all placed in the "old campus" area west of Main Street, effectively ceding the eastern realm to the theological seminary. This division of the grounds into the academy to the west and the seminary to the east perhaps explains why Bulfinch

Hall was abandoned as an academic building in the 1860s and relegated to other purposes—first as a gymnasium, then as a dining hall.

The Andover campus of the mid-to-late nineteenth century is a layer of the palimpsest that has been largely erased. Due to changing architectural tastes in the early decades of the twentieth century and a decision by the trustees to employ colonial revival styles, many of the Victorian-era buildings were demolished, especially during the redesign of the campus in the 1920s.[50] A substantial period of the school's history has been largely effaced. Two fine buildings, Graves and Phillips Halls, have survived, perhaps because they stand on the less prominent west side of Main Street. There are also the fine Victorian structures on the former Abbot Academy campus.

THE RESIDENTIAL ACADEMY

It has been said that Phillips Academy's history falls into two periods: the first hundred years, when the school was essentially conservative—still "an eighteenth-century institution," according to Frederick Allis—and its more progressive development after 1873 when Cecil Bancroft was named principal.[51] During Bancroft's 28-year tenure, he made sweeping reforms: modernizing the curriculum, strengthening the faculty, down-playing the rigid Calvinism that had dominated the school, and improving students' living conditions. Bancroft was eager to solve the problem of student housing. Most students still roomed and boarded in private houses in town, and those who lived on campus were largely housed in the old student-run Latin Commons. There was increasing concern that these types of unsupervised housing contributed to serious disciplinary problems, including drunkenness, vandalism, hazing injuries, and even the accidental killing of one student by another.[52] Bancroft also looked to such newly founded academies as Round Hill in Massachusetts, St. Paul's in New Hampshire, and Lawrenceville in New Jersey, which were raising the standards for student housing in private secondary schools. Bancroft did not want Andover to be left behind.[53]

Phillips Academy eventually built collegiate-style dormitories. But first, in the early 1890s, it erected four "cottages," each housing a small number of students and a supervising

Eaton and Andover Cottages, with Farrar House, the Power Plant, and the English Commons in the distance, 1903. Courtesy of the National Park Service, Frederick Law Olmsted National Historic Site [Frederick Law Olmsted NHS, hereafter]

instructor. These were Andover Cottage, Draper Cottage, Pemberton (formerly Taylor) Cottage, and Eaton (formerly Bancroft) Cottage—which together housed about forty students.[54] Paid for by several donors and designed by at least three architects, the cottages represented two distinct styles of architecture.[55] Andover Cottage had the Victorian-Gothic character of the previous nineteenth-century Andover, while the other three cottages were designed in a simplified classical style, signaling the architectural direction that would come to dominate the campus.

All four cottages were sited in the southwest corner of a new access road, a continuation of Old Campus Road, and Phillips Street, with Draper Cottage on the site of one of the old English Commons that had been destroyed by fire. The Latin and English Commons, now deplored as dangerous and substandard (lacking plumbing, for example), would soon be demolished. But the fact that the cottages that began to replace them were a similar type of small-scale housing, though better in quality and with supervision, suggests that the academy had an abiding preference for a domestic scale of housing, whether run by private families, the students themselves, or the academy.

The involvement of the firm of Frederick Law Olmsted, the great park and town planner, on the Andover campus is worth noting. Starting in the 1860s Olmsted advocated that colleges and universities be developed with a "cottage system" of student housing, arguing that it would be more humane and beneficial than "barracks" dormitories.[56] The Andover trustees engaged the Olmsted firm in 1891 to create a comprehensive plan for the academy's campus; that plan provided the guidelines for the siting of Draper, Pemberton, Andover, and Eaton Cottages.[57] While no documentary evidence exists, it is possible that Olmsted's views were known to those at Andover who preferred the domestically-scaled cottage housing for students. It is also intriguing to speculate that Olmsted's cottage system was originally inspired, at least in part, by his knowledge of the housing patterns at Andover, since as a young man, Olmsted spent the year 1837–38 on the Andover campus.

The academy finally began to provide seriously for the students' housing and boarding needs during the period from 1900 to the First World War—the last years of Bancroft's principalship and the first part of Alfred E. Stearns's tenure (1903–33). In 1902 Bulfinch Hall on Salem Street, gutted by fire, was rebuilt as a dining commons—the first "proper" dining hall for the school, thereby departing from the earlier pattern of students' taking meals in many different places.[58]

The academy also began building dormitories on a large enough scale to house most students (although not all the students until 1930). Bancroft Hall, consisting of three cottage-sized dorm units strung together within one large facade, was erected in 1899 on Phillips Street.[59] In 1902 the academy rented Bartlet Hall from the theological seminary, which was failing and virtually student-less.[60] When the seminary finally left Andover in 1908 and sold its campus to the academy, Foxcroft Hall was also used for students.[61] But these old structures were inadequate (Foxcroft was declared unsafe in 1911 and temporarily scheduled for demolition).[62] A series of new dormitories was constructed from 1910 to 1913: Day Hall, in line with Bartlet Hall; and Bishop, Adams, and Taylor Halls to the west of Main Street, forming two sides of what became West Quadrangle.[63]

Other non-academic facilities were constructed during this period: Borden Gym and York Pool (1902 and 1911, now part of Memorial Gym); Isham Infirmary (1913), now Isham Dormitory; and the Robert S. Peabody Museum of Archaeology (1901–03).[64] These buildings were designed by Boston architects in the neocolonial style—the dormitories following the pattern of simple New England college dorms, the other buildings having ornamental Georgian references. They signaled an allegiance to early-American imagery that would dominate the academy's architectural development during most of the twentieth century.

The siting of these buildings, however, betrayed the difficulties facing the academy in its development of a coherent campus.[65] In 1903 the administration determined to consolidate the academy campus farther up the hill from Academy Hall, on the west side of Main Street on axis with Bulfinch Hall, where the West Quadrangle is today. Even in 1908, the purchase by the academy of the seminary campus and buildings did not deter the continued planning for the academy campus on the west side.

The art of creating "development plans" for existing campuses became a concern among American architects and planners in the early decades of the twentieth century.[66] In 1919, Guy Lowell, the academy's architect, adapting the Olmsted Brothers' proposals, produced a master plan for new structures: dormitories, a Memorial Tower, and a large auditorium and classroom building, to honor the academy's heroes of World War I.[67] These buildings were to form a large rectangular space west of Main Street (extending from the "West Quad" dorms to Phillips Street), and set back from the highway "to prevent disturbance by trucks and street-cars."[68]

ABOVE: **Academy Hill, 1912. Map by Jane Garvie**   BELOW: **Guy Lowell, Proposed Master Plan for Campus West of Main Street, 1919**

Debate continued about the siting of the academy campus and buildings, and whether seminary land should or should not be used. In 1920, when suggestion was made to site the academy's new administration building along Main Street on an axis with Salem Street, Lowell wrote to the trustees, revealing campus-planning thinking of the period: "I would like to see the school have a center all its own that it would not share with the Town's streets nor the Public's highway. . . . It is now the modern theory of college planning that the important buildings should turn their faces to the center of college life, the campus, and not to the outside world."[69]

If the west side plans of Lowell had been executed, the functional and psychological center of the academy would have remained on the west side of Main Street. This did not occur. In the early 1920s, one of the boldest schemes in campus-planning history was to turn the development of the academy in a new direction.

THE CAMPUS RESTRUCTURED

The major transformation of the Andover campus was made possible by several fortunate conditions, especially the desire of wealthy alumni to support their school, and strong architectural direction. A successful fund-raising campaign in 1919–20, conducted mainly by alumni, made it possible to implement bold campus development plans.[70] Trustee George B. Case, with the assistance of other New York alumni, argued fervently for campus development on the east side of Main Street, which would relate to the old buildings of Seminary Row.[71] As principal Alfred Stearns recalled, the debate between the "East Siders," those who joined Case's arguments, and the "West Siders," who felt "that the western slope offered most attractive opportunities for an extensive and attractive development," was "continuous and heated for several years."[72] To find a way out of the disagreement, the school consulted with New York architect Charles A. Platt, who suggested three plans. The trustees chose the one that located development on the east side behind Seminary Row. To accomplish this, Pearson Hall was moved in 1922 to the south end of a new quadrangle, and in 1924 the new main academy building, Samuel Phillips Hall, was erected to form the eastern focus of this quad.[73] Memorial Tower, originally planned for the West Quad, was constructed on a prominent site at the corner of Main and Salem Streets.[74] Guy Lowell designed both the tower and Samuel Phillips Hall. These major shifts in the campus's location and focus marked the first stages of what would become Platt's reshaping of the Andover campus, the most extensive in its history.[75]

Charles Platt specialized in the design of country houses and gardens, as well as public buildings and college campuses, employing the Renaissance and Beaux-Arts traditions he had studied in Europe.[76] An accomplished painter and print-maker, Platt embodied a highly aesthetic view of architecture and its role in society. He reportedly summarized his vision of a new Phillips Academy this way: "Why not surround [the students] with the very best in architecture and nature and the fine arts? . . . a really fine library, a topnotch art gallery, a good Colonial church with an organ . . . broad vistas, . . . lawns and terraces, . . . lectures and concerts—all instruments of culture."[77]

This high artistic ideal was a world apart from the Phillips family's founding virtues of Calvinist modesty and self-denial. But it was in tune with upper-class aspirations of the early

ABOVE: **Foxcroft, Samuel Phillips,
and Bartlet Halls, 1946** RIGHT: **Memorial
Bell Tower, 1923** FAR RIGHT: **George
Washington Hall and Samuel Phillips
Hall, circa 1926**

twentieth century, as well as a pedagogical trend toward education of the "whole child."[78] And it aroused the fervent support of Thomas Cochran, wealthy alumnus and trustee of the academy, who provided extraordinary funds for executing Platt's vision of the campus beautiful.[79] From about 1922 to 1932, the architect and the financier worked closely to reshape Andover and to give it, in Cochran's words, "the most lovely school buildings in America surrounded by the most lovely grounds."[80]

Many substantial structures were erected as part of this program: George Washington Hall (1925–26); Samuel F. B. Morse Hall (1927–28); Paul Revere Hall (1928); Oliver Wendell Holmes Library (1928–29); The Commons (1928–30); Addison Gallery of American Art (1929–31); and Cochran Chapel (1930–32).[81] As significant as the individual buildings, however, was the grand spatial organization that Platt created with them: a pattern of axes and cross-axes, sequences of spaces, vistas, and orderly landscaping—all of which integrated the east and west parts of the school for the first time and gave the campus the character of a highly structured park.

The main axis of this parkland runs east–west, from Samuel Phillips Hall in the Great Quadrangle through The Lawn, crossing Main Street to a tree-lined allée which originally led the eye all the way to the hills in the west. (Today it ends in trees that have grown in the middle distance.) Secondary north–south axes include that defined by the Great Quadrangle and extending into the Flagstaff Quadrangle to the south, and another that runs the length of The Lawn, from Memorial Tower at the south to Cochran Chapel at the north. Platt's siting of the new library and art gallery created a kind of forecourt between The Lawn and the Great Quadrangle.

These monumental spaces exemplified the Beaux-Arts principles that dominated much of American campus planning of the period.[82] They also reflected Platt's background as a designer

The Vista from the tower of Samuel
Phillips Hall, 1929

Pearson Hall being moved, 1922

of country estates and gardens. Many American campuses were designed around axes, but they were normally axes of approach and circulation. The main function of Platt's principal axis at Andover was simply to create a view—the Vista—from Samuel Phillips Hall through the sequence of quadrangles and allées to the distant hills to the west. This was a characteristic of Baroque French gardens, as at Versailles, and it was a pattern Platt had employed in many of his designs for the grounds of lavish country houses.[83] Thus, like the early academy that had been integrated into the domestic life of Andover, the new campus could also be seen as having a domestic character—though it was now the domesticity of an estate rather than that of a New England village.

The importance that Platt and Cochran, aided by the school's treasurer, James Sawyer, attached to this artistic remaking of the campus was demonstrated by the extraordinary efforts they expended to achieve it, most specifically their willingness to demolish or move incompatible existing buildings.[84] The two most prominent nineteenth-century structures on the campus, Brechin Hall and Stone Chapel, were torn down in 1929–30 mainly because of their objectionable Gothic styling and because their locations "destroy[ed] the balance" that Platt was creating.[85] The top floors of Foxcroft and Bartlet Halls were removed in 1929, "to conform to the architecture of the surrounding buildings."[86]

20

Academy Hill, 1932. Map by Jane Garvie

Platt and Cochran's other method of dealing with troublesome buildings was to move them. This was not unprecedented. It had been done occasionally at both Phillips and Abbot Academy, but usually for practical rather than aesthetic reasons.[87] And in 1909, the architectural critic Montgomery Schuyler had written about Harvard's campus and had suggested that vistas could be created there by moving several of the buildings; but this was not taken seriously there or elsewhere.[88] Only at Andover, it seems, was the idea carried out on a large scale. From 1922 to 1929, at least nine buildings were relocated as part of Platt's master plan for Andover.[89] Four of these—Pearson Hall, Tucker House, Bancroft Hall, and Pemberton Cottage—were moved in order to open the space, along the central east-west axis, which became the Vista.

These demolitions, relocations, and new buildings transformed the campus so radically that they inspired school legends of alumni revisiting the academy and finding it completely unrecognizable.[90] But if Platt and Cochran were in effect creating a new campus, they also attempted to forge ties to the school's past. This is seen especially in the architectural styles of the buildings designed by Platt: like those of Guy Lowell they were neoclassical, and even more directly alluded to early American architecture to emphasize the venerable origins of the academy.[91] Several of Platt's buildings, including the Commons and Cochran Chapel, made reference to the Federal style of Charles Bulfinch, either in detailing or general feeling.[92]

Commons, circa 1930

The homage to Andover's architectural past was selective. The new chapel, for example, while modeled on early American architecture on the exterior facade, was given an opulent, Christopher Wren-style interior, hardly in tune with the ascetic Calvinism of the early academy.[93] The image of prestige, affluence, and culture that the academy now wished to project prevailed over its austere historical presence. Platt's architecture and landscape served present purposes perfectly. As architectural historian Keith N. Morgan has stated, Platt's works "are icons of self-conscious economic, social, and cultural intentions. . . . projections of a new American landscape of power, wealth, sophistication, and public benefaction."[94]

RECREATIONAL AMENITIES

As the transformation of the central campus was occurring, the school also focused on developing facilities for sports and socializing. Around 1900 land was purchased for the creation of football and baseball playing fields; several years later a running track and other facilities were added. In 1909 students organized a fund-raising campaign to construct an indoor pool, which was added to Borden Gym in 1911.[95] And in 1922, a 32-acre tract of farmland was purchased to the south, to provide additional playing fields.[96] Similar to American colleges, most preparatory academies, including Andover, by now accepted athletics as a desirable activity, and the large areas of land needed to accommodate it would henceforth constitute a significant proportion of the campus grounds.

In addition to athletics, the other major expression of student extra-curricular activity at Andover was the "secret society" phenomenon. Here, too, the practice had originated at colleges, where in the early and mid-nineteenth century, students had created various kinds of social clubs, most of which were disapproved by the authorities and often had to exist in secret, but which were gradually accepted and ultimately produced the Greek-letter fraternity system.

Andover was apparently the only secondary school in which this phenomenon manifested itself in a major way.[97] Starting in the 1870s, Phillips Academy students founded a large number of societies—such as Kappa Omega Alpha (KOA), Auctotitas Unitas Veritas (AUV), and Pi Alpha Epsilon (PAE)—which the trustees banned at first but in the 1880s grudgingly acknowledged and attempted to regulate. The singular success of these groups at Andover may have been due partly to the unusually strong tradition there of students' running their own extra-curricular lives, as seen for example in the autonomy of the Latin and English Commons starting in the 1830s and in the student-managed "eating clubs" created in the 1850s.[98] These societies thrived at Andover, despite periodic attempts by the administration to suppress them; they were finally abolished in 1950.

The importance that students attached to these societies, as well as their considerable affluence, is revealed by the buildings created for them. The societies at Andover served only for

Borden Gymnasium, 1902

Alumni House, before 1950, postcard

socializing, not for housing (as at most colleges), yet they acquired substantial and even lavish structures.[99] The first societies bought private houses in the vicinity of the academy, then began erecting their own buildings. Eventually seven societies built houses, several on land purchased from the academy.[100] These structures, designed by different architects with distinctive architectural traits, all tend to be exuberant and individualistic, probably reflecting the members' youthful enthusiasm and their desire to make each house stand out from the rest. Alumni House (KOA house), built in 1901 by architect William C. Brocklesby, is a classical temple form with a robust portico and columns, while Graham House (AUV house), built in 1915 by Codman & Despradelle, and Benner House (Alpha Gamma Chi or AGC house), built in 1928–29 by Bogner & Billings, represent versions of the Baroque style, with opulent, curvilinear forms and ornament. Davison House (Phi Lambda Delta or FLD house), built in 1928 by Perry, Shaw & Hepburn, is a sophisticated rendition of a picturesque Tudor cottage. The strong personalities of these houses were due perhaps to the students' desire to give each society an individual identity on a campus where most of the early buildings had a strong ascetic character.

The society houses added a new tone to the campus architecture while they reinforced the domestic nature of the academy environment. Like the many private houses on the campus, in which faculty lived and students boarded, and like the Latin Commons, the English Commons, and the four cottages built in the 1890s, the society houses added to the domestic scale that characterized Phillips Academy since its founding.

THE ANDOVER PROGRAM

Following completion of Cochran Chapel in 1932, twenty-five years passed with little architectural activity at Phillips Academy.[101] This hiatus, broken only by a minor and occasional building project, was due not only to the economic depression of the 1930s and to the Second World War, but also to the fact that Cochran and Platt's construction frenzy of the 1920s had provided fully for the academy's physical requirements.[102]

By the 1950s, new dormitories, a science building, increased library space, and an arts facility were among the school's main needs, and the resulting "Andover Program" campaign brought modern design, somewhat belatedly, to the campus. The new structures were sited mostly at the edges of the campus—especially to the north and east of the Great Quadrangle—thereby preserving the integrity of the earlier architecture and spaces. For these additions, the academy engaged Benjamin Thompson of The Architects Collaborative (TAC), the Cambridge architectural firm founded by modernist pioneer Walter Gropius.[103] For nearly a decade between 1957 and 1966, Thompson produced four new dormitories for the Rabbit Pond area—Stearns, Stevens, Fuess, and Hale Houses—which broke with the earlier patterns in both their siting and their architectural style. In contrast to the formality of Guy Lowell's and Charles Platt's master plans for quadrangles, axes, and vistas, Thompson located the new structures in irregular patterns along a curving road adjacent to Rabbit Pond in an area that was carved out of the Moncrieff Cochran Bird Sanctuary.

These dorms, built of reinforced concrete, are infilled and partly covered by red-brick walls that echo the ubiquitous material of the traditional campus buildings. TAC's modernist tendencies during this period were tempered here by a desire to mediate with the older academy buildings—an early example of architectural contextualism, also seen in the gable roofs of most of the dorms (only Hale House has the typically flat, international-style roof).[104]

Adding to the informality of the buildings' siting in the woods is the irregularity of their individual plans, combining various one-story and two-story shapes and a relatively small scale. The resulting appearance of this complex of dorms—including the wood-sided Elbridge H. Stuart House, added in 1971 and designed by Pietro Belluschi—suggests a suburban group of private houses, or perhaps vacation homes. The Rabbit Pond complex perpetuated the domestic quality of Phillips Academy since its earliest years, of which only vestiges survived. These dormitories, while largely modern in architectural style, thus revive a distinctive trait of the academy's early days.

The other major building projects of the Andover Program were Thomas M. Evans Hall, the science building, and the Arts and Communications Center, both designed by Benjamin Thompson.[105] Sited closer than the dorms to the center of the campus—Evans Hall behind Samuel Phillips Hall, and the Arts and Communication Center linking George Washington Hall with the Addison Gallery of American Art—they nevertheless are forthrightly modern in their use of reinforced-concrete structure, expanses of glass, and asymmetrical massing. These buildings also embodied new planning concepts that emerged in the postwar years. In contrast to classical principles of proportion and proper distances between buildings, the new guidelines allowed

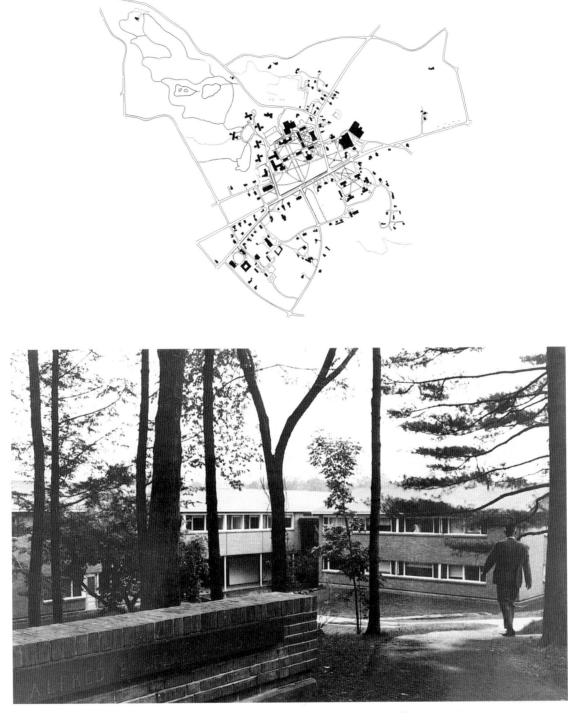

TOP: **Academy Hill, 1971. Map by Jane Garvie**   BOTTOM: **Alfred P. Stearns House, 1959**

asymmetry, the connecting of existing buildings with new construction, and even the placement of buildings in the middle of spaces rather than at their edges.

Most American colleges and universities were strongly affected by these new planning principles in the post-war decades.[106] Andover, while adding some examples of the new manner, kept them peripheral and thereby preserved to a remarkable degree the character of its earlier campus. Another important addition to the academy campus during this period, however, resulted not from new construction but from the acquisition of Abbot Academy and the absorption of its campus.

ABBOT ACADEMY

The 1973 merger of Phillips Academy and Abbot Academy, the girls' preparatory school, ended the long single-sex histories of these institutions. The two campuses merged, Abbot's contribution being relatively small but certainly distinctive. The Abbot environment was stable and centered on the same spot throughout its history, in contrast to Phillips's shifting and centrifugal campus.

Abbot Female Academy, founded in 1828 by a group of Andover citizens that included officials from Phillips Academy and Andover Theological Seminary, was built on an acre of donated land on School Street, northwest of the Phillips Academy property.[107] Until 1863, Abbot possessed only this one acre; then it added to the grounds.

Abbot Hall, first known as the Academy Building and erected in 1828–29, was designed in the neoclassical manner complete with columned portico. It was thus more up to date and ornamented than any of the Phillips or theological seminary structures of the time, and it suggested a less ascetic ideology than that of the male schools—even though the Calvinist faith was ostensibly just as important at Abbot.[108] The building contained two large classrooms and an assembly hall, but no living quarters. Similar to the boys' academy, Abbot provided no housing; students either were local and lived at home, or boarded in private houses.[109] As out-of-town enrollment increased, the trustees realized that Abbot Academy had to provide room and board for students. In 1854 Smith Hall was erected, a large wooden dormitory accommodating about sixty students on the upper floors, with a dining room, kitchen, music room, and matron's apartment on the first floor.[110] This building was located behind the main building, and the students' entry to the latter was shifted to its rear away from the street, making the academy environment more private and protected.[111]

These two buildings contained virtually all Abbot Academy functions; together they thus operated like the type of structure that was developing in the mid nineteenth century for the new women's colleges in America—a single large building containing all collegiate functions to assure students' safety.[112] In 1865 Abbot acquired the two private houses flanking Abbot Hall, South Hall and Davis Hall, to provide additional housing, but the institution retained its protective compactness—reinforced by fences that were erected around the property.[113] By the 1880s, Abbot's facilities were no longer adequate in size and quality. The academy in 1886 commissioned a plan for new buildings, recognizing the need to compete with other women's institutions. Designed by the Boston architectural firm of Hartwell & Richardson, the master plan called for demolition of the four Abbot structures and the construction of four larger edifices, in the then fashionable Richardsonian Romanesque style.[114] These buildings were to be asymmetrically composed and arranged around a quadrangular space open to School Street. Fund-raising efforts were less successful than hoped, and only the central structure, Draper Hall, could be built.

But in order to site it where the master plan specified, and to create the new quadrangle, extraordinary measures had to be taken: the relocation of three of the existing structures. Between 1887 and 1889, Smith Hall was moved farther from School Street, the Academy Building (renamed Abbot Hall) was rotated ninety degrees and moved to form the south-east side of the new quadrangle, and South Hall was divided in two and moved to separate locations to serve as private residences. Draper Hall, erected in 1889, contained a multiplicity of functions: dormitory suites, dining rooms, kitchen, laundries, servants' quarters, a library, reading room, parlors, offices, the Principal's suite, and eleven music rooms. In 1903, the building projected by the master plan for the north-west side of the quadrangle was finally built, in a modified version of the "Romanesque" style of Draper Hall. This was McKeen Memorial Hall, containing classrooms and a combination auditorium-gymnasium. This group of buildings—Abbot Hall, Draper Hall, and McKeen Hall, and the quadrangle they created—remain the heart of the Abbot Academy campus. Even with new structures added in the twentieth century—the John-Esther Art Gallery (1906–07), Taylor Infirmary (1913–14), Abbey House dormitory (1939), and Abbot Gym (1955–56)—the central campus space and its buildings came increasingly to embody the character of the school.[115]

Indeed, "the Circle," the space defined by the circular road that had been laid out around the quadrangle after Draper Hall was erected—gradually assumed a powerful mystique for Abbot

Abbot Academy, 1885, left to right, **South Hall, Smith Hall, Abbot Hall, and Davis Halls**

students and alumni, a symbol of the school's nurturing qualities.[116] This implies an awareness of the distinctive architectural nature of the place. By about 1900, when Phillips Academy was denigrating its Victorian buildings and asserting classicism as the only proper style, Abbot Academy's "circle" and surrounding structures, especially Draper and McKeen Halls, retained the irregular, asymmetrical, picturesque, and rounded forms.

Abbot with its distinctive environment narrowly escaped destruction in the 1930s, when the school engaged the architect and campus planner Jens Frederick Larson to remodel its architecture.[117] Larson's ideal was classical regularity and uniformity, even if it meant destroying a school's physical heritage.[118] For Abbot he proposed new buildings in a "Bulfinch" style, and a new façade for Draper Hall in the same mode.[119] If executed, this plan would have transformed Abbot into a miniature version of Charles Platt's classically-restructured Phillips campus. Only the failure of the ensuing fund-raising campaign saved the historic Abbot campus that exists today—thus preserving the picturesque architecture that Phillips Academy largely erased from its own campus.

ANDOVER'S PLACE AMONG AMERICAN CAMPUSES

The campus of Phillips Academy retains some vestiges of its modest beginnings. But the growth of the Andover campus, through most of its history, has reflected principles derived largely from the planning of colleges, so it can be seen as part of the history of the American collegiate campus. Phillips Academy belongs to a very small group of institutions—whether colleges

Abbot Academy, circa 1922, postcard, left to right, **John-Esther Gallery and Abbot Hall, Draper Hall, Merrill Gate, and McKeen Hall**

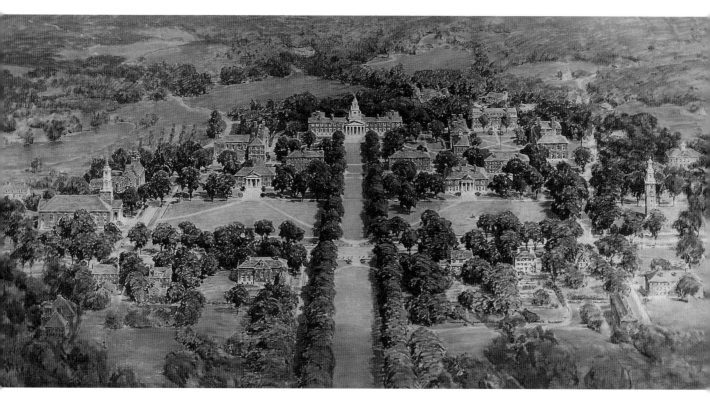

Charles A. Platt, Completed Andover Campus, 1932–33. The Vista runs vertically from Samuel Phillips Hall at the top. In front of "Sam Phil" is the Great Quadrangle; Flagstaff Quad is to the right. At center, parallel to Main Street, is the Great Lawn, from Cochran Chapel on the left to the Memorial Bell Tower on the right

or academies—whose campuses date from the time of the American Revolution or earlier.[120] Its buildings and grounds thus bear witness to a long evolution. Furthermore, the Andover campus has a more complex history than that of perhaps any other American academic institution. Even Harvard's campus, which is considerably older and larger, developed over the centuries in a relatively straightforward manner compared with that of Phillips Academy.

The convoluted history of the Andover campus is due largely to the fact that it has resulted from the merger of several institutions, whose individual traits were embodied in their buildings and grounds: the modest domesticity of the early Phillips Academy, the Yale-like pattern of Andover Theological Seminary's Row, and the intimate character of the Circle at Abbot Academy. Further complexity was created by the nineteenth-century relationship between the academy and the theological seminary and the academy's awkward, bifurcated existence on both sides of Main Street.

Also remarkable is the fact that several of the campus patterns produced at Andover are exemplars of their types. The three aligned buildings of Seminary Row, at the upper edge of the expansive quadrangle, epitomized this early-nineteenth-century type of the "college on the hill." The sophisticated pattern of buildings, axes, and spaces created by Charles Platt in the 1920s is one of the finest examples of Beaux-Arts campus planning. And Abbot Academy is the embodiment of the nurturing ideals of the traditional female academy in America. Andover could be used to illustrate many of the distinctive forms in American campus history.

While the Andover campus is exemplary in these ways, it also reveals idiosyncrasies. Most peculiar, perhaps, was the school's propensity to move buildings from place to place, either for practical or aesthetic reasons. The most extraordinary example was the wholesale relocation of structures during the Platt-Cochran redesign of the campus, but it had also been done at earlier times, notably Abbot Academy in the 1880s. This suggests the unusual emphasis that each of the Andover institutions has placed on the shaping of its environment. The multi-layered palimpsest that is the Phillips Academy campus serves both as an ideal representative of the American campus in general, and as the highly individual embodiment of a unique school.

David Chase

To Promote True Piety & Virtue

DEVELOPMENT OF THE PHILLIPS ACADEMY CAMPUS, 1778-1838

WHAT MAKES A PLACE MEMORABLE? In the case of the Phillips Academy campus it was, first, topography. There was nothing noteworthy about the acreage donated in 1778, save that it was hilltop farmland. It was, according to geographer and Andover trustee Jedidiah Morse, *a delightful eminence encompassed with a salubrious air.*[1] It was a beginning. That beauty of location is largely unseen now; trees obscure it. But to this natural asset was added in Andover's first sixty years an abundance of gifts, and the form and focus and feel of the core of the campus embody decisions made in those decades of the late eighteenth and early nineteenth centuries. We inherit that legacy. Even with the overlay of twentieth-century revisions and additions—artful, handsome, and impressive as they are—the campus today is recognizably the campus that existed in 1838. The making of this seemingly timeless New England place reflects happenstance and mischance, yet also collective will and personal vision, effort, planning, extraordinary philanthropy, and the marks of craft and design tradition. In particular, the early campus was the product of a continuity of inspired leadership that was only to come into play again at Andover in the early years of the twentieth century.

The public road system traversing the center of campus has not changed since the 1830s: Main Street, Phillips Street, and Salem Street remain essentially as they existed. Then as now the hub was the "Seminary Common," today's Great Lawn. Fronting the high road, the common extended almost 1,100 feet from Chapel Avenue on the north to Salem Street on the south. A fence surrounded the common on three sides, just as today a stone wall surrounds it. In 1838 young elm trees bordered the common along Chapel Avenue, Main Street, and Salem Street. On the east side of the common, facing the main road and set up on a broad terrace, stood a row of three dignified brick buildings, the one in the center topped by a tall cupola. An axial, tree-lined path, nearly 500 feet in length, led to these buildings from Main Street. A second path, "Elm Arch," crossed the common side-to-side.[2]

In 1838, as today, everything on and around the Seminary Common belonged to the trustees of Phillips Academy. Unlike today, the 1830s campus accommodated three educational

Francis Alexander, Theological Seminary, Andover, 1827–1829, lithograph. Andover Historical Society, Andover, Massachusetts

33

ABOVE: **Andover Theological Institution & Teachers' Seminary,** circa 1834, engraving, left to right, **Teachers' Seminary, Samaritan House, Stowe House, Foxcroft Hall, Pearson Hall,** and **Bartlet Hall.** Collection of the Addison Gallery of American Art, Phillips Academy [Addison Gallery, hereafter]

BELOW: **Andover Theological Seminary,** after 1832, engraving, left to right, **Foxcroft Hall, Pearson Hall, Bartlet Hall, Bulfinch Hall, Hardy House, Blanchard House, Moses Stuart House, Printing Shop,** and **Mansion House.** Addison Gallery

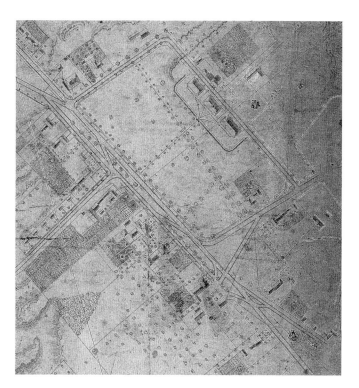

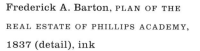

Frederick A. Barton, PLAN OF THE
REAL ESTATE OF PHILLIPS ACADEMY,
1837 (detail), ink

institutions, each with its own faculty and students, all under the aegis of one board: Phillips Academy, founded in 1778, then referred to on campus as the Latin or Classical Academy; Andover Theological Seminary, founded in 1808; and the English Academy and Teachers Seminary, founded in 1827. Andover Theological Seminary dominated. Appropriately, it was housed in the brick buildings along the east side of the common. Phillips Hall (1808–09) on the north, now Foxcroft Hall, was a dormitory. The central building, Bartlet Chapel (1817–18), today called Pearson Hall and moved, contained a chapel, library, and classrooms. The south building in the row, Bartlet Hall (1820–21), was a dormitory. In 1838 the Classical Academy occupied Bulfinch Hall (1818–19). Although 200 feet south of Salem Street, the brick schoolhouse stood on an elevated site that was terraced and visible from the common and Main Street. The so-called "Stone Academy" (1828–30, destroyed by fire 1864), which faced the common from the northeast corner of Main Street and Chapel Avenue, housed the English Academy and Teachers Seminary; it too set upon a terraced site. The fact that three schools occupied one campus was signaled only by the fact that the main building of each—Pearson, Bulfinch, and the Stone Academy—had a belfry. Along the north, Chapel Avenue side of the common stood Samaritan House (an infirmary built in 1824, since moved), and the seminary workshop (1828, now Stowe House and relocated). East, behind Seminary Row, was a dining hall (1809–10, moved), a farm, and a community cemetery. South of the common stood Blanchard House (since moved), an eighteenth-century dwelling within what are now the bounds of the Great Lawn. It faced Hardy House (1804–05) across Salem Street,

Printing Shop and Mansion House, circa 1880

home to the Classical Academy's principal. At the southeast corner of Salem and Main Streets was the Training Field, open and treeless, a sort of junior common. South of the Training Field was Newman House (circa 1807). Along the west side of Main Street, facing the common, was Faculty Row. Opposite Newman House was Moses Stuart House (1810–11). North up Main Street was a brick printing office (1833, demolished) and the Mansion House. Built in 1782–85 by Samuel Phillips Jr. as his home, the Mansion House served as an inn (and occasional dormitory) from 1812 until burning in 1887. Next north was Pease House (1815–16), then Phelps House (1809–10). A house at the southwest corner of Main and Phillips Streets (since moved off campus) served as the dining hall for the Classical Academy. Across Phillips Street, facing Main, stood Farrar House (1811–12, moved west down Phillips Street). Next was the brick Park House (1833–34), and, opposite Chapel Avenue, a two-family dwelling, "Double Brick" (1829–30). West of Faculty Row in 1838, off Main Street, were farms where poor but industrious students could work to help pay for their education and could live in modest frame dormitories. The six Classical Academy dormitories (1830–32, 1835, demolished) lined the north side of Phillips Street; six identical English Academy dormitories (1834, 1835, demolished) formed a row off School Street, behind Clement House, which housed their dining commons.[3]

Withal, it was a neat, pleasing, and ample but unpretentious physical plant, village-like in character, impressive in its completeness. Although diverse architecturally, there was a certain commonality, more so than today. The campus registered as a whole—the verdant common, the understated "public" buildings overlooking it, the "private" buildings framing it on three sides. Thanks to the Andover Theological Seminary—both famous and infamous as the epicenter of New England Puritan orthodoxy, training, and missionary zeal—views of the campus were published repeatedly in the 1820s and 1830s. Remarkably, in them we see a place we can recognize.[4]

LEADERSHIP

Andover's early-nineteenth-century campus was the product of six decades and three interconnecting generations of leadership.[5] All the major players, save one, were trustees. All were observant Puritans, many were Congregational ministers, and eight were members of the Phillips family. Trustees were elected for life, and most chose to remain until they died. It was very much a Harvard-educated board, very much an Andover–Boston board. The trustees were comfortably fixed; a few were wealthy. Public service was common. The first era of board leadership began in 1777, before the academy opened; its prime mover was Samuel Phillips Jr. The second commenced in 1802, with the election of Eliphalet Pearson to succeed Phillips, and ended when Pearson stepped down as president in 1821. This period is the most critical to the formation of the early campus. Pearson was heavily involved, but he had three key partners in this work: Col. John Phillips, son of Samuel Phillips Jr.; Samuel Farrar, treasurer of the board; and William Bartlet, a major donor who, despite his philanthropy, was never a trustee. In the third period, from 1821 through the 1830s, treasurer Farrar took the lead.

Samuel Phillips Jr. (1752–1802), founder of Phillips Academy, followed his father and grandfather at Harvard, graduating in 1771. He also followed them as a strict Calvinist, a businessman, and as a public figure. He became town clerk, and began representing Andover in the state legislature in 1776. He held public office continuously thereafter, for many years leading the state senate and serving as lieutenant governor at the time of his death. During the Revolution, Samuel Phillips Jr.'s best-known endeavor was producing gunpowder for General George Washington's troops. Although a leader in the rebellion, Phillips, his family, and associates were troubled by the associated social upheaval. He decried "the prevalence of ignorance and vice, disorder and wickedness" abroad in the land. And concluded, "[an] earnest solicitude to find the source of these evils and their remedy; and a small acquaintance with the qualities of young minds . . . evidences that Youth is the important period, on the improvement or neglect of which depend the most important consequences to individuals themselves and the community." The response, which Samuel Phillips Jr. formulated and led, was to found an academy (and, he hoped, soon other academies) that taught ancient virtues. According to the Phillips Academy Constitution of 1778, the object was not only to provide students instruction in "English and Latin Grammar, Writing, Arithmetic, and those Sciences, wherein they are commonly taught, but more especially to learn

Samuel Phillips, frontispiece from John L. Taylor, A MEMOIR OF HIS HONOR SAMUEL PHILLIPS, LLD (Boston, 1856), mezzotint

them the Great End and Real Business of Living." His wealthy father and uncle, Squire Samuel Phillips and Dr. John Phillips of Exeter, provided funds to establish the school, paying for land and creating an endowment. Samuel Phillips Jr. purchased the site and made all the practical arrangements. He oversaw the physical development of the school until his death.[6]

Eliphalet Pearson (1752–1826) succeeded Samuel Phillips Jr. as leader of the board. They attended Governor Dummer Academy together in the 1760s, then Harvard. Pearson came to Andover to teach in the town grammar school. Soon he was engaged as amateur chemist, assisting Phillips to make gunpowder. Pearson was principal advisor to Samuel Phillips Jr. in formulating the constitution for Phillips Academy, and he became the first schoolmaster, holding that post until he moved on to Harvard in 1786 to serve as Hancock Professor of Hebrew and Oriental Languages. He labored on behalf of Harvard, and rose in academic circles, being appointed acting president in 1804. He hoped to gain that post permanently, but Pearson was very conservative, he was not an easy man, and he had many enemies. He not only lost out in his presidential bid, he lost in the choice of a divinity professor. Pearson and fellow Calvinists were aghast. Where would new ministers train in the old orthodoxy? Liberal religious thinking was spreading quickly, Unitarianism was now ascendant at Harvard and the old guard felt threatened. Pearson determined to create an ultra-orthodox Calvinist institution at Andover. It would be the nation's first

Protestant theological seminary. Pearson had been appointed a founding trustee of Phillips Academy in 1778 and remained on the board throughout his Harvard career. He served as board president after Samuel Phillips Jr.'s death, and set about creating the seminary, an entity of the existing board. Dr. Pearson resigned his Harvard professorship and moved to Andover in 1806 to launch the seminary. Upon learning that a Newburyport group had a similar plan, Pearson lobbied intensely and persuaded the Newburyport faction, led by Rev. Samuel Spring, to join the Andover group as "Associate Founders." He enlisted donors to fund professorships and buildings, and Pearson continued to shape the campus until he resigned the presidency in 1821. He was recalled by former pupil and fellow trustee Josiah Quincy, in a letter written after the first Andover board meeting following Pearson's death, in 1826. Quincy stated his respect for Pearson's achievements, but continued, "Dr. Pearson was coldly remembered. Those who fill the places he created feel little gratitude toward him. I cannot blame them, considering all the trouble and vexation his Papal humor caused to the occupants of those chairs." Dr. Pearson was a man of discerning taste. Edwards Park, student and later professor at the theological seminary, recalled Pearson's reputation as "an adept of the fine arts. He had a musical ear, and an architect's eye and forecast."[7]

Colonel John Phillips (1776–1820) had a meteoric career as an Andover trustee. Elected in 1801, he was the first graduate on the board. As son and heir of Samuel Phillips Jr., and someone heavily engaged in constructing buildings for his own account, he must have expected to someday take charge of the campus. In 1802 Phillips superintended alterations to the second academy building. In 1804 he contracted to build Hardy House for the board. John Phillips and his mother built the theological seminary's first buildings in 1808–09, he playing more than the usual donor role and serving as his own general contractor. He should have had a long and important role as a shaper of the campus, but his influence was cut short by reckless investments, and perhaps more. Col. Phillips went bankrupt upon completion of the seminary buildings. According to Salem minister and diarist William Bentley, writing in October 1809, "The Theme of Conversation is the Insolvency of John Phillips of Andover, son of the late Lieut. Governor. . . . Some of our Salem friends have suffered. . . . [It] was thought there was no end to his money. He has been very irregular in his habits & this is the true cause of his sufferings." Col. Phillips' career was eclipsed. He remained a trustee until his death in 1820, but really had no significant role to play.[8]

William Bartlet (1748–1841), Newburyport shipowner, merchant, and textile manufacturer, was an exacting, teetotaling Calvinist. A member of Rev. Samuel Spring's parish, Bartlet was induced by Spring to support the theological seminary. This he did liberally. Starting in 1808, he donated $160,000 over the course of four decades. Nearly half of that money he spent erecting five buildings: Phelps House (1809–10), Moses Stuart House (1810–11), Pearson Hall (1817–18), Bartlet Hall (1820–21) and Park House (1833–34). In each case save the last, Bartlet served as his own contractor, hiring builders, purchasing materials, and paying the bills. Bartlet enjoyed building, understood the process well, and was comfortable making decisions.[9]

Samuel Farrar (1773–1864) was a trustee of Phillips Academy for 44 years, and treasurer from 1803 to 1840. He first arrived in Andover in 1797 as a recent Harvard graduate to teach in the academy, and returned in 1803 after training in the law, this time to become heavily involved in local business and civic affairs. He was frugal, obsessive about order and routine, devout, an appreciator of sacred music, a practical man, and at times bold. He supervised every construction project on campus during his 37-year tenure as treasurer. In the case of any major project, he was paid a fee for his efforts. The treasurer added to the campus by using profits from the seminary dining hall to buy land surrounding the Seminary Common and beyond. Squire Farrar used the Prize Fund, which he created in 1807 with his own donations and from which no prizes were ever awarded, to hire singing masters and to provide capital for a variety of building projects, including the infirmary and twelve dormitories. By the 1870s, Farrar was being criticized for his architectural tastes. Claude Moore Fuess, in the first comprehensive history of Phillips Academy, went further, asserting Farrar functioned as the architect of many Andover buildings, and was "obsessed by a craving for simplicity (and) created a style . . . all his own, not Grecian or Gothic or Colonial, but essentially 'Farraresque.'"[10] Fuess's criticism was not based on fact. Farrar did not design the buildings he had responsibility for, and many of the buildings he superintended through planning and construction were handsome—Pearson Hall and Bulfinch Hall among them. Although apparently conservative in all else, Samuel Farrar took a real interest in educational innovation. He played a key role in founding the Andover Theological Seminary, as well as the English Academy & Teachers Seminary and the nearby Abbot Academy, the girls' school launched in 1828.[11]

BUILDERS & ARCHITECTS

In addition to the continuity of leadership Phillips Academy enjoyed during its first sixty years, a second source of continuity in campus development was the builders and craftsmen. The trustees employed skilled mechanics to construct Andover buildings in the first decade of the nineteenth century, people who continued to work for them and for William Bartlet into the 1830s. The mark of their skill lives on to this day. Two young Newburyport carpenters, David Rice and David Hidden, came to Andover to work for Bartlet on Phelps House in 1809 and stayed on to do countless jobs on campus. Hidden's ledger survives, documenting no fewer than fifteen major campus construction projects he worked on through 1835, and scores of small projects. For example, on October 12, 1819, Hidden charged Professor Moses Stuart $0.25 for "fixing a place for your coffee mill." David Rice received $7.40 in December 1810 for fabricating and hanging blinds. In 1834–35, in partnership with Benjamin Clement, Rice was general contractor for six dormitories. In 1817–18, and again in 1824, Rice and Hidden were partners; they contracted with William Bartlet for the carpentry work in Pearson Hall, and with Samuel Farrar to build Samaritan House.[12] Simeon M. Marshall, a Newburyport bricklayer and stonemason, also came to Andover at the behest of William Bartlet. He served as chief mason for Pearson Hall, Bulfinch Hall, and Bartlet Hall. Between times, he repaired chimneys, set up stoves, and did whitewashing. Surviving records indicate that Marshall never worked as a designer, while Rice and Hidden designed mostly small projects and only occasionally an entire building, such as Samaritan House.[13]

Architects as such played a minor role in the development of the Andover campus through the 1830s. No professional worked on a master plan or on the siting of individual buildings.

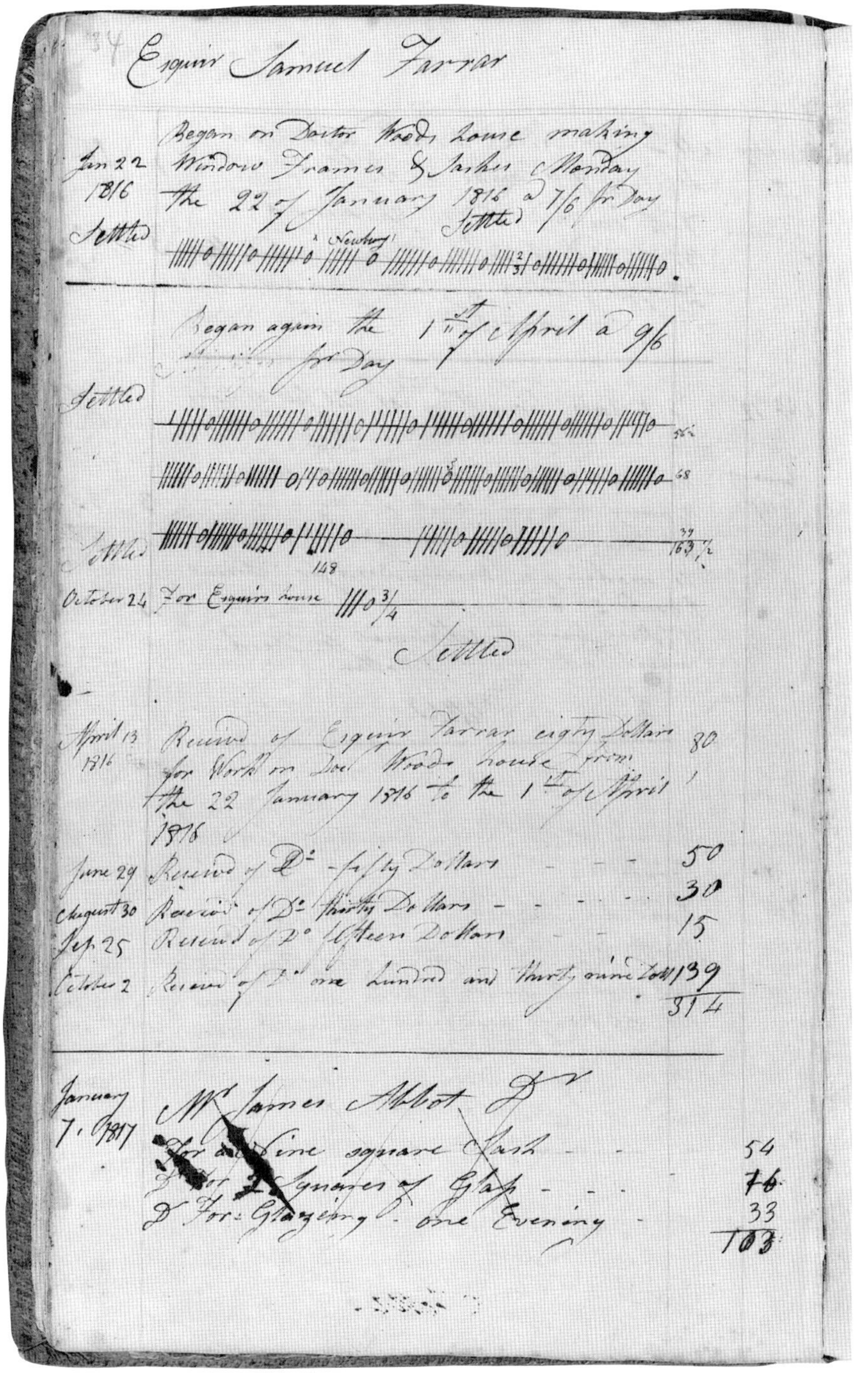

Esquire Samuel Farrar

Jan 22
1816
Settled

Began on Doctor Woods house making
Window Frames & Sashes Monday
the 22 of January 1816 @ 7/6 pr Day   Settled

Newbury

Began again the 1st of April @ 9/6
for Day

Settled

56

58

Settled

163½

148

October 24   For Esquire house

Settled

April 13
1816

Received of Esquire Farrar eighty Dollars
for Work on Doc Woods house from
the 22 January 1816 to the 1st of April
1816   80

June 29   Received of Do fifty Dollars   50
August 30 Received of Do thirty Dollars   30
Sep 25   Received of Do fifteen Dollars   15
October 2 Received of Do one hundred and thirty nine 139
                                                        314

January
7. 1817   Mr James Abbot Dr
           for nine square Sash   54
           Do 9 Squares of Glass   76
           Do For Glazing one Evening   33
                                            103

David Hidden, Ledger 1816–1817, ACCOUNT OF SAMUEL FARRAR. Andover Historical Society

In contrast to what occurred in the late nineteenth century and continued through the 1960s at Andover, the academy's leadership never developed a long-term relationship with an individual designer. A different architect designed each of Andover's five public buildings erected between 1809 and 1829. Most of those designers were and remain obscure, and two of the five were carpenter-builders, such as Rice and Hidden. Oliver Holden designed Foxcroft Hall (1808–09), Charles Bulfinch created Pearson Hall (1817–18), Asher Benjamin designed Bulfinch Hall (1818–19), William Chase designed Bartlet Hall (1820–21), and William Sparrell designed the Stone Academy (1828–30). Oliver Holden, who had business ties with Col. John Phillips, was a Charlestown carpenter, speculative builder, and sometime poet and writer of popular hymns. His role in building Foxcroft was akin to that of Rice and Hidden at Samaritan House and like them he took on odd jobs when he could.[14] William Sparrell of Boston was a housewright turned architect. He designed one off-campus dormitory for Harvard, and many brick rowhouses. How he came to the notice of the Andover trustees is unknown, but he was hired by Samuel Farrar to design the Stone Academy as well as the faculty residence, Double Brick, built just across Main Street at the same time.[15] William Chase was a Newburyport carpenter employed by William Bartlet to design and build the Andover Theological Seminary dormitory bearing Bartlet's name. Like Rice, Hidden, Marshall, and Holden, William Chase took on the occasional odd job for Squire Farrar.[16]

Bulfinch Hall, circa 1880

One can only guess why Charles Bulfinch, the leading New England architect of the day, designed but one building on the Andover campus. He was known to the trustees personally, professionally, and in his capacity as the leader of Boston municipal government. A Harvard graduate, Bulfinch designed two buildings for the Cambridge campus; at least five Phillips board members held office on the Harvard Corporation while these buildings were being planned and built; for a portion of this period, Eliphalet Pearson was Harvard's acting president. Andover's trustees turned to Bulfinch for their most important project, Pearson Hall, in 1817. Yet Bulfinch was disappointed the following year when the trustees only consulted with him about the new academy. Ironically, the building has been misattributed to Bulfinch so long it has carried his name since the 1930s.[17] While Asher Benjamin, another carpenter-turned-architect, was a great admirer of Charles Bulfinch, and occasionally worked with him, it was Benjamin who designed Bulfinch Hall. On May 5th, 1818 Samuel Farrar recorded in the academy's cashbook, "Pd. Mr. Asher Benjamin for Plan of Acad:—15." Although renowned for architectural publications, when Benjamin designed Andover's third academy building he was working primarily as a property manager and paint store operator. Here again there is no known connection between architect and client. Benjamin's task was restricted to designing the exterior; an on-campus committee determined the plan, and construction details were left to the masons and carpenters (Simeon Marshall, David Rice, and David Hidden). Asher Benjamin had no other role in shaping the Andover campus, yet the handsome structure to which he gave form should not be named for another architect.[18]

FARMSCAPE TO TOWNSCAPE

The campus came into being through the initiative of Samuel Phillips Jr., "master-spirit of the enterprise." In 1777 and early 1778 he purchased parcels of farmland totaling 141 acres straddling present-day Main Street, which comprise the heart of campus. Phillips intended to locate the academy several miles away, in present-day North Andover, but the property available at the preferred site was not large enough, and thus Andover Hill was chosen by default. This acreage was of mixed quality, improved as planting fields, pasture, and woodland. What made it suitable was accessibility. In the late eighteenth century, Salem Street, Phillips Street, and School Street were important thoroughfares and their intersection a node of some consequence. The fact that a training field for the local militia was sited here bears this out. A remote location would not do; it had to be accessible to day students, it had to be accessible from houses scattered around the neighborhood where out-of-town students boarded.[19] Having acquired a strategic site, ample land, and a dwelling for schoolmaster Pearson, the next task was providing a schoolhouse. Phillips moved a joiner's shop acquired with the land to the northwest corner of Main and Phillips Streets, fitting it up with belfry, benches, and stove. From the first, this cramped and rude facility was considered temporary. Little action was taken until 1784, however, when a committee was created, including Samuel Phillips Jr. and the senior Phillips brothers—Squire Samuel, Dr. John Phillips of Exeter, and William, a successful Boston merchant; their charge was to determine a site for a new academy and to build. They chose the northeast corner of Main and Salem Streets, the most visible point along the main road over Andover Hill, across Salem Street from the militia's training field. The lot belonged to Samuel Phillips Jr., who in 1782 had acted on the board's behalf as well as his own by purchasing the hilltop real estate. Phillips supervised construction of the handsome academy building, which was occupied in January 1786 just as Eliphalet Pearson departed for Harvard. The schoolhouse was paid for in equal shares by the three senior Phillips brothers, and title passed to the trustees six years later, in 1792.[20]

Samuel Phillips Jr. had also acquired the Blanchard property adjacent to the academy building, as well as the Asa Towne house, the Training Field, and, opposite these, the acreage on which he built his own residence (1782–85), later to become the Mansion House inn. Phillips was an improver. In the mid 1780s he planted elms in front of the Mansion House and around the new academy building. This was the beginning of the extensive use of elm plantings to provide visual structure and to ornament the campus. In the 1790s Phillips took in hand the crooked north-south "road to the meetinghouse"—which ran in front of the Academy, the Training Field, and his imposing house—and re-aligned it to run roughly parallel to (but a bit west of) the present Main Street. He built walls along either side, and rebuilt the walls down Phillips Street at the same time; the trustees partially paid for the work.[21]

President Washington, newly elected, passed this way in November 1789 during an official tour of the northeastern states. He was accompanied on this leg of his journey by Samuel Phillips Jr., then president of the Massachusetts State Senate. Andover Hill was well on its way to being transformed from a picturesque bit of rural farmscape into a place of real distinction. Washington described the setting as beautiful. In the same year Salem's Rev. William Bentley claimed the new Academy building impressive, noting that its site atop Andover Hill made the schoolhouse visible for miles around. The campus-shaping legacy of Samuel Phillips Jr. was summarized by a board colleague, Rev. Jedidiah Morse, in his *American Universal Geography* of 1793. The academy, he wrote, is "accommodated with a large and elegant building, erected at the expense of the founders. . . . It is situated on a delightful eminence, near the mansion house of the Honorable Samuel Phillips [Jr.], its distinguished patron. . . . [It] is encompassed with a salubrious air, and commands an extensive prospect. The lower story contains a large school room, and two other apartments for a library, and other purposes; the upper story consists of a spacious hall . . . designed for exhibitions and other public occasions."[22]

Eliphalet Pearson followed Phillips as president of the board in 1802, holding the post until 1821. In large measure, Andover's campus today reflects the major developments accomplished during Pearson's presidency. The first project was not an academy initiative: it was the Essex Turnpike, promoted by Col. Phillips. The turnpike was a business venture intended to facilitate travel between Boston and towns to the north in Essex County; shareholders hoped to recoup their investment from tolls. Begun in 1804 and opened in 1806, the turnpike is now Route 28—Main Street through Andover. While the road turned out to be a poor investment for its sponsors, it was a boon to Phillips Academy. The school was more accessible, stagecoach service ran to Andover Hill, and the road attracted further landscape development. Surveyed rifle-shot

Foxcroft, Pearson and Bartlet Halls, before 1875, frontispiece in Henry K. Rowe, HISTORY OF THE ANDOVER THEOLOGICAL SEMINARY (Newton, Massachusetts, 1833)

straight across the campus, it paralleled the "road to the meeting house" earlier straightened by Col. Phillips' father. The intervening strip of land, from the Moses Stuart House on the south to the future site of Double Brick on the north (a distance of 1,650 feet), was treated as a mall. Stone walls built by Samuel Phillips Jr. in the 1790s were moved. Street trees again became a preoccupation. In 1806 the trustees voted to have "the Committee of Exigencies cause the elm trees in all the avenues upon the land in the neighborhood of the Academy annually to be dug 'round at least two feet from the roots and for such as are dead to be replaced." Two years later in 1808 they voted that "superfluous trees in the Mall be removed and vacancies be supplied by the Committee of Exigencies." The mall and the old right-of-way on its west flank have been eliminated, but they survive in vestigial form in the wide breadth of Main Street as it bisects campus.[23]

Eliphalet Pearson returned to Andover in 1806 to bring the theological institution into being. To create this "great object," he engineered an accord with the Newburyport group, donors pledged support, and in June 1807 the trustees sought legislative approval to increase capitalization under the terms of Phillips Academy's charter. Col. Phillips lobbied on behalf of the board, and the petition was approved. At the end of August Col. Phillips and his mother signed an indenture binding them to construct buildings for the theological institution (the matter of location left to the trustees); their pledge was accepted in September. Eliphalet Pearson appointed a committee to confer with the Phillipses. Progress was slow and the board met on December 31, 1807 to deliberate again and reconstitute a committee to continue discussions. This time, Pearson chaired the committee. Exactly when agreement was reached is unknown, but construction started in 1808. The Foxcroft Hall site was on a ledge at the top of the wet, rocky academy pasture. The ridge was more than 500 feet east of Main Street, and about 12 feet above the level of the roadway. Considering Foxcroft's Main Street facade (so understated, and devoid of a central focal element) and the topography (which drops off sharply just to the north), one may deduce this "college" was conceived from the first as the northern-most structure in a row to be continued southward. In addition, the Seminary Common, in concept, became the basis for planning by 1808. The west side of the common, Faculty Row, probably was part of this initial plan as well, and it certainly was an element by 1811.[24]

Who produced the grand design for the Andover Theological Seminary campus—the expansive common beside the turnpike, the terraced row of public buildings on the east, Faculty Row on the west? For a century, historians have ascribed the overarching plan to Eliphalet Pearson; a nineteenth-century anecdote is attached to this attribution. Dr. Pearson's son Henry recalled that his father shinnied up a large oak tree east of the future Seminary Common and, perched there, proceeded to lay out the campus. Without doubt, Pearson had much to say about what was executed, and he could well have been author of the plan. What is lacking is the mark of a designer with substantial training, and much indicating that it was a communal effort. Were there specific models on which the Andover campus plan was based? Similarities to artist John Trumbull's 1792 design for Yale Row suggest it may have been a model, but if so it was not the only source. Two colleges were visited by members of Andover's campus planning committees during the period they were engaged in their work: Harvard and Brown. The basic planning unit for Harvard's campus was the quadrangle defined by closely spaced dormitories and academic buildings. That concept is not reflected at Andover. The visit to Brown late in 1807, although prompted by the desire to examine the all-purpose building housing the institution, may have provided inspiration for Andover's campus plan; here was an embryonic hilltop campus with its first building set on rising ground aside a large, fenced green, with later buildings added incrementally in a row along the green. But placing the main campus buildings on an elevated terrace was not to be seen at Yale, Harvard, or Brown. Similar examples are actually a bit later and much grander. There are no other early-nineteenth-century examples of a college common bordered on one side by dormitories and academic buildings, and on the other by a row of professors' houses. The Andover layout was unique, and related as much to town planning as it did to campus planning.[25]

Consideration for landscaping the common began in 1808, but action was slow and the grounds took years to complete. Dr. Timothy Dwight, a booster of the seminary, characterized the unimproved Seminary Common as "an open green." An unvarnished description was given by a new Andover Theological Seminary student in September 1810: "Arrived in Andover, and was landed off the stage upon the turnpike opposite Phillips Hall [Foxcroft], at a point where there was an opening in the wall to a foot path leading through a bush-pasture, clothed with wild shrubbery, up to the college. . . . I gathered up my luggage and followed the muddy pathway,

Elm Arch looking north, 1880s

striding over sloughs from stone to stone, neither few nor far between, and landed myself and baggage in Divinity College." Had this student matriculated a year later, he would have found the muddy track replaced by a plank walk, paid for by the seminary faculty, who were no doubt frustrated by the condition of the grounds and the trustees' inaction. The trustees were mindful of the need. At a board meeting on November 21, 1808, the trustees asked Dr. Pearson, Squire Farrar, Col. Phillips, and Rev. French to develop "a plan for leveling and laying out the grounds around the building." If they drew up a landscape plan, it was not executed. Perhaps the financial embarrassment in which Col. Phillips found himself curtailed this initiative. In August 1811 the trustees addressed the matter again, creating a new committee "to report a plan for laying out and improving in the best manner the lands in front of Phillips Hall." As both resolutions stated, the area under consideration was limited to the northern portion of the Seminary Common. Finally, in the summer of 1813, existing elms were cared for and seeding took place.

     The primary thrust to make this area presentable occurred in the summer of 1815, with grading, fertilizing, and planting of additional elms.[26] Major improvements came in 1817 and 1818, when Bartlet Chapel (Pearson Hall) was under construction. It was necessary to continue the terrace surrounding Foxcroft Hall, which turned out to be a considerable undertaking.

Samaritan House on Chapel Avenue, before 1929

William Bartlet, the building's contractor, used the term "levying" to describe the embankment created for the building in the summer of 1817 by a crew of 16 farmers hired by Samuel Farrar. At the same time Farrar employed a twenty-year-old academy student, Harvey Peet, to remove brush and trees and clean up the rest of the common, not cleared when only Foxcroft Hall was standing. Farrar removed the stone wall surrounding the common, replacing it with a painted, four-rail fence. The wall was new, but it was not in keeping with the changed use. It had to be replaced to define the former pasture as an ornamental public space. Farrar and Bartlet consulted on laying out the central walk from Main Street to Bartlet's chapel, agreeing it should be "level with the ground" and that a flight of stone steps would lead from the lawn up to the terrace occupied by the seminary buildings. In March 1820 work began on Bartlet Hall, which was completed in 1821. The layout of the common was largely fixed. The terrace begun in 1808, extended in 1817, was again extended southward by levying. Additional tree planting took place, and one final ornamental element was added in 1821 at William Bartlet's expense: a distinctive line of tall octagonal granite bollards, linked by double swags of wrought-iron chain, ringing the Seminary Row terrace.[27] Like the campus' overall plan, the common's early-nineteenth-century landscape design evolved over several years, the product of successive committees. There is a generic, anonymous quality to it: a great lawn surrounded and transected by elm-shaded walks intended as much for recreation as practicality. This is most true of Elm Arch, a promenade leading nowhere.[28]

Samuel Farrar—"the good, old, wrinkled, immemorial Squire"[29]—expanded and enhanced the institution he loved. He had a particular benevolent devotion to making schooling

George Kendall Warren, Stone Academy, 1857, salt print. Addison Gallery

on Andover Hill available to poor, "hopefully pious" young men. During the 1820s and 1830s, he pursued this objective continuously and creatively, and in doing so added facilities around the Seminary Common and beyond—almost none of which survive. During this time the board was presided over first by William Phillips, and following Phillips' death in 1827, by Samuel Hubbard. Both were in Boston busy with government, business, and the affairs of charitable institutions; they gave Farrar the freedom to lead Andover's board in new directions. As treasurer, Farrar assisted the well-intentioned but impecunious Samaritan Female Society, established in 1817 to care for sick students at the academy and seminary, particularly charity scholars. The group wanted a building, and in 1824 Farrar had Rice and Hidden build Samaritan House on Chapel Avenue, using his Prize Fund for mortgage capital. The English Academy & Teachers' Seminary, projected in 1827–28, was largely Farrar's creation. Funded with income from an unrestricted endowment bequest left by William Phillips, Farrar was the only individual to sit on all three committees that deliberated on what to do with the legacy, and he had personal charge of planning and erecting the Stone Academy.

Between 1829 and 1835 Farrar put in place an ingenious set of facilities designed to assist poor students attending Andover. Using his Prize Fund, he built no-frills dormitories and dining halls for students in the Classical Academy and the English Academy & Teachers' Seminary who could ill-afford the private boarding houses surrounding campus. Farrar did everything possible to make room and board fees as low as possible. To assist further, he operated a farm for each academy where students could work to earn their keep.[30] Annual promotional brochures for the English Academy and Teachers' Seminary described its facilities in detail:

Connected with this Institution is a convenient Boarding-House, and a farm under good cultivation, affording to such as may desire it an opportunity for manual labor as a means of preserving health and defraying, in part, the expenses of board. . . . All who board . . . are provided with neat and convenient rooms, duly furnished for study and lodgings. For the use of rooms and furniture, each occupant is charged one dollar a term. . . . To provide these rooms, six three-story buildings are erected near the Boarding-House, affording apartments sufficient for the accommodation of from seventy to one hundred students.[31]

BUILDINGS

A full account of the buildings on Andover's early-nineteenth-century campus lies beyond the scope of this essay. Two detailed survey maps dated 1836 and 1837 delineate more than 90 campus structures, including six academic buildings, eight buildings housing support facilities (including dining halls, the theological seminary's students workshop, and a model school operated in conjunction with the teachers' seminary), 12 dormitories, 24 dwellings (several rental properties), and a host of barns, shops, chaise houses, sheds, woodhouses, and miscellaneous structures. Among the 50 primary structures on campus in the late 1830s, about half of them survive; the trustees or William Bartlet erected 35 out of the 50. Of roughly 40 early-nineteenth-century outbuildings, four or five survive. Here it is possible to discuss only the key extant buildings: Hardy House, the houses of Faculty Row, Bulfinch Hall, and Seminary Row—Foxcroft, Bartlet, and Pearson Halls.[32]

Hardy House, begun in 1804, makes an appropriate starting point from an historical perspective, since it was the first structure erected by the trustees and marks the beginning of the building activities of Eliphalet Pearson, Col. John Phillips, and Samuel Farrar. Visually, emblematically, it invokes the institution's colonial heritage. It reads as an eighteenth-century building. Externally, in form and detail, gambrel-roofed, two-and-a-half-story Hardy House—with its tall end chimneys, tight proportions, 12-over-12 sash and pedimented central entrance—could as well date to 1754 as to 1804. Entirely a vernacular expression, it bespoke extraordinary conservatism in design and construction. The interior tells a more complicated story, very much the tale of Andover in transition—from an institution devoted to preparing pious youth for college to one centered on a graduate school training Puritan clerics. When planned by Pearson and his colleagues, Hardy House was not to be a house, but a Spartan dormitory for scholarship students in the academy. Originally grafted to a humble mid-eighteenth-century cottage, the tall, narrow proportions of Hardy House reflected that purpose. Its three floors each had two rooms opening off a plain, cramped, yet delightful Federal-style central stairhall. The six identical dormitory rooms had fireplaces and minimal trim. Treasurer Farrar paid Col. Phillips $1,600 to build Hardy House, plus $105.17 for "extra work ordered by the trustees." That was Hardy House as completed

Hardy House, circa 1860

in 1805, when Pearson (still a professor and acting president at Harvard) and his colleagues ruminated on establishing a theological seminary. By March 1806 all was at a fever pitch to move ahead. The trustees invited Pearson to return, to devote himself full-time to the seminary, and occupy the still empty dormitory rent-free. Pearson accepted. Puritan and Spartan are not synonymous, however, and a charity student dormitory was not fitting for the president of the board. Farrar fenced the yard and repainted the exterior. The old Asa Town cottage became a kitchen, fireplaces were dressed-up with crossetted overmantels, rooms repainted and papered. The Pearson family occupied Hardy House until 1810; through the years the theological seminary was planned, laid out, built, and opened. Visible from Main Street, across Training Field and the common, this up-sprouting bandbox of a building today recalls the school's colonial origins. It marks the start of the transformation of the campus during the first third of the nineteenth century, and stands as a sort of cherished parenthesis amid the quiet grandeur of Andover as recast in the first third of the twentieth century.[33]

Faculty Row, on the west side of Main Street facing the Seminary Common, although modified repeatedly, retains today the character established between 1809 and 1835. All the faculty houses built in that period exist—from north to south, Double Brick (1829–30), Park House (1833–34), Phelps House (1809–10), Pease House (1815–16), and Moses Stuart House (1810–11). So too does the Newman House (circa 1807), opposite Moses Stuart, which has functioned as a faculty residence since 1818. To achieve the ambitious goals set for the theological seminary, a distinguished faculty was a prerequisite. When Rev. Spring was courting Moses Stuart to join the faculty in the professorship sponsored by the Newburyport Associate Founders, Stuart's New Haven congregation protested: he could not be spared. "We do not want a man who can be spared," Spring responded. To attract outstanding faculty, good housing had to be provided. Jedidiah Morse corresponded with prospective professor Leonard Woods in 1807 on behalf of the seminary. Woods repeatedly brought up the question of housing: "If houses could be built by the trustees for the professors it would add to the beauty of the seminary, and to the convenience of the professors, and be an alluring circumstance to those who shall be appointed from time to time."[34]

Given the common purpose of the five early-nineteenth-century residences built for seminary faculty, they form a surprisingly heterogeneous row. The first built, Phelps House (1809–10), was imposing and stylish. Possibly designed by Anglo-American builder-architect Peter Banner, the elaborately finished Main Street elevation had a two-story central pavilion and single-story flanking wings.[35] It represented the sort of Federal style country house a wealthy Boston merchant might have built. By contrast, the second professor's house, Moses Stuart (1810–11), now much altered, was large but unpretentious, and eccentric in form. The house and main entrance faced east, gable-end to the street, with a highly visible service ell and barn. The third professor's

LEFT: **Phelps House, 1999, by Walter Smalling Jr.**; RIGHT: **Pease House, 1880–1890**

dwelling, Pease House (1815–16), built for Leonard Woods, was ample and formal yet plain. It was built as a square box of a dwelling—three stories, low hip roof, twin interior chimney stacks, five-bay front with an unassuming central entrance. The fourth and much later house, Double Brick (1829–30), was faced with pressed brick and a smooth-finished granite foundation, and marked with granite lintels and sills. The entrances were centered in the six-bay, three-story street elevation; the twin end gables carried up to form chimney stacks. This was the one faculty house for which the architect was known—William Sparrell. It is no wonder Double Brick resembled a pair of middle-class city rowhouses, for that was the bread-and-butter work of Sparrell's Boston-based practice. The last of the five professor's residences, Park House (1833–34), was also faced in pressed brick with a granite foundation, and trimmed with brownstone around windows and doors. The two-story, five-bay dwelling featured a central entrance and, although different in form, was as substantial and correct as Double Brick.

Given the fact that William Bartlet was patron of three of these buildings, and Samuel Farrar supervised construction of all five, one might expect them to be less diverse. Except in the case of Double Brick, however, each was built for a specific individual, and each professor was given considerable latitude to erect a house suiting his own requirements and preferences. In most cases, everyone was satisfied. Leonard Woods thanked the trustees for his Faculty Row residence, writing, "The neat simplicity of the style in which the work is done exactly corresponds with my wishes."[36]

William Bartlet's three Faculty Row dwellings lacked any unifying architectural elements. His views regarding the last, Park House, went unrecorded. He remarked of the second, erected for Moses Stuart, "This is exactly such a house as a professor ought to have." His assessment of his first

LEFT: **Double Brick House, circa 1890**   RIGHT: **Park House with Professor and Mrs. Park and Miss Agnes Park, circa 1885**

53

Andover building project, Phelps House, was the stuff of legend: Bartlet grew heart-sick, the story goes, as bills mounted; he insisted that treasurer Farrar take over as general contractor, pay the bills, and say no more. It is a wonderful tale, but largely apocryphal. Like all useful tales, it helps to explain the inexplicable, in this case how a hard-nosed Newburyport merchant came to build a spectacular modern house for a preacher he hardly knew. Phelps House was grand. It was no bigger than other theological seminary faculty residences, but it did possess a commanding presence engendered by the massing, the manipulation of scale, and the knowing use of fashionable detail.

Why such pomp? William Bartlet intended to install a brilliant Calvinist orator as the first Bartlet Professor of Pulpit Eloquence, and he was willing to go to great lengths to achieve this purpose, starting with the domicile of such a teacher. He chose Edward Dorr Griffin (1770–1837). A famed preacher, Griffin championed orthodoxy and the new missionary movement. Bartlet was captivated, but others were not.[37] Bartlet's own minister, Samuel Spring, leader of the Newburyport Associate Founders group, wrote to Rev. Jedidiah Morse:

> Alas! Alas! What a Mammoth of an orator have we. . . . If we do
> not confine the monster within the firm walls of the Institution,
> all will be up. . . . I can bear tolerably well to be equaled . . . but to
> be so astonishingly outdone![38]

By physical standards for average adults of the day, Griffin was mammoth. He stood six feet three inches tall and weighed 250 pounds. In a well-modulated voice Griffin preached hellfire and damnation. To Bartlet's chagrin, Griffin was not convinced he should join the Andover faculty, nor disposed to forsake the act of preaching in order to teach the art. Bartlet agreed to allow Griffin to spend much of his time preaching in Boston, and he offered a house, suggesting Griffin send a plan. The preacher was intrigued. After further negotiations and hand-ringing, Griffin finally arrived in May 1809. In July the trustees sold Bartlet a three-acre house lot and he quickly sent over a Newburyport crew led by the town's finest builder, Andrews Palmer. Bartlet promised Griffin the house would be complete within a year. On December 29, 1809, Bartlet wrote Dr. Griffin about the house, reviewed progress, and expressed thanks for the theologian's concern about the expense. Bartlet dismissed any thought of scaling back. The costs were indeed greater than anticipated, particularly for terracing the garden, but he reassured the professor, "I hope you don't think I have been reluctant. I have never complained to any person of the expense being beyond what I am cheerfully willing to defray." Despite Bartlet's generosity of spirit and purse, Edward Dorr Griffin never came to terms with his fellow faculty members, nor with living in quiet Andover. He resigned Bartlet's professorship after only two years, never having occupied the house built to his standards, which was intended to lure him and to keep him on Andover Hill.[39]

When the Phillips brothers' second academy building burned to the ground on the night of January 30, 1818, Eliphalet Pearson could not help but get involved in rebuilding. This had to be a fast-track job, it had to be done in a manner consistent with the scale and quality of the seminary. Pearson appointed himself chair of a three-man building committee that included treasurer

Farrar and schoolmaster John Adams. It would have been natural to build on the site of the destroyed second Academy, at the corner of Main and Salem Streets, but Pearson determined to devote the entire high road frontage, from Salem Street to Chapel Avenue, to the seminary common. Consequently, the new schoolhouse was placed at a good but considerably less prominent location south of Salem Street. Asher Benjamin was architect of the exterior only, and that is all that survives from the 1818 building. The two-story structure, originally 80 by 40 feet, had a large schoolroom and two smaller rooms on the ground floor, the latter variously used as classrooms, library, museum, and office. The hall above accommodated examinations, services, and graduation exercises—fixtures of the academic year. Pearson, Farrar, and Adams produced the plan in March. They based it on the 1785 Academy. For $15 Benjamin drew up the exterior design for their new schoolhouse. The Main Street elevation was seven bays wide, with a three-bay, pedimented central pavilion projected very slightly. The composition resembled Benjamin's Rhode Island Union Bank, Newport (1817), which shared a cognate Benjamin detail: a pediment fanlight with muntin bars resembling the lines scribing latitude and longitude on a globe. Atop the hipped roof rose a handsome, octagonal open belfry with a gilded weathervane. Because it was oriented to face Salem Street and the Seminary Common, Bulfinch Hall's north front has always been a major elevation, and the doorway there the primary entrance. Benjamin chose to dignify it by framing the north door with a rusticated granite architrave. It was beautifully executed as was all stonework and brickwork. Simeon Marshall was the mason in charge. Brought to Andover in 1817 by William Bartlet to build Bartlet chapel (Pearson Hall), Marshall was an outstanding craftsman, a known quantity, and available when it suddenly became necessary to erect a new academy. Withal, the decision was made to build in brick.[40]

In contrast to Phelps House, Asher Benjamin's Bulfinch Hall (1818) struck a comfortable balance between purpose and built form; suitability has never been an issue. Like Phelps House, Bulfinch Hall has long been admired.[41] Its misattribution to, and naming for Charles Bulfinch, manifest that regard. The fit between form and purpose went beyond a merely functional design. There was something synchronous, apt in the clarity and primness of Benjamin's third Academy, a sense that all that was needed was done, and no more. There was a seriousness that harkens back to the real teaching going on:

> The purpose of this Institution is declared to be the promotion of true piety and virtue.[42] It shall ever be considered, as the first and principal duty of the Schoolmaster, to regulate the tempers, to enlarge the minds and form the Morals of the Youth committed to his care.[43]

If Faculty Row gave to early nineteenth-century Andover a village-like aspect, Seminary Row (Foxcroft, Bartlet, and Pearson Halls) stamped it as campus. Changes to the buildings that occurred in the 1920s make it difficult today to assess the original visual impact of these structures: Pearson Hall was relocated; Foxcroft and Bartlet had their fourth stories removed; the Addison

August 18. 1818 —

50 Sundry Accounts D: to Cash —
61 New Academy —

Paid Benj: Jenkins for carting boards — Ap: 27. — 5.14
Paid Samuel Jenkins for carting boards — " " — 6.
Paid Benj: Jenkins for carting boards — May 5. 4.50
Paid Flagg & Gould for printing Circular Letters — 12.
Paid Asher Benjamin for Plan of Acad: — 15.
Paid Isaac Blunt for use of horse May 5. 2.0
Paid Joseph Chandler for carting boards May 8. 6.0
Paid Samuel Jenkins for carting boards " " 9.89
Paid Samuel Jenkins for carting boards May 9. 6.30
Paid W. E. & I. Hacker for boards — July 13. — 420.
Paid David Hidden for Carp: work " 22. 101.10
Paid James Butterfield for timber — " " " 274.43
Paid James Butterfield for sawing joist — 12.54
Paid Sher: Hunt for carting boards July 24. 12.60
Paid Sher: Hunt for carting boards " 28. 9.60
Paid Eben: Jones for carting stones " 29. 4.50
Paid Obadiah Horton for timber — " " 5.
Paid M: John Adams's bill of expenses — Aug: 42.0
Paid Isaac Chandler for laling stones " 8. 6.17
Paid John Goodhue for carting boards " 10. 22.24
Paid John Averill for boards Aug: 13 — 33.60
Paid Thomas Read for stones — Aug. 14. 38.50   1049 35

44
51 Salaries & Grants D: to John Adams
for his salary & grants to the end of
the current year. ————   1200

47
53 Sundry Accounts D: to Charity Scholars
His Honor William Phillips's Contribution
for the support of Charity Scholars. — 500.
59 Boston Female Ed: Soc: their Contrib:ⁿ } 154.43
for the same object ———   654 43

Sundry Accounts listing payment to Asher Benjamin "for Plan of Acad;" in JOURNAL ACCOUNT BOOK FOR PHILLIPS' ANDOVER ACADEMY, 1818

Gallery and Oliver Wendell Holmes Library were added as flankers, in advance of the old Seminary Row terrace. Nineteenth-century views suggested the three-building ensemble was reticent yet still impressive. Seminary Row was a tripartite set of buildings, an orchestrated sequence, its unity contrasting with the disparateness of Faculty Row across the common. Foxcroft Hall (1808–09) and Bartlet Hall (1820–21) still register as the pair they were. In massing, materials and detail, both reflect long-established norms for American college design. The line of descent is direct from buildings like Harvard's first Stoughton Hall (1697), Yale's Connecticut Hall (1750), Princeton's Nassau Hall (1764), Brown's University Hall (1770), continuing through Peter Banner's Berkeley Hall (1802) at Yale and Bulfinch's second Stoughton Hall at Harvard (1804): sober, sturdy, four-story, rectangular brick buildings with hip roofs, massive chimney stacks, multiple entrances, regular fenestration, and minimal ornamentation. In contrast to most earlier examples, however, neither of the two "colleges" at Andover had a central cross gable accenting the primary elevations—the better to focus attention on what was the central element in Seminary Row, Pearson Hall. Seminary Row's layout evolved as Eliphalet Pearson and his colleagues worked with Col. John Phillips on plans for the original seminary buildings during the closing months of 1807 and the opening months of 1808. Initially Col. Phillips and his mother pledged to build a three-story dormitory accommodating fifty students and a second, two-story building to house the chapel, library, dining hall, kitchen, and steward's quarters; the program implied that both were to be brick. The trustees accepted the Phillipses' offer and Pearson appointed a committee he chaired "to confer with them upon the plan of the same." On December 21, 1807, Pearson reported to Jedidiah Morse that Col. Phillips and his builder-architect, Oliver Holden, were about to go to Providence to inspect the building (today called University Hall) that then housed all of Brown's required facilities. It was to be the model from which "we shall attempt to draw a plan of a building to be presented to the trustees." The board met on December 31; the plan was discussed at length, but not accepted. A final plan was agreed to early in 1808, and construction was completed in 1809. That September the board voted to release Col. Phillips and Mrs. Phillips from their 1807 indenture and accept the project as built: "[On] land belonging to Phillips Academy, a brick building 90 feet long, 40 feet wide, & four stories high . . . containing, besides a Chapel & an apartment for a Library, 29 lodging rooms . . . [also] a wooden building, near the aforesaid brick building, calculated & intended for the accommodation of a Steward & his family, containing, in addition to a hall 40 feet by 20, a kitchen and five chambers, together with a barn 40 by 25, and a contiguous woodhouse 50 by 18, [all] gratuitously erected by himself and his mother."[44]

The very first seminary faculty annual report, submitted in September 1810, asserted that Foxcroft Hall, only one year in service, was inadequate and too small. Classes were being held in dormitory rooms and faculty houses, the chapel was cramped, and the nascent library had little space for expansion. The professors urged the trustees to erect a building that housed a proper chapel and an adequate library and lecture rooms. Subsequent reports continued this theme and flagged additional needs—providing heat in the dining hall; building a workshop, "where some cleanly mechanical business" might be performed by seminary students for exercise during inclement weather; and, as enrollment rose, building a second dormitory. Pearson Hall provided the required chapel, library and lecture space; Bartlet Hall ("South College") became the second dormitory.[45]

When completed in 1818, Bulfinch's Pearson Hall became the focus of campus, functionally and visually—the centerpiece of Seminary Row. The board and the Newburyport-based Associate Founders all realized such a facility was required, but it took William Bartlet to bring it into being. He initially offered a gift of $5,000 to start a building fund, but no other donors stepped up, and he quickly determined to proceed, writing to the trustees February 10, 1817 with his offer to build a chapel "three stories high, which stories shall be such as to bring it to proper height for symmetry with the Colleges; to be placed so as to project in front sufficiently to break the line of uniform appearance and preserve symmetry; making . . . a room for public worship . . . with a gallery, . . . a library room over it . . . and three public lecture-rooms, etc., etc."[46] The board accepted Bartlet's proposal four days after he submitted it. And there was no discussion of siting: it would stand south of Foxcroft Hall and north of the planned, but as yet unbuilt "South College." No building committee was needed. Bartlet set to work immediately, in partnership with Samuel Farrar, the two in almost daily communication. The earliest surviving correspondence, from Bartlet to Farrar, is dated February 26th, 1817:

> I notice you wish to employ Messrs. Rice & Hidden about the carpenter work for the new Chapel. . . . I think them well acquainted with the business & will answer the purpose. There is a number in this town [Newburyport] that would be glad to join them, & good workmen [too], but they will not be wanted yet. I should like to see the plan of the building when it can be made convenient. I think you would do well to know [for what price] you can have the timber hauled to the spot from the woods 'round Andover, & if not, to be had as cheap as it can from up the [Merrimack] River. . . . I have seen Mr. Simeon M. Marshall who is a Mason & is recommended as a suitable man to undertake the oversight of laying the Bricks, who will undertake [the work] for himself & Boy at $3.25 per day. . . . I should like not to have a drop of spirituous liquor drunk within the [building] or one hundred feet from it. It is a foolish practice of drinking liquor and it is much better to let it alone. As to the Bricks, I wish to have those of the best kind. If such can be had at Andover, that will be best. I wish to know whether they can or not. . . . I wish you to write me every mail if you have anything to communicate. I will endeavor to meet your wishes.[47]

Farrar journeyed "to Boston to see Mr. Bulfinch" two days later, on February 28th. The building program outlined in Bartlet's original letter to the trustees did not change, but the size was altered (it was built 94 feet by 40 feet) and the exterior (at that point not designed) did not break forward in the center. Rather, the nine-bay front was essentially flat, with only the most subtle projection of the third and seventh bays, creating a five-part elevation. The cornice line was equal to that of Foxcroft Hall (and later Bartlet Hall), but the unusual fenestration resulted from the complexities of creating a symmetrical facade for a building that incorporated three floors on one end and two floors in the rest of the building. To give the building greater presence, Bulfinch designed a paneled balustrade rising from the cornice over the central five bays of the west (Main Street) front. In the center of the balustrade was a large clock; above it rose a tall, domed octagonal belfry. The design represented a scaled-down version of Bulfinch's University Hall at Harvard (1813).[48]

By March 6, 1817, Bartlet was writing Farrar to find out what size timbers Bulfinch planned to specify. Where will the timber be had? Do not worry about procuring shingles, wrote Bartlet, I intend to slate the building: "The man I propose to slate it . . . has done my House and store & they are very tight & handsomely done." Bartlet went on to discuss brick, and the possibility of using brick produced at Andover's Poor Farm: "Mr. Marshall confirms my opinion that the clay at Andover is not fit to make the Bricks for the outside [of the building]. I will get them . . . here." On March 10th Bartlet received Bulfinch's first drawings: "I see nothing extravagant in [the design] & believe it will not be considered so by people of moderate taste." Bartlet returned the drawings to Farrar within the week, so they could be completed. He wondered to Farrar if perhaps freestone (brownstone) might be substituted for marble for the window sills, springing blocks, keystones and belt course, save on the Main Street front. This was a subject Bartlet returned to several times, deciding by the end of March that all the ornamental stonework would be freestone, painted white to resemble marble. In April Bartlet asked Farrar to thank the seminary students who volunteered to dig the cellar. In May Bartlet reported to Farrar that Charles Bulfinch planned to visit the building site when they were ready to begin framing the floors. In June he told Farrar about the number of brick posts he wanted in the cellar to support the first floor; about cutting glass for the sash; about the "levying" around the building. By September he and Farrar corresponded about landscaping, and in November, Bartlet returned to the subject of painting the freestone trim. It was fabricated in Newburyport, Bartlet had gone to see it, and Bartlet liked it as it was: "The caps & stools were made very handsome, the door pillars [too]. A great deal of pain was taken to have them look well. I at present don't think paint would add to their appearance." The stonework was beautifully executed, but the brown of the freestone was so close to the brick's tone the trim had no impact from a distance. Bulfinch's contrasting accents would have made the building appear much better from the highway, across the seminary common. But Bartlet won out. The freestone trim has never been painted, and when Bartlet Hall was built, its trim was free stone too.[49]

Eliphalet Pearson took it upon himself to select the chapel bell. He wrote to the Revere foundry, stating that he would shortly come to listen to the bells they had for sale: "Our new Bell [should] be strong & musical, such as will gratify the nicest ear, and compose the most delicate nerves, in a word, such as will harmonize the soul, and prepare it for the exercises of devotion."

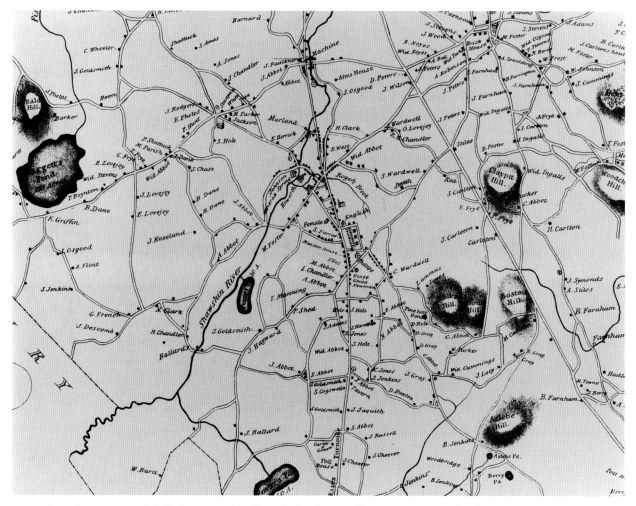

Moses Dorman Jr., detail of A Plan of Andover Taken for the Town, 1830, reproduction from map in collection of Andover Historical Society

The theological seminary chapel was dedicated September 18, 1818. It cost Bartlet $23,374. Rev. Ebenezer Porter (successor to Griffin as Bartlet Professor) preached the dedicatory sermon. William Bartlet insisted that he not be mentioned by name: "Is it then the hand of enchantment that spreads this scene before us? It is the hand of God, operating through honored instruments, who ascribe, and require us to ascribe, all the glory to Him." William Bartlet wrote to the trustees: "Responding to your appeal, it is done. The Foundation was laid, the walls built, its covering put on, the ceilings & apartments finished, the furniture put in place, & it is now offered for your acceptance." The trustees accepted Bartlet's "elegant and capacious" new building with thanks, and informed him they planned to name it in his honor. They also requested that he sit for his portrait. Bartlet declined.[50]

The trustees addressed the need for a second dormitory incrementally with temporary measures, awaiting the day another college would be built. It was necessary to let "theologues" board in private houses. The faculty objected, insisting this hurt the "habits and attendance" of the student body as a whole.[51] It was inevitable that Farrar would go to William Bartlet again. He requested his assistance in December 1819. Bartlet responded:

> I received your friendly letter. . . . Oh, how wonderful! Providence is trying us by prospering us beyond what we could have any prospect of when we first thought of the undertaking; and are we suitably thankful and humble? I cannot say but I have had thoughts of making another attempt to make things more convenient; but I have had thoughts that hinder me. What will the world say?[52]

Bartlet's concerns were soon allayed, and he petitioned the board in March to allow him to erect a new dormitory. The board accepted; Bartlet, again with Farrar's assistance, began to build. His carpenter-architect William Chase and master mason Simeon Marshall followed the massing of Foxcroft, but chose details more eighteenth-century in character than did the earlier dormitory. Bartlet equipped his college well, installing fancy painted furniture, hearth brushes, and hat racks. In turn, he insisted that students living in the new college's fifty rooms be responsible for care of the building and its contents. He had Farrar number all the dormitory rooms, and all the furniture in the rooms, to make it easy to assess damages. Bartlet specified that the school inspect the building each term, to ensure continued good repair. Bartlet Hall was dedicated in September 1821. Students were delighted, and faculty hailed the "elegant building . . . amply furnished throughout. . . . [The] plan and workmanship reflect the most refined taste." The trustees accepted Bartlet's "great donation" with enthusiasm, voted to name the building Bartlet Hall, and again asked him to sit for his portrait. Again Bartlet declined.[53]

David Chase

Liberal Advantages:

THE FOUNDING OF ABBOT ACADEMY

It is the design of this institution to afford the most liberal
advantages for the solid education of females.
~ ABBOT ACADEMY CIRCULAR, MARCH 13, 1829[1]

IN 1829 ABBOT FEMALE ACADEMY joined the extensive hilltop campus developed in the late eighteenth and early nineteenth centuries by the trustees of Phillips Academy for the education of men and boys. For 144 years Abbot and Phillips stood side-by-side; they have been united since 1973. In contrast to Phillips Academy, Abbot began on a single acre of ground, but in a beautiful and imposing building, Abbot Hall.

Although a half century separates the founding of the two schools, a sentimental tale links the inception of these institutions. As told by Samuel Farrar in 1854, when Samuel Phillips Jr. determined to found Phillips Academy, his wife, Phebe Foxcroft Phillips, was not happy about removing to the country and living in the old George Abbot house on Andover Hill. Her husband promised that if she would assist in creating the new academy for boys, he would one day join with her in founding an academy for girls. Both died before the girls' school came into being, but Squire Farrar, who was devoted to Mrs. Phillips, played a pivotal role in creating Abbot Academy. Edwards Amasa Park, professor at Andover Theological Seminary and Abbot Academy trustee, recalled in his address at the Abbot Academy graduation ceremony in 1878, that although Farrar was "constitutionally free from romance," he had been electrified by Madame Phillips, and was the "conducting wire" from her to Abbot Academy.[2]

The late 1820s were a period of social and political ferment. In 1828 Andrew Jackson was elected president, and even conservative Andover was experiencing broadened interest in innovation, especially in education. Locally, Squire Farrar and others were laying plans for Andover's English Academy and Teachers' Seminary. In the field of women's education, 1828 was the year in which two nationally significant women's seminaries opened, Catharine Beecher's in Hartford, Connecticut, and Zilpah Grant's in Ipswich, Massachusetts, twenty miles from Andover. In keeping with the democratization that characterized the period, Abbot Academy was launched not as

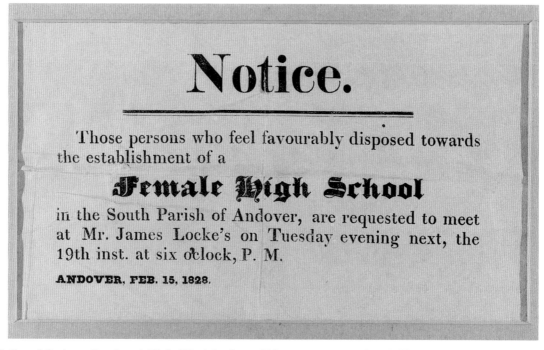

Notice of first meeting to establish Abbot Academy, February 15, 1828, handbill

the public act of a private family, but as a community initiative. Just who began the effort to create this academy for girls in Andover is unknown. But we do know that several professors and schoolmasters on Andover Hill had daughters and wives who believed in formal education for all children. Local mill owners and entrepreneurs wanted the same. These citizens looked to the schools to sustain traditional New England values in the face of change.

In February 1828 handbills appeared all over town announcing an open meeting to discuss the merits of creating "a FEMALE HIGH SCHOOL in the South Parish of Andover." South Parish Deacon Mark Newman, formerly the principal of Phillips Academy and at the time a bookseller, moderated the meeting. Response to the proposal was favorable and an organizing committee was formed—all community leaders, all men. It met March 4th, and chose three members, the Rev. Milton Badger of Andover's South Parish, the Rev. Samuel Jackson of the West Parish, and Squire Farrar to draw up a constitution. The committee also determined to erect a two-story brick schoolhouse on Main Street. Meeting ten days later, the organizing committee selected Mark Newman to be president pro tempore, and designated Newman and local lawyer and businessman Hobart Clark as its building committee. The organizing committee next met four months later, on July 4, 1828; it approved the constitution drafted by Farrar and the Reverends Jackson and Badger, and approved the plans presented by Newman and Clark for the schoolhouse on Main Street.

Soon mothers of prospective students let it be known they did not approve of the site selected. They did not want their daughters walking up and down Main Street, for "Theologues and Academy boys" frequented it. Mrs. John Adams and Mrs. Moses Stuart circulated a petition of protest, which they presented to the organizing committee. This setback, and fund-raising difficulties, caused the committee to meet July 24 and vote "That it is not expedient to erect a building for a Female Academy on our present plan, with our present means." But Samuel Farrar and Mark Newman would not let the matter rest there. Newman called his committee back for a second session later in the day. Farrar announced that a client whose financial affairs he managed, Madame Sarah Abbot (widow of Phillips Academy's first treasurer, Nehemiah Abbot), offered a gift by bequest of $1,000, contingent on the committee locating the proposed girls school off Main Street. Mark Newman offered to donate a one-acre parcel on School Street (the old "road to the meeting house") as the schoolhouse lot. Both offers were accepted. The organizing committee applied for an act of incorporation on behalf of "Abbot Academy" to honor Sarah Abbot.[3]

The organizing committee closed out the fateful second July 24 meeting with a vote to move ahead with the building plans previously approved, modifying them as required by the circumstances of the new School Street site. The architect of Abbot Hall is unknown, as are details about suppliers or the masons. But David Hidden and a new partner, William Saunders of Cambridge (a seasoned and skilled mechanic), had charge of carpentry work, and that portion of the project is well documented through Hidden's ledger. The carpenters arrived on site August 29, 1828, and worked on Abbot Hall more or less continuously through spring, until April 3, 1829. Additional work was ordered by the Abbot trustees in August 1829 when they decided to create a chemistry laboratory in the basement of Abbot Hall; special projects executed by Saunders & Hidden continued into September of that year.

Abbot Hall as originally built was a two-story, hip-roofed brick structure, 70 by 40 feet, with four end-wall chimneys. A pedimented portico carried on four giant Ionic columns dominated the facade. Pediment and columns projected from the plane of the facade, but the volume of the two-story portico was recessed into the mass of the building. Large, tripartite windows with granite lintels flanked the portico on each floor. In an attempt to create a dignified approach and break from the residential streetscape, the building was set back perhaps 100 feet on its terraced site. Imposing and public, almost official in character, everything about the original Abbot Hall design reflects its origins—that it was designed not to be hidden away on School Street. Conceived for the original Main Street site, the building proclaims with dignity and conviction that educating girls was valued in this community.[4]

More than monumentality distinguishes Abbot Hall from the buildings erected just up the hill by the Phillips Academy trustees for the Classical Academy, Andover Theological Seminary, and the English Academy and Teachers' Seminary. The most telling comparison is between Abbot Hall and the so-called Stone Academy, home to the English Academy and Teachers Seminary, begun in 1829, before Abbot Hall was completed. Stone Academy and Abbot Hall were almost the same size and had the same general massing. Both were imposing masonry structures with slate hip roofs and four end-wall chimneys. Many of the same craftsmen worked on both buildings. And both were handsome. There the similarities end. The Stone Academy represented a late and essentially vernacular expression of the Federal style, made imposing in

William Sparrell's design by the building's scale, simplicity, bold detail, and muscular stonework. Sparrell's design was very much of its moment, while the Abbot Hall design was curiously more traditional and yet more advanced, reflecting both the Palladian tastes of past generations and the new interest in correctly copying ancient architectural forms that produced the Greek Revival style of the 1830s and 1840s. The facade of Abbot Hall derived from the tripartite, Ionic-porticoed designs that Andrea Palladio developed for Italian country villas in the late sixteenth century, designs which became the *sine qua non* of advanced architectural aesthetics in England and the British colonies in the eighteenth century. The Ionic order of Abbot's portico is that preferred by Palladio, yet the extraordinary care William Saunders took to execute the columns, capitals, and bases correctly, spending three-and-a-half weeks on the work in his shop beside the Charles River in Cambridge, suggests the Greek Revival. So too do details like the Greek key fretwork ornamenting the portico soffit.[5]

There is about Abbot Hall a degree of design sophistication that is unique in Andover during this era. It may be in large part the product of Abbot Academy's educational mandate of Abbot Academy. The Abbot charter approved on July 4, 1828, set forth the purposes of the new institution:

> The primary objects to be aimed at in this School shall ever be to regulate the tempers, to improve the taste, to discipline and enlarge the minds, and form the morals of the youth who may be members of it.[6]

"To improve the taste"—an object foreign to Phillips Academy, or any boys' school in this era. This would have been one of the "liberal advantages for the solid and complete education of females" advertised in the prospectus issued by the Abbot Academy trustees in March 1829. That promotional piece went on to state that the school would be under the direction "of a gentleman," Charles Goddard, whose "character, education, manners and experience" would inspire confidence in all. Goddard was a man of refinement, who among other subjects taught drawing—using drawing boards and stools built for the purpose by Saunders and Hidden. Abbot was not a finishing school. Goddard and his colleagues taught a comprehensive program, including ancient and modern languages, English, history, geography, mathematics, even chemistry. Yet, in this academy for girls, refinement of taste had its place too, and Abbot Hall reflected that.[7]

McCormick, Banjo Club, circa 1886

Roger G. Reed

The Lost Victorian Campus: 1838–1908

ACADEMY HILL RETAINS LITTLE EVIDENCE of the radical changes in architectural style that took place in America in the nineteenth century. At the height of the early Victorian era, from 1840 to 1865, no new construction occurred at Phillips Academy or the Andover Theological Seminary. The picturesque and romantic Gothic and Italianate styles are almost entirely absent. A flurry of activity in the decade following 1865 produced three fine late Victorian Ruskinian Gothic buildings, all of which were demolished in the twentieth century.

The Greek Revival style, exceptionally popular in New England during the second quarter of the nineteenth century, appeared only on the Abbot Academy campus. In 1829 just before the Phillips Academy trustees built the boxy Stone Academy to house the Teachers' Seminary on the corner of Main and Chapel streets, Abbot's founders were erecting their fashionable Greek Revival academy building along School Street. It was one of the earliest Greek Revival public buildings in Andover, and it far surpassed the architectural conservatism of Phillips Academy and Andover Theological Seminary. Twenty-five years later Abbot again architecturally led her brother institutions with the erection of Smith Hall, designed by Boston architect John Stevens in the Italianate style. Although not architecturally ornate, it demonstrated a willingness on the part of the Abbot trustees to enlarge the school and respond to new architectural fashions. Its construction provided a dramatic contrast to the vernacular English and Latin Commons, which housed Phillips Academy students.[1]

At Andover Theological Seminary in the 1850s, the new architectural fashions were expressed only in a few domestic buildings. Professor Calvin Stowe was appointed to the faculty in 1854, and Harriet Beecher Stowe, his wife, supervised a major renovation to the old stone house on Bartlet Street for their residence. Erected in 1828 as a workshop for the exercise of seminary students, the original building was characteristic of the austere architecture built under the supervision of Samuel Farrar. Mrs. Stowe added a polygonal porch and wooden blinds in a picturesque manner made fashionable by the books of Andrew Jackson Downing.[2]

Academy Hall, 1872

TOP: **Smith Hall, April 9, 1865, inscribed "The Day Richmond Surrendered"**   BOTTOM: **Stowe House, before 1929**   RIGHT: **Stone Academy, after fire of December 21, 1864**

ACADEMY HALL

    A single catastrophic event propelled the Phillips Academy trustees into the new age of Victorian architecture. On December 21, 1864, the Stone Academy, then being used by the academy's English department, was gutted by fire.[3] When the trustees decided to replace the building, they chose a site across Main Street at the juncture of School Street, evidently concluding that efforts should be made to establish a campus for Phillips Academy distinct from the seminary. In fact, during the remainder of the nineteenth century the trustees would focus their efforts at creating a new campus on the west side of Main Street, an effort that only ended in 1922, many years after the seminary's 1908 move to Cambridge, Massachusetts.

    With the burning of the Stone Academy, concerned Phillips Academy alumni gathered forces to aid the school in fundraising and rebuilding. The trustees, giving hearty approval to the alumni effort, appointed a building committee and authorized it to solicit plans. On June 5, 1865, the committee, consisting of Alpheus Hardy, president of the board of trustees, John Lord Taylor, treasurer, and Samuel H. Taylor, headmaster, approved the plans and authorized construction of a building to the design of Charles A. Cummings.[4]

    No information has come to light indicating how Cummings was selected, or if the designs of any other architect had been considered. It is likely that the decision was made by Taylor, reputedly an autocratic headmaster. Cummings had only been in practice for about seven years, and little is known about his early career. Indeed, Academy Hall is his earliest identified commission. Born

Baseball Field with English Commons and Academy Hall, before 1882

in Boston in 1833, he received technical training at the Rensselaer Polytechnic Institute in Troy, New York, where he graduated in 1853. He then received practical training in the office of Boston architect Gridley J. F. Bryant, followed by travel in Europe and Egypt. It may have been during his travels abroad that he acquired a taste for Venetian Gothic architecture, advocated by English art critic John Ruskin. He designed the three Andover buildings, as well as his best known work in Boston, in this style.[5] Samuel Taylor and the trustees may have known Cummings through his writings; he published articles in various periodicals, including the *Christian Examiner*.[6]

Academy Hall was dedicated on February 9, 1866. It had cost $49,000, of which $21,000 had been raised by alumni and other supporters. The four-story building featured an "exhibition hall" for recitation on the top floor.[7] No greater contrast with the old Stone Academy could have been provided than the design of the new building. Its dimensions, 50 feet by 90 feet, were not particularly large but the exterior had a pronounced verticality. In addition to the use of Gothic lancet-arched windows and doors, there was a mansard roof capped by a steeply pitched hip and an imposing entrance pavilion. This pavilion featured flanking staircases, a gable roof, and bellcote that suggested the appearance of a chapel wing projecting from the center of the building.[8]

Academy Hall was set back from School Street against a large open yard that accentuated the building's prominence as the centerpiece of the campus. Directly behind Academy Hall on

Academy Hill, 1875. Map by Jane Garvie

either side of a large open field were the two rows of wooden dormitories—the English Commons on the north and the Latin Commons on the south. Before Academy Hall was completed, the trustees voted in November 1865 to grade this field for athletic use. The location of the new building, and subsequent actions taken over the next two decades, confirm that it was the intention of the trustees that Phillips Academy would emerge from the shadow of the Andover Theological Seminary at a location opposite that school.

BRECHIN HALL

As the construction of the academy proceeded, the seminary also engaged in new building. The Reverend John L. Taylor served on the building committee for both Academy Hall and the seminary—perhaps the reason Charles Cummings was selected as the seminary's architect. John Smith, Peter Smith, and John Dove, local Andover mill owners from Brechin, Scotland funded Brechin Hall in large part. Constructed as a library for the seminary, the large, open second floor contained the traditional arrangement in which open alcoves for books surrounded the reading room. On the ground floor were rooms devoted to exhibit space, including a Missionary Museum and a model of Jerusalem.

Brechin Hall, circa 1865

Brechin Hall Library, circa 1865

Accounts of the dedication on August 2, 1866, tell that Brechin Hall was built of locally quarried stone with trim of brick and Gloucester granite.[9] The roofs were embellished with a polychromatic slate laid in horizontal bands. Cummings designed a rectangular structure with an entrance tower in the center of the long facade. The proportions of this building accentuated the vertical features of the Venetian Gothic style in a manner more pronounced than Academy Hall. Brechin Hall was only 70 feet long and 43 feet deep, 20 feet shorter than the Phillips Academy building. A steeply pitched hip roof topped the central 93-foot entrance tower, while the roof over the library formed a steep-pitched gable. In addition, each corner of the building had small buttressed towers with conical roofs. The narrow vertical proportions of Brechin Hall suggest that the patron or the architect planned it with the intention of future additions. Indeed, an elevation by Cummings & Sears dated June 1881 illustrating proposed additions for Brechin Hall has been recently uncovered in the academy archives. This proposal, a rare surviving drawing by the firm, called for a small two-story wing linked at the second floor by an enclosed bridge. It was part of the appeal of Gothic architecture in the nineteenth century that it could be designed so that it appeared to have been built across several generations. Brechin Hall lent itself to future additions and conveyed the appearance of a venerable institution.

Cummings & Sears, Sketch of proposed Additions to the Library of the Phillips Academy, Andover, June 18, 1881, ink

Sited well away from Seminary Row near the intersection of Main and Salem Streets, Brechin Hall faced north toward the open lawn. The proposal for future additions offers logical explanation for the building's relatively isolated location. Although the streets and paths that defined the Andover Theological Seminary campus did not conform to a rigid symmetry, the placement of Brechin Hall provided a strong axial relationship with Samaritan House on Chapel Street.

The Venetian Gothic design for the two buildings at Andover in 1865-66 was atypical for the Boston area. Gothic architecture for college buildings had been advocated since the early nineteenth century, but this polychromatic style remained uncommon in New England. Ware & Van Brunt's Gothic masterpiece, Memorial Hall at Harvard, dated from 1866. Outside of New England a major collegiate work was Lehigh University in Bethlehem, Pennsylvania, by New

York architect Edward Tuckerman Potter. Potter's 1865 design was the same year as Academy Hall. In the Boston area a major example of Venetian Gothic collegiate architecture first appeared in 1874, when Wellesley College built College Hall, designed by Hammatt Billings. Charles Cummings' two Victorian Gothic buildings at Andover were important early examples of the style, and demonstrate the trustees had turned away from the conservative building tradition established by Square Farrar.[10]

With two buildings to his credit, Andover's trustees turned to Cummings again in renovating two existing buildings. The third academy building, alternately known as Old Brick or the Brick Academy (now Bulfinch Hall), had been built in 1818–19 for classrooms. With the construction of the Academy Hall, the trustees decided to convert Bulfinch into a gymnasium. Cummings' analysis determined that the first story would not accommodate the use; writing to Alpheus Hardy, he suggested, "by taking out the ceiling of the second story and getting the benefit of the height between the roof-trusses, I think we should do very well."[11] These alterations were made and the building served as a gymnasium until fire gutted it in 1896.

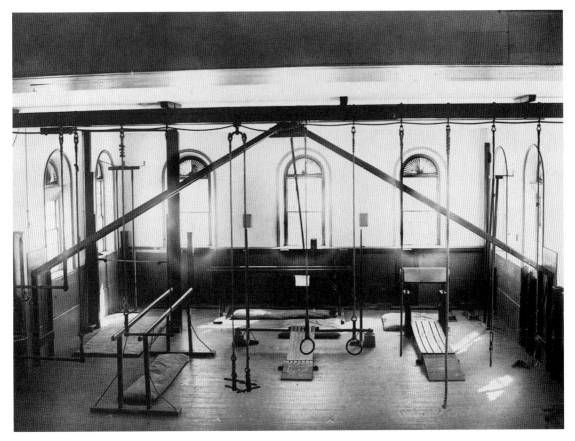

Bulfinch Hall as gymnasium, circa 1865

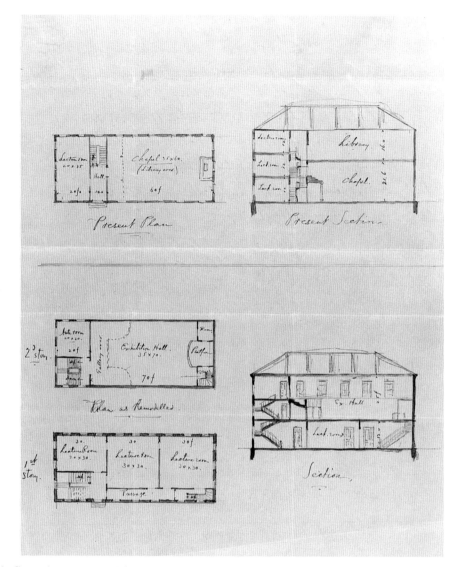

Charles A. Cummings, proposal for renovation of Pearson Hall, January 31, 1865, sketch in letter to Alpheus Hardy

The second building the trustees proposed to renovate was the seminary's Pearson Hall, which had served as both the school's chapel and library. With the library scheduled to move to Brechin Hall and a new chapel being discussed, alternate uses needed to be found for the 1817–18 building by Charles Bulfinch. Cummings supplemented his report with sketches of existing room layouts and proposed changes—an extensive reworking of the interior that changed the height of the second floor, replaced the first-floor chapel with three lecture rooms, and substituted an exhibition hall for the second-floor library.[12] Cummings' plan was not implemented.

ABBOT ACADEMY

In the early 1870s Abbot Academy's two most active trustees, Warren F. Draper and George F. Smith, began efforts to improve the landscaping of the girls' school campus. They added new walks, built stone walls and fences, and planted ornamental trees. When Smith Hall had been built in 1854, the total grounds of Abbot consisted of only one rugged acre. From the 1850s onward, the school had slowly increased its land holdings and in 1870 the trustees could claim that "a stretch of poor, stony pasture-land had been converted into a broad, soft lawn."[13] In 1877 the trustees acquired an additional 14 acres of the Abbot estate on Phillips Street, to bring the total grounds to 22 acres.[14] A year later in 1878 the trustees hired civil engineer Charles W. Gay, of Lynn, Massachusetts to coordinate improvements and prepare a landscape plan. Gay based his scheme on the existing structures, rather than introducing a new master plan for the campus. He added formal drives and paths to connect the buildings. Behind Abbot Hall, Gay reserved a tree-lined semi-circle, the forebear of the present Abbot Circle. Smith Hall, on the site of the present Draper Hall, faced this open space, as did the rear of Abbot Hall with its 1842 verandah. Gay plotted the "Maple Walk" and envisioned it continuing all the way to the intersection of Phillips and Abbot Streets, with a series of curvilinear trails in the woods. A pavilion, or gazebo, was also planned for the western edge of the woods on a high point of the terrain.[15] In 1879, the academy added the stone wall along Abbot Street.

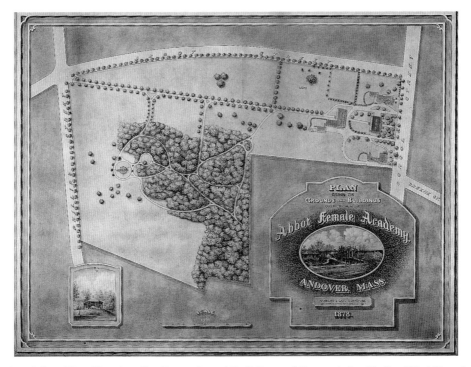

Hammond and Gay, Plan Showing the Grounds and Buildings of Connected with the Abbot Female Academy, Andover, Mass., 1878, ink

Stone Chapel, circa 1876

Stone Chapel interior, circa 1876

ANDOVER THEOLOGICAL SEMINARY

Back up the hill, further building was in progress. The trustees again hired Cummings, this time to design a chapel for the Andover Theological Seminary. Cummings had formed a partnership in 1867 with Willard T. Sears, an architect he had met in Gridley Bryant's office. In Boston's post-Civil War building boom the new firm rose to become one of the leading architects in New England, particularly noted for their work in the High Victorian Gothic style—churches and commercial structures, such as the Macullar-Parker Building, the Mason & Hamlin Building, and the Montgomery Building.[16]

The seminary chapel was coincident with the firm's work on Boston's Old South Church. Money for the Andover building was being raised as early as 1873, and work began in the summer of 1875.[17] The building was dedicated on October 6, 1876. Whether due to the influence of Willard Sears, or simply the maturity that comes with greater experience, the design for the Andover Theological Seminary chapel showed none of the awkward or exaggerated picturesque character of Academy Hall and Brechin Hall. The chapel was constructed of locally quarried stone and embellished with Connecticut and Ohio sandstone to achieve a polychromatic effect. The traditional Gothic design consisted of a nave with a gable roof, an arcaded entrance porch, and a flanking bell tower. In the rear corner opposite the bell tower was a smaller narrow stone spire that provided balance in the design.[18] The interior was not exceptionally ornate, consisting

FROM LEFT TO RIGHT: **Foxcroft, Pearson and Bartlet Halls, 1907; The Sanhedrin, after 1922; Leonard Woods monument, Chapel Cemetery, 1999, photograph by Walter Smalling Jr.**

of exposed wood lancet arched trusses constructed of ash and rows of pews flanking a center aisle. In the rear of the sanctuary, beneath the stained glass windows was a balcony with organ.[19]

The chapel stood at the north end of the Elm Walk, well forward of Seminary Row. With two Victorian buildings standing at each end of the Elm Walk, the seminary trustees then decided to remodel Pearson Hall by adding a tower at the center of the facade facing Main Street. The addition of this tower in 1878 was intended to provide visual continuity between the older Seminary Row and the two new buildings.[20]

With the Andover Theological Seminary expanding its public buildings, the trustees also added utilitarian buildings to the campus. In 1880 they constructed a farmhouse for Deacon Holbrook Chandler, the superintendent of real estate, located behind the chapel at the end of Chapel Avenue. Local contractors Abbott & Jenkins designed it as a traditional farmhouse.[21] The next year a laundry and bathhouse designed by Boston architect Edgar Allen Poe Newcomb was erected behind Seminary Row. A Queen Anne style building of brick and shingles called the Sanhedrin, it was moved in 1922 west of the site of Paul Revere Hall, where it was later demolished.[22] Both the farmhouse and the laundry occupied locations that were out of view, as did the cemetery that sat on a rise behind Seminary Row. Established by the trustees in 1810, the cemetery had served as a resting place for many of the illustrious alumni and ministers of the seminary. In 1872 a group formed the cemetery association, perhaps coincident with the erection of stone walls around the lot. And in 1878, the Gothic style monument built in honor of Theological Seminary president Leonard Woods, the most ornate feature in the cemetery, was dedicated. On the strength of stylistic character, it might well be the work of Cummings & Sears.

TOP: **Tucker House on Main Street, 1880s** BOTTOM: **Churchill House, 1880s** RIGHT: **Hardy House, after 1886.** THE PHILLIPS BULLETIN 10 no. 2 (January 1926)

As if in response to the new Victorian structures built on the seminary campus on the east side of Main Street, houses arose on the west side designed in the fashionable picturesque manner. Residences for William J. Tucker, professor of sacred rhetoric, and John W. Churchill, professor of elocution, represented very fine works of the Queen Anne style. The old Federal style Farrar House was moved down Phillips Street from the corner of Phillips and Main Streets to make way for Churchill's house. The architects of the Tucker house (1880) were John F. Eaton and Otis Merrill of Lowell; the Churchill house (1882) was the work of E. A. P. Newcomb, who designed many elegant residences in the suburban communities of Brookline and Newton, just outside of Boston. The Churchill house, characteristic of Newcomb's work, was richly embellished on the inside and outside, and featured a variety of woodwork and decorative treatments characteristic of the style.[23]

On the south side of Salem Street the old Adams house was remodeled for Professor Graves in 1885 by William Ralph Emerson, an architect known for his strong interest in vernacular architecture of the American colonial period. The oldest part of the building, a one-story unit, was demolished for a new two-story wing; the main section, built in 1804–05, was modestly remodeled with neocolonial features, such as the portico with built-in benches over the entrance on the principal façade.[24]

These 1880s improvements were the last to occur on the Andover Theological Seminary campus, as enrollment declined steadily through the end of the nineteenth century. At the same time, both Phillips Academy and Abbot Academy began significant campus improvements on the west side of Main Street. Phillips began the process of capital development with Academy Hall in 1865; further improvements slowed during the 1870s with the drop in enrollment and the need to retire debt incurred by the cost of Academy Hall.

BIRD'S EYE VIEW OF
NEW BUILDINGS FOR
ABBOT ACADEMY
ANDOVER MASS.
H.W. HARTWELL & W.C. RICHARDSON · ARCHITECTS
68 Devonshire St. Boston.

ABBOT ACADEMY

In 1884 the Abbot trustees, led by Warren F. Draper, hired the Boston firm of Hartwell &
Richardson to develop a master plan for the campus.[25] Four Romanesque style buildings were
proposed to replace all of the existing structures and create an open quadrangle on School Street.
On the north side a new classroom and assembly building faced the street. A large main building
was to replace the original academy building. Containing student and faculty rooms, parlors,
music and art studios, it would connect with two other dormitories, French and German Houses,
where students could converse in the respective foreign language. A central kitchen provided
meals for three dining halls, one in each dormitory.

Hartwell & Richardson, Bird's Eye
View of New Buildings for Abbot
Academy, Andover Mass. 1886,
reproduced in Annie Sawyer Downs,
"Abbot Academy, Andover, A Sketch
of Its History, and of the Plan for
Erecting a Group of New Buildings,"
reprint from THE NEW ENGLAND
MAGAZINE (1886)

This was an ambitious plan, which was modified due to financial restraints. Instead of constructing the French and German Houses, Abbot Hall was retained and moved back and turned 90 degrees on the south side of the quadrangle. The Greek Revival style of Abbot Hall, now in the 1880s prized with the reemergence of neoclassical architecture, was modified only with a new basement level above grade; this raised the building to a monumental presence facing the quadrangle. Draper Hall, the large L-shaped dormitory begun in 1888 and named in honor of its principal donor, trustee Warren F. Draper, arose on the west side of the quadrangle facing School Street.[26] In preparation for the new construction, Smith Hall was moved back out of the way in 1887 and it continued in use for another ten years before being demolished.

Draper Hall's handsome Richardsonian Romanesque design features round arches and a prominent asymmetrical tower. Yet the facade facing the quadrangle stresses a classical symmetry, and the two wings have wood-shingled gambrel roofs. This hybrid of Romanesque and shingle style is unusual, and probably an effort to emphasize the largely domestic dormitory use, which was then called a "living-house".[27]

McKeen Hall completed the Abbot quadrangle in 1903-04. Designed by Hartwell, Richardson & Driver, the building provided Abbot with an assembly hall and gymnasium.[28] The architects designed a granite and brick structure that was architecturally compatible with both Draper and Abbot Halls. The massing of McKeen suggests the Romanesque style, yet the masonry and detailing is neoclassical. Ten years later, Abbot trustees commissioned Hartwell, Richardson & Driver to design a small laundry building behind Draper, a modestly domestic Renaissance revival structure.

The John-Esther Gallery of 1906-07 filled the last open space facing the quadrangle, on the south side between Abbot Hall and School Street. In 1904 Abbot alumna Mrs. Esther H. Byers gave to the academy her art collection and a bequest for a gallery to house it. The Boston firm of Andrews, Jaques & Rantoul was hired to design the John-Esther Gallery, named in honor of Mrs. Byers and her husband John, a past trustee of Abbot. The Renaissance styled gallery, ajoining Abbot Hall, was an extraordinary addition for a small New England girls' school. Indeed, at this time it was the rare college that even had its own art gallery in a separate building.[29] Although additional structures, including the Antoinette Hall Tayler Infirmary (1913-14), Abbey House (1939), and George E. Abbot Gymnasium (1955-56), were added behind Draper Hall, the core of the Abbot Academy campus was essentially complete by 1907.

LEFT: **Hartwell & Richardson, Draper Hall, circa 1887**   TOP: **McKeen Hall, circa 1904**   BOTTOM: **John-Esther Gallery and Abbot Hall, circa 1907**

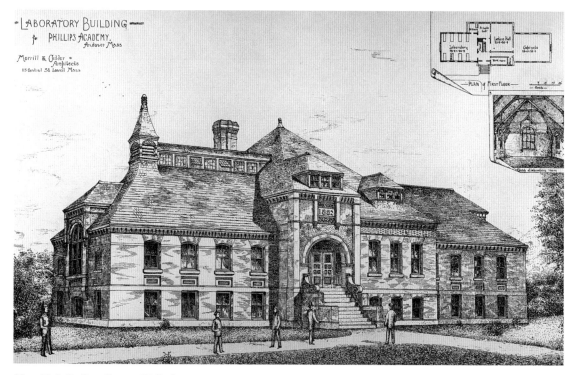

Merrill & Cutler, Graves Hall, from AMERICAN ARCHITECT AND BUILDING NEWS (December 30, 1882).
Fine Arts Department, Boston Public Library; reproduced Courtesy of the Trustees of the Boston Public
Library of the City of Boston

GRAVES HALL, PHILLIPS ACADEMY

Progress on Phillips Academy proceeded more slowly in the 1880s and 1890s. The first major addition was a laboratory building for the physical sciences, which principal Cecil Bancroft argued for at an 1880 trustees meeting. The increasing demand in colleges for science courses prompted Phillips Academy to keep abreast of these changes in curriculum. It was also a safety measure, as the existing laboratory space lacked proper lighting and ventilation. The trustees appropriated funds for the new laboratory building, Graves Hall, on June 19, 1882, and retained Merrill & Cutler, a Lowell, Massachusetts, architectural firm. This firm's selection may have been due to the fact that Arthur S. Cutler, the junior partner, hailed from Andover. Otis A. Merrill had been in practice since 1873, and had been previously hired by the theological seminary to design Tucker House. Graves Hall in 1882 was among the partners' earliest projects, a design published that year in the architectural journal *American Architect and Building News.*[30]

Constructed of brick with Nova Scotia sandstone trim and a granite base, Graves Hall was designed with a mixture of Queen Anne and Romanesque style elements. The building went up in two phases: the original east wing was completed in 1882-83; the center section and west wing were built in 1891. As completed, Graves Hall featured a central Romanesque entrance section with open porch. The main-floor chemical laboratory received natural light by a combination of tall windows and lantern in the roof. Seven ventilators under the side windows and a minimum of combustible materials for interior finishes were important safety features. Graves Hall was sited just south of Academy Hall and was thus the second structure to be built as part of a new campus center.[31] Graves was set with its narrow east end facing School and Main Streets, and its entrance facade looking north toward Academy Hall. When the latter building was demolished in 1927, the logic of Graves' orientation was lost, further obscured by the subsequent growth of foliage.

DORMITORIES, DINING HALLS, AND FRATERNITIES

Several projects competed for funds after the east wing of Graves Hall had been built. The trustees took up principal Bancroft's long-standing call for a single dining facility where all the academy boys could have their meals. They solicited plans from Merrill & Cutler of Lowell and Van Brunt & Howe of Boston in June 1885.[32] Two years later the trustees asked both firms to revise their drawings. Despite Bancroft's conviction that the lack of a single commons facility put Phillips Academy at a disadvantage with other private schools, no decision was made to construct a new building, evidently due to the lack of funding.

Space for academy administrative offices had long been inadequate. Edward Taylor, Phillips Academy treasurer during 1868-89, donated funds to erect an office building in 1885. Merrill & Cutler were again hired to prepare plans for Phillips Hall, a brick Romanesque style building with sandstone trim. It contained offices for the treasurer and the principal, as well as a vault and a trustees room.[33] Its prominent location on the south side of Academy Hall, accessed by a separate curved drive off School Street signified that the Phillips Academy trustees were committed to development of a campus separate from Andover Theological Seminary.[34]

Under the supervision of science professor William Graves, the large open field between the English and Latin Commons was surveyed and graded to improve drainage in the summer of 1886, partly in anticipation of the dining hall to be built opposite the baseball field. Work continued in the summer of 1887 and a road was built between Phillips Street and the last building in the row of Latin Commons, providing access along what was then the back of the campus. By this time there were many demands for improvements. In addition to the dining hall and the completion of Graves Hall, the need for new dormitories to replace the commons, and for new athletic facilities were fervently desired for the academy campus.[35]

Only a fraction of academy students were housed in dormitories. Most boarded locally in private residences and rooming houses. Demands for onsite student housing may have factored into the trustees' decision to tolerate secret fraternal societies. After the school gave up attempts to ban them in 1883, fraternity houses opened their doors near the school.[36] Kappa Omega Alpha (KOA), the first secret society at Andover, led the way with a shingle style house on Locke Street. Designed in 1892 by George W. Cole, this building showed the influence of Shepley, Rutan & Coolidge, where Cole apprenticed.[37]

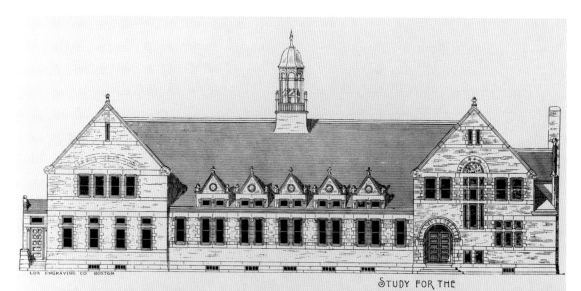

PRINCIPAL ELEVATION

STUDY FOR THE
DINING HALL.

VAN BRUNT & HOWE · ARCHITECTS ·
BOSTON · MASS · & KANSAS CITY · MO

PHILLIPS' ACADEMY · ANDOVER · MASS ·

LEFT TOP: Van Brunt & Howe, Study for the Dining Hall, 1890, reproduced in THE MIRROR 37 no. 1 (December 1890)   LEFT BOTTOM: Merrill & Cutler, Proposed Alumni Dining Hall Building, 1887, reproduced in THE MIRROR 33 no. 2 (March 1887)   ABOVE: Phillips Hall, circa 1885

AUV/Graham House, 1915, ink. Plan Room, Office of Physical Plant, Phillips Academy

Other fraternities followed KOA's example. A different architect designed each secret society building, and, as on most college campuses, these buildings represented a variety of architectural styles. AUV sold its original woodframe house at 123 Main Street and constructed a new brick building designed by Codman & Despradelle on Wheeler Street in 1915. After renting an old Gothic revival style house at 131 Main Street, PAE constructed the colonial revival brick building near Borden Gymnasium in 1908. Phi Lambda Delta (FLD) constructed the last secret society building on Old Campus Road, designed by Perry, Shaw & Hepburn in 1928.[38]

The trustees formed a new committee on real estate and buildings in June 1889, to which they referred "all matters relating to Real Estate, including the rebuilding of the mansion House, new Dining Hall, and a comprehensive plan for the grounds and buildings required by the institutions."[39] The committee handled various campus and building improvements, including a grandstand for athletic activities, erected in 1889, and the completion of Graves Hall in 1891.

In 1891 the trustees made two significant decisions that would affect the future of the campus. They finally agreed that the old wooden English and Latin Commons structures should be replaced with new small, cottage style dormitories. And on June 9, 1891, the trustees authorized the real estate committee "to consult with Frederick Law Olmsted with reference to the location of the proposed new buildings, and the other buildings required by the institutions, and the exercise grounds of the students."[40]

TOP: PAE/Cooley House, circa 1925   BOTTOM: FLD/Davison House, 1928

OLMSTED'S "COTTAGES"

F. L. Olmsted & Co. prepared a master plan to guide the siting of new buildings and the future development of the Phillips Academy campus.[41] Notes of the committee indicate that the Olmsted firm presented two proposals. The first, characterized by the committee as a "dignified symmetrical and impressive display of the largest and most important buildings of the institution," included the provision that academy buildings would gradually displace the faculty row houses occupied by seminary professors as the growth of the school demanded more space. This proposal was rejected—because of the expense and because of the opposition from the occupants of the houses. The committee approved Olmsted's second plan, which organized the new campus in an

> irregular, picturesque manner . . . based upon the fundamental idea of a grouping of the buildings according to their uses; embodying . . . a series of irregular, park-like plots of land beginning at Main Street near the junction of School Street, including the triangle between them and the present Academy buildings, extending in a curve around, through land west of the present professor's dwellings, to Main Street again and ending at the historical brick building [Bulfinch Hall] now temporarily used as a gymnasium.[42]

This was a dramatic and comprehensive plan for the development of a significantly larger campus that could provide recitation and administrative buildings, dormitories, and faculty houses well into the future.

With the Olmsted plan in hand, construction of new brick cottages began, each to provide accommodations for approximately ten students and a faculty member. Each building was designed by a different architectural firm and funded by a different donor. In 1891 alumnus Melville Day donated $8,000 for the construction of the first cottage. Sited facing Phillips Street at the corner of Old Campus Road, Pemberton Cottage was designed in a simple neocolonial revival style by architect Alexander Wadsworth Longfellow, head of the Boston office of the Pittsburgh firm of Longfellow, Alden, and Harlow.[43] Next came Andover Cottage in December 1892, designed by George W. Cole and Joseph Everett Chandler. Town residents funded Andover Cottage, which was perhaps the reason Cole, an Andover native, was selected. The son of a prominent local contractor, George Cole trained in the Boston office of Shepley, Rutan & Coolidge. He had been working in New London, Connecticut, on projects for the Shepley firm and decided to start his own practice there. Cole took on Chandler as his partner, an association that terminated with Cole's early death in 1893.[44]

The third dormitory, Draper Cottage, was funded by Warren L. Draper and completed by January 1893.[45] Draper was the only one of the four to be built behind Academy Hall on the site of one of the English Commons that had burned. The neocolonial revival design of this structure,

F. L. Olmsted & Co., Phillip's Academy, Andover, Mass., Preliminary Study, 1891, drawing. Frederick Law Olmsted NHS

TOP LEFT: **Pemberton Cottage, circa 1892**   TOP RIGHT: **Andover Cottage, circa 1893**   LEFT: **Draper Cottage and English Commons, circa 1898**   RIGHT: **Eaton Cottage, after 1900**

whose architect remains unknown, was very similar to Longfellow's design for Pemberton.[46] Eaton was the last of the four cottages, another colonial revival design by architect George C. Harding of Pittsfield, Massachusetts. Melville Day was the benefactor.[47] All four cottages differed in interior plans and finishes, although recent remodelings have left no evidence of the original interior fabric. *The Phillipian,* reporting on the new cottages, commented that Andover Cottage had "a much more pleasing exterior" than the other three, which were in the "old Colonial style." George Cole's design was in the simplified English Tudor manner and unlike any other building in Andover. According to his partner Chandler, the idea was to suggest the old English school buildings at Eaton and Oxford.[48] The others, with their three-story facades and colonial revival ornament, complemented the large Federal style mansions along Main Street, no doubt appearing less modern to students.

In 1899 plans were commissioned from A.W. Longfellow to meet additional dormitory needs.[49] This time, instead of free-standing cottage units, the new Bancroft Hall's three-story brick facade united three smaller cottage-sized units, each with its own entry, into one large building. Conflicts between the architect, client, and landscape firm arose immediately. The Olmsted firm strongly objected to Longfellow siting Bancroft Hall parallel to Phillips Street, which would violate their 1891 campus plan that created a long open view from Draper Cottage at the north to behind Faculty Row at the south, now the site of the West Quadrangle. Although construction of Bancroft Hall had already begun, the Olmsted firm urged that the building be relocated to sit perpendicular to the street. When the school replied that it was too late, Olmsted Brothers wrote a strong letter to trustee and former client Robert Bishop, claiming that "Mr. Longfellow has on more than one occasion shown his indifference to matters of landscape design, and he would certainly be reluctant to do anything that would make it appear that he was not right." They followed with another letter stating that the present location "will be utterly out of harmony" with the plan, and "the building will be a [sic] abominable eyesore."[50] Bishop and the school administrators prevailed and Bancroft continued to be built as sited by Longfellow. The Olmsted firm's position proved correct when Bancroft Hall was moved away from the Phillips Street site in the 1920s.

The acquisition of the theological seminary property in 1908 offered dramatic possibilities for expanding the campus. The west side of Main Street remained the focal point until the trustees in the early 1920s set forth drastic changes in campus development plans. As these shifts were made, the fate of many of the nineteenth-century buildings changed too. Over the first decades of the twentieth century, these structures would be either moved or demolished in the great redesign of the campus. Only a shadow of the nineteenth century remains on Academy Hill.

Bancroft Hall, circa 1900

ONE QUARTER OF GRILLE
¾" = 1'-0"

NOTE:- THIS DRAWING SUPERSEDES THE DETAIL OF
RECTANGULAR GRILLE SHOWN ON SHEET #110.

REVISED DETAIL
OF
ORGAN GRILLES

REVISIONS

Susan C. Faxon

Forces of Change:

THE TRANSFORMATION
OF THE CAMPUS, 1900–1932

AS ONE APPROACHES PHILLIPS ACADEMY along Main Street in Andover today, it is easy to believe that this picture-perfect campus has always been thus. It is also easy to assume that the central quadrangle, with the blue clock face in the tower of Samuel Phillips Hall beaming toward Main Street, is the limit of the campus. Yet, it is only one part of the 500-acre holdings of the school; it is also the most formal. Other campus areas, other configurations of buildings and landscape, tell a far more diverse and complex story.

The story to be told in these pages is about the first thirty years of the twentieth century, focused primarily on one of the institutions on Academy Hill—Phillips Academy. There are many colorful stories told about these years, some of them embellishments of fact. One tale suggests that the present campus design sprang full blown in the minds of two people, Thomas Cochran, trustee, investment banker, and the school's most generous benefactor, and Charles A. Platt, debonair New York architect of classical revival country estates and campuses. While Cochran and Platt, aided by school treasurer and trustee James C. Sawyer, were prime movers in the 1920s and 1930s development, the history at this time is one of different voices—of conflicting personalities, of many starts and stops, of thirty years of debate and thought. Even after the final plan was set in the late twenties, with factions having been brought into uneasy alignment and major construction begun, the result was not totally conceptualized. Buildings were going up, buildings were being razed, buildings were on rollers moving across campus, letters were being sent, plans were being re-drawn, and the design was being formed in the midst of frenzied activity.

BEGINNINGS OF A PLAN

The roots of Phillips Academy's architectural future were actually planted in the 1870s, nearly fifty years before Cochran, Platt, and Sawyer formed their partnership. Following a long line of stern and pious headmasters, Dr. Cecil Bancroft, headmaster from 1873 to 1901, set himself apart by initiating comprehensive plans for the school. His first tasks were to achieve financial stability,

Charles A. Platt, Revised detail of Organ Grilles, Administration Building [auditorium, George Washington Hall], 1926, drawing. Avery Architectural & Fine Arts Library

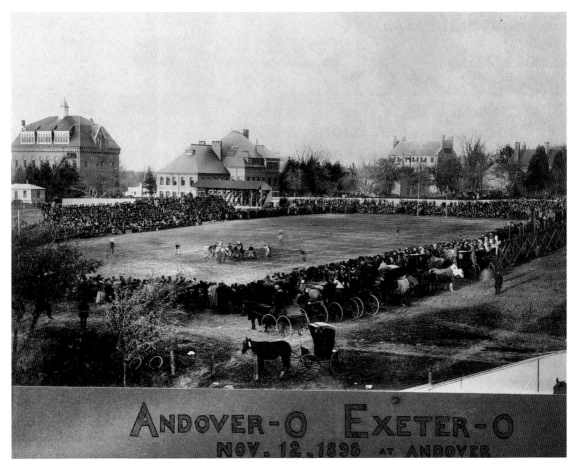

Andover-Exeter Game on playing fields of Phillips Academy, November 12, 1898, left to right, **Academy Hall, Graves Hall, bleachers, Double Brick and Park Houses**

improve the faculty, increase Phillips' prestige and recognition, and capture a wider distribution of students. Improvement of the academy's physical plant followed close behind. In 1879 Bancroft reported to the trustees, "As soon as we have funds I shall desire a few improvements and changes."[1]

Those changes were to involve improvements to the new main Academy Hall; an addition to the science building to accommodate laboratories; the construction of an administration building; and eventually, a comprehensive plan for the development of a new campus by landscape architects F. L. Olmsted & Co., and the construction of four small dormitories, or "cottages" to house the academy students as the first steps in the execution of that plan.

Bancroft's death in 1901 was a blow to the school, which had gained much in reputation and physical improvement under his leadership. But others on Academy Hill shared his vision. Shortly after Bancroft's death, the trustees offered the principalship to James Hardy Ropes, a trustee and faculty member in religion at Harvard. Ropes wrote a thoughtful response to the board that outlined issues facing the school and the conditions under which he would accept the post. Crediting Bancroft for providing the school "an opportunity to hold a place at the head of American schools which I believe lies before no other school in this country," he echoed his predecessor's concerns:

> In the essential matter, however, of the housing and boarding of the boys, the Academy is, I believe, behind every other important boarding school in this country of which I have knowledge. Only 70 boys out of a total this year of about 340 boarding-pupils, have proper rooms provided by the Institution. The sanitary and other evils of the old Commons are well known to the Board, and are intolerable. The demoralizing arrangements of the Commons dining-hall, the only provision for the boys' meals which the Academy can at present make, have lately been vividly set before the Board by the Treasurer. In consequence the daily life of the greater part of the boys is largely out of the control of the administration of the School, with the result of serious moral evils and constant danger of greater ones. I believe it is absolutely essential to any successful administration of the Academy and to the retaining of public confidence in the School that the boys' life should be brought again into the hands of the authorities of the School by the institution of sufficient dormitories and of a suitable dining-hall, in which at any rate the larger part of the School, and not, as at present, only the poorest boards, shall board, and where the influences shall be civilizing and not the reverse.

He challenged the board to develop an effective plan, determine the funds necessary, and begin active fundraising efforts "sufficient to assure a complete change from the present system of caring for the boys." He also urged resolution of the greatest uncertainty facing the school at the time, the question of whether the theological seminary would remain in Andover.[2]

Even though Ropes' assessment was fair, the trustees were unwilling to commit themselves and Ropes declined the offer. Instead, the board appointed thirty-two-year-old Alfred Stearns, Bancroft's nephew and his uncle's assistant, as vice-principal in 1902; after a successful trial year, he was elected the ninth principal in 1903. When he took over, as a later colleague pointed out, the physical plant of Phillips Academy

> occupied an area on the west side of Main Street, owning the old Main Building, eleven wooden Commons, Graves Hall, "the four" splendid new brick dormitories,—Andover, Pemberton, Eaton, and Bancroft,—a few scattered residences, and the executive office, which then contained three small rooms.[3]

Phillips Academy campus in winter, from Abbot alumna photo album, 1890s, cyanotype

For Stearns, the deficient facilities at Phillips must have been a great concern. By contrast, just down the hill at Abbot Academy and on other campuses, building plans were underway. Abbot, under the leadership of Miss Philena McKeen, had taken the first steps in the realization of a major new campus that would rival the latest in campus design for female colleges. Bancroft's fellow principals, Dr. James C. Mackenzie at Lawrenceville School in New Jersey, and the Reverend Endicott Peabody at Groton School, just a few miles southwest of Andover, were developing entirely new and modern campuses with the assistance of the Olmsted firm and the Boston architects, Peabody & Stearns.

GROWTH OF THE ACADEMY

Change at Phillips Academy, however, faced an important stumbling block—the uncertain future of Andover Theological Seminary. Phillips Academy and the seminary had stood together on Academy Hill for nearly eighty years. They shared the same founding family; the land owned by each was inexorably entwined; and the same board of trustees governed the two schools. But as the seminary's annual enrollments continued to dwindle (ten students in 1902), it had too much space; the growing academy, meanwhile, had too little.[4] The academy moved forward with various stop-gap measures: it rented Bartlet Hall from the seminary for the use of academy students; it demolished the old (and long-despised) Latin Commons along Phillips Street; it voted to renovate Bulfinch Hall, built in 1818–19 and gutted by fire in 1896, from a gymnasium to a dining hall; and it built a new archaeology building.[5]

The school turned to Boston architect, Guy Lowell, for the archaeology building and the Bulfinch Hall renovation. The archaeology building, at the corner of Main and Phillips Streets, a generous gift of Robert Singleton Peabody in 1901, was to house Peabody's extensive collection, the department of archaeology, and a social center for the school in the basement. It was the first in a long line of buildings that Lowell would design for Andover over the next 27 years.[6] Lowell, brother-in-law of trustee James Hardy Ropes, was a young and promising architect in 1901. Lowell's training made him an inspired choice, since the academy was poised to commission not only buildings but also to embark on the development of an entire campus south of Phillips Street. He had studied at Harvard and the Massachusetts Institute of Technology, and trained in architecture and landscape architecture at the École des Beaux-Arts in Paris. Upon his return to the states, he cultivated a growing number of wealthy clients from Massachusetts to Pennsylvania for whom he designed elaborate estates with mansions, outbuildings, and gardens. In the archaeology building, Lowell applied his hallmark "strength of restraint, dignity and restfulness of repose and rhythm," to the development of a new colonial revival building that he believed would "harmonize with the traditions of the institution."[7]

Lowell's first challenge in designing the building was the existing two-and-a-half-story Queen Anne style house occupied by seminary professor, John Wesley Churchill, that stood on the site.[8] Churchill House was rolled several doors down Main Street to stand on the other side of Pease House. This began what was to become a prevalent practice on the Andover campus well

TOP: **Robert S. Peabody Museum, under construction, 1902. Frederick Law Olmsted NHS** BOTTOM: **View of Phillips Academy campus, circa 1902,** left to right, **Hardy House, Bulfinch Hall, and Borden Gymnasium**

into the 1930s. Buildings that did not fit the immediate plan or space needs were moved and/or removed. No building and few sites were sacred.

After Bulfinch Hall's use as a gymnasium was ended by fire in 1896, the school raised $50,000 for a new gymnasium, the fully outfitted Borden Gymnasium. Bulfinch was then renovated to accommodate the long-awaited dining hall. In a pattern that was to continue throughout the next two decades, the Olmsted firm was asked to work with Lowell to site, grade, and landscape the grounds around the archaeology building as well as to assist with the siting of the new Borden Gymnasium and the renovation and addition to Bulfinch Hall.

The trustees awarded the gymnasium commission to prominent Boston architects Peabody & Stearns. Olmsted suggested a site at the edge of the playing fields that trustee George B. Knapp had recently purchased for the school's athletic programs. The brick and limestone building, designed in the colonial revival style, featured a projecting central pedimented bay and twelve-over-twelve windows; its columnar entrance door approached by a rise of stone steps. Both these projects, the Borden Gymnasium, satisfying Stearns's fervent desire to establish the "new Athletic System" that ensured physical training for every academy boy, and Bulfinch Hall, fulfilling Bancroft's long-standing call for adequate dining facilities, moved the school several steps forward in its master plan.

At the same time that Borden Gymnasium was opening its doors, Miss Philena McKeen's master plan for the Abbot Academy campus was moving forward with the construction of another building, McKeen Hall. Designed by Hartwell, Richardson & Driver, the successor firm to the one that had developed the comprehensive campus plan for Abbot in 1884,[9] it was completed in 1904, and named in honor of the headmistress and her sister who had died in 1898. With the addition of the Italian Renaissance style John-Esther Gallery to Abbot Hall in 1907,[10] Abbot Academy's campus plan was completed. Abbot's three main buildings, set in the formal U-shaped, open quadrangle, presented an impressive and imposing sight. The quadrangle enclosed a green, ceremonially approached from a circular drive that looped from a gate at School Street around in front of all three buildings. Behind Draper Hall the majestic Maple Walk led westward from the school's buildings across a rolling field, past a remarkable grove of oaks, to Phillips Street. It was 1907; Abbot enjoyed a fine and a carefully planned campus and Phillips Academy was still grappling with what to do.

PLANS FOR A NEW CAMPUS

Five years before, in 1902, the never-ending inadequacy of Phillips's Academy Hall had come to a head when the building was declared unsafe. Principal Alfred Stearns remembered the moment when the engineer from Guy Lowell's office opened up the assembly hall floor to expose structural beams that had separated from the supporting walls:

> We were ordered to vacate the building without an hour's delay
> and we did. Arrangements were promptly made for the removal

of the treacherous top floor. . . . The following year, with the
lower stories suitably reinforced we were able to resume classroom activities in the three lower floors. A little later the familiar
porch had to be removed and the old Academy Building assumed
a new and unfamiliar form.[11]

Stearns and the board were now faced with a virtual crisis, the need to move forward with plans
for a new building. The trustees saw this as a moment to rethink the whole campus. Frederick
Law Olmsted Jr., the Olmsted firm's partner-in-charge of Phillips landscape design, reported that
the trustees on February 10, 1903, were leaning toward a decision "to move the centre of the school
life up toward the top of the hill, away from the village and the present academy building. . . . to
concentrate the school buildings more compactly for the sake of convenience and discipline; to get
the school life a little further from direct contact with the village." He enumerated the needs of
the school: a new academy building, "the best site for which seems to be on the west side of the
main street on the axis of the dining hall [Bulfinch]," an infirmary, one or two recitation buildings,
and a library. He went on:

> For the sake of economy and discipline—a dormitory system
> instead of a cottage system is expected. . . . The sentiment seemed
> to be decidedly in favor of a group—perhaps a quadrangle—
> extending west of the proposed site for the academy building.

Olmsted's notes also defined the current thinking about the limits of the campus. "The future
development of the school and the area for which a tentative study is now wanted will not

FROM LEFT TO RIGHT: **Academy Hall, 1888**;
Academy Hall, circa 1903, showing building
after removal of top floor; Academy Hall, circa
1911, showing building after removal of porch

extend north of Phillips Street, south of the gymnasium or west of Taylor [Pemberton] Cottage."[12]

Today, with the contemporary academy campus sitting so solidly on the east side of Main Street, it is hard to imagine that for thirty years the academy's plans focused on the opposite side of Main. The essential reason for this, of course, was that the land owned exclusively by Phillips Academy consisted only of plots on south of the seminary, on the west side of Main Street, and along the wide swath of playing fields and open land behind Faculty Row.

THE SEMINARY DEPARTS

The Preliminary Plan that the Olmsted firm drew in 1903, transforming the campus into rectangular blocks to follow trustees' desire for a residential quadrangle, abandoned the picturesqueness of their 1891 plan. An addendum plan showed faculty housing in large lots serviced by a looping road through what is now known as the Hidden Field area.[13] As these plans were being developed, the trustees continued to study the possible move of the seminary and the ways to separate the two schools. The question of where the seminary might relocate and with what institution it might be associated was complicated by the obligation that it remain in Massachusetts. With the more theologically sympathetic institutions located only in Connecticut and Maine, there was little choice but Harvard, whose liberal theology had been a prime cause for the founding of the Andover seminary in the first place.[14] Finally an arrangement was struck with Harvard for the purchase of land in Cambridge and the erection of a seminary building with the proceeds from the sale of its land holdings in Andover to the academy.[15] It was not until May 1908 that the two schools hammered out a purchase agreement. The academy acquired sixteen parcels of land from the seminary for a total price of $200,000.

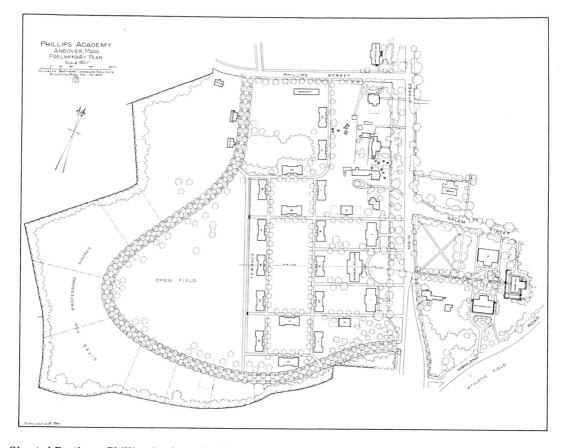

Olmsted Brothers, Phillips Academy, Preliminary Plan, 1903, drawing. Frederick Law Olmsted NHS

Many years later, Stearns defined the challenge faced by the academy at this juncture, providing a succinct description about what became a long and complicated debate that continued for another twelve years.

> The acquisition of the seminary property, mostly located on the
> east side of Main Street presented the trustees with a wholly new
> and difficult problem—on which side of this dividing artery
> should the school of the future develop? Heretofore, barring the
> Dining Hall later known as Bulfinch, and the Borden Gym-
> nasium, the academy's future had been visualized as a continua-
> tion of its existing location on the westerly fringe of its holdings
> [behind Faculty Row]. Plans had already been drawn and
> accepted for a row of buildings extending from the old campus in
> a semi-circle up to the Stuart House on Main Street. On the

basis of this plan Taylor, now Pemberton, Andover and Eaton cottages had already been erected. Should these now be left on the outskirts in favor of an easterly development? This was a puzzling question and the trustees split into two groups whom we commonly termed "East Siders" and "West Siders." The majority were enrolled in the latter group who felt strongly that the western slope offered most attractive opportunities for an extensive and attractive development believing that the cemetery and unsightly stone ledge behind the seminary buildings gave us no change for further growth in that direction and that the main campus [on the east] itself should not be cluttered with buildings.[16]

Even with the addition of the seminary dormitories—Foxcroft and Bartlet—to the existing facilities, the school was still pressed for student housing. As the Olmsted notes and plans attested, the school was now determined to build large dormitory style buildings. Lowell's design for a new dormitory was presented to the board and Melville C. Day, the alumnus who had financed three of the 1890s cottages, took up the call, donating money for one building and allowing the school to contemplate a second. Ground for Day Hall was broken in late 1910 and the building completed to Lowell's design in 1911. For this building, the architect carefully coordinated both site and design with the impressive early-nineteenth-century seminary buildings and especially with Pearson Hall, designed by Federal-era architect Charles Bulfinch. Guy Lowell designed his new dormitory in a spare and somewhat idiosyncratic colonial revival style to sympathize with the old buildings; he sited it to the south of and in line with Seminary Row. The school erected Bishop Hall that same year, again designed by Lowell. Adams Hall in 1912 and Taylor Hall

Panorama of Andover Theological Seminary, circa 1900, the seminary as it was when Phillips Academy purchased the property, left to right, Samaritan House, Phillips Inn (incorporating Stowe House), Stone Chapel, Harrington House (partial view), Foxcroft, Pearson, and Bartlet Halls, Blanchard House (partial view), Bulfinch Hall (partial view), Hardy House, and Brechin Hall quickly followed in 1913. The latter three buildings were placed according to the quadrangle arrangement defined on the Olmsted campus plan for the west side.

Notwithstanding the great generosity of Melville Day, who sponsored three of the four new dormitories, financial support by alumni was generally modest. The school had faced serious difficulties in raising money to purchase the seminary buildings and the administration was wary of the efforts required to realize their new campus goals. The key to success, they felt, was the alumni and their close and generous involvement. In 1913 the alumni fund committee, a group of eleven prominent alumni, was formed, charged with increasing annual giving.[17] For at least two of the members, Thomas Cochran and George B. Case, this was only the first step to more important involvement with the school in the years to come.

THE WEST SIDE CAMPUS

Except for the Phillips Union, built in 1915 behind the archaeology building as a student grille, only interior renovations, maintenance, and essential repairs were carried out in the next

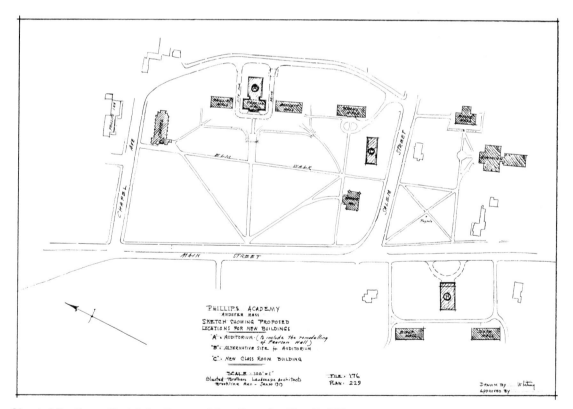

Olmsted Brothers, Sketch for Proposed Locations for New Buildings, 1919, drawing. Frederick Law Olmsted NHS

few years as the school's attention was focused on the ongoing war effort.[18] Early in January 1919, the trustees once again turned their attention to new campus buildings, now with the noble purpose of erecting a "Memorial Building as a tribute to former members of the school who have given their lives during the great war."[19] Again they asked Olmsted to assist in planning. The firm submitted three alternative locations for an auditorium building, two on the east (seminary) side of Main Street, one on the west. Although the Olmsted firm was enamored of the east side solution that aligned the new building with Pearson Hall at the architectural center of Seminary Row, the trustees voted for the site on the westerly side of Main Street.[20]

By April of that year Lowell had designed a grand administration building to be set in the center of the new west campus, surrounded by dormitories. The scale of Lowell's proposed building was enormous, since it was conceived to accommodate administration offices, recitation rooms, as well as an auditorium for the entire school, all under one roof. Lowell also designed a memorial tower to stand in front of the main building on axis with Bulfinch Hall across the street. This axis was carefully planned to link the new development with the cluster of academy buildings that already existed on Salem Street—Bulfinch, Borden Gymnasium, and Hardy House. With plans in hand, Stearns and Sawyer consulted with the New York representatives of the Alumni Fund who agreed to take on the fundraising efforts for the project. The Fund reconstituted itself as the building and endowment committee, with Stearns, Sawyer, and English teacher Claude Fuess added to represent the academy, and set their goal, as their stationery proclaimed, to raise "$1,500,000 for Andover Before January 1, 1920." Of that ambitious amount, $500,000 was for the Assembly and Recitation Hall, the remaining one million was to fund increased salaries for faculty.

In spite of the trustees' clear vote, the debate between west siders and east siders intensified. As Stearns stated, "The arguments were continuous and heated for several years."[21] Some argued about practical matters—a group of the faculty thought noise from the trolley lines along Main Street would be objectionable. Other arguments were based on aesthetics. It was at this moment that George Case stepped into a leading role in the debate, and through his perseverance altered the course of events.[22] In a letter to Sawyer of May 1919, Case expressed his feeling that the proposed buildings were pretentious. He also disagreed with their placement.

> While the bell tower proposed is handsome, it seems to me it is out of keeping with the needs of the school in other directions, and perhaps with the surroundings of the site proposed. The site proposed slopes downward, and it is rare that you see a group of buildings with monuments, etc., at the foot of any slope. I know you will pardon the above coming from a rank layman, but I think you are entitled to know just how I feel, for it may be that many others rankly ignorant as I am may feel the same way.[23]

Sawyer urged Case and the others to reserve judgment until the full and final plan was developed. After all, he added, the tower was "practically a duplicate of the steeple of the Old South

Model of Lowell's master plan for the campus on the west side of Main Street, circa 1919–20

Meeting House on Washington Street, Boston, which design seemed entirely appropriate for our hill top."[24]

Further debate brought a proposal that the center of the new campus be moved north from its place in axis with Bulfinch in order to align it with the seminary buildings on the east side. Lowell, a ready compromiser, was willing to try the new site, but he was seriously concerned about the suggestion. He wrote a long and earnest letter to president Alfred Ripley in May 1920, explaining why he felt the original plan was far better.

> If the Memorial Building is placed facing Main Street, to the North of the continuation of Salem Street, it can be made dignified and monumental, but it will be of necessity a building standing by itself and will not be helpful in opening up a new center of school activities in the land now undeveloped to the west of Main Street. . . . It would hold the same isolated position as does a town hall standing by itself or a local high school, contributing nothing to and gaining nothing from the surrounding buildings. It is now the modern theory of college planning that the important buildings should turn their faces to the center of college life, the campus, and not to the outside world.[25]

It was clear that trustees, the administration, and the designers had serious and growing disagreements about the best path for the school to take in developing its new campus.

George Case continued to believe that the Lowell plan was flawed and he wrote again, this time to Claude Fuess, in March 1920,

TOP: Guy Lowell, drawing of Memorial Campus, circa 1919–20, showing proposed Memorial Tower and Memorial Building BOTTOM: Guy Lowell, drawing of Memorial Campus, circa 1919–20, showing proposed Memorial Tower in relation to dormitories

> I never can quite get it out of my mind that the establishment of
> the new buildings with the important center which they will cre-
> ate on one side of Main Street, with the theological grounds,
> gymnasium, church, etc. on the other, would be unfortunate.

While he admitted that it was hard to think of the best location on the east side, he went on to suggest, "The only one that has occurred to me is the knoll back of the present line of the Seminary
Dormitories, which slopes down towards Rabbit Pond."[26] He recounted conversations with other
New York alumni, who were in agreement with him. Even Samuel Fuller, the alumnus who had
been identified to fund the memorial tower, agreed that the location in front of the proposed administration building on the west side was problematic. Two days later, Case was back to James Sawyer.
"I hate to be stubborn," he started. "Nevertheless, I am convinced that in time we will be sorry that
we put these buildings in the place indicated by Mr. Lowell and the Olmsted brothers, and with the
broad expanse on the top of the hill to choose from, I think it ought to be gone over again."[27]

The trustees felt compelled to listen to Case, now a member of the board of trustees, since
he and his New York cohorts were the ones who were raising the money. As a way out of the
dilemma, the trustees formed a committee consisting of Thomas Cochran, Oliver Jennings, Fred
C. Walcott, Samuel Fuller, and Philip Reed. The trustees' letter to Cochran on February 2, 1921,
explained,

> It is also expected that the committee will select one or two
> architects of distinction to serve as consulting architects with Mr.
> Lowell in order that the plans finally adopted may have been
> studied from different and the best possible angles.[28]

The Olmsted firm drew up plans of the existing campus without any indications of where the proposed buildings might be placed, so that the consultants would be able to advise on the logical
location for further development with a clear and impartial eye.

CHARLES PLATT AND THE EAST CAMPUS

Ultimately only one consulting architect was enlisted: Charles Adams Platt, New York artist,
architect, and landscape architect.[29] Platt was a prestigious choice for Phillips Academy. Like Lowell,
Platt had an established reputation. In fact, in testament of his appreciation of Platt and his work,
Lowell had included several of Platt's design for country estates and their grounds in his elegantly
produced book, *American Gardens,* published in 1901.[30] Platt's list of wealthy, socially prominent
clients was impressive and his experience with campus planning ideally suited to the task at hand.[31]

Olmsted, at the trustees' request, sent the campus layout to Charles Platt on September
22, 1921. Shortly after, Platt came back with several proposals for sites, as Olmsted partner Percival
Gallagher's notes recounted,

Platt's first recommendation was to place Academic Building at southerly end of the old Elm Walk and related to Gymnasium and Dining Hall [on the site of the present Hardy House]. But this was disapproved of by Trustees for several reasons, primarily because it intruded upon the old Common [the training field at Salem and Main Streets], concerning which there is restriction against using it for buildings. His next suggestion was site east of Pierson [sic] with the removal of latter. As to this idea I gave cordial approval.

Gallagher, revealing concern about the Olmsted firm's future relationship to the academy, added,

Mr. Sawyer is not at all disturbed by recent criticisms of the New York Alumni and apparently has not lost confidence in our advice given heretofore with respect to locating buildings. I was gratified to find that my original suggestion to concentrate buildings at Pierson [sic] Hall site was not forgotten.[32]

George Case and the "East Siders" had won the point. The decision was made to pursue the second plan and Platt's involvement with the school quickly increased. By June 1922, the trustees asked Platt to develop a comprehensive plan for the development of the campus on the east side. This departed from Olmsted's role during the last thirty years in which the firm had served as close advisors on matters of landscape, campus planning, and specific building sitings. Now, with very little debate, Platt was asked to step into the role. When Sawyer explained the building committee's action to Gallagher, the Olmsted partner was gracious: "I told Mr. Sawyer it was well that Mr. Platt was to make a general plan as it would permit him to more satisfactorily complete his work." With this new role for Platt, the future of Phillips Academy's campus development took a giant step in a new direction and the dynamics of the relationship between Olmsted, Lowell, and the school irrevocably changed.

Platt's plan for the east side incorporated the Andover Theological Seminary campus as the core of the new development. Fifteen months after Olmsted Brothers had drawn the Memorial Campus Design on the west side of Main Street, they drew a new plan, this one plotting buildings on the land behind the three original seminary buildings. Platt's plan required moving Bulfinch's central seminary building, Pearson Hall. It was lifted from between Foxcroft and Bartlet, moved back and to the south and turned ninety degrees to rest at right angles behind Bartlet. Importantly, this was the first step in creating a rectilinear quadrangle on the crest of the seminary hill. It now allowed the new administration building to stand to the rear and center of the quadrangle, facing west toward Main Street through the newly opened up Vista created by the removal of Pearson.

The Memorial Bell Tower that had been planned for the west side then moved across the street to the training field at the corner of Salem and Main Streets, where George Washington

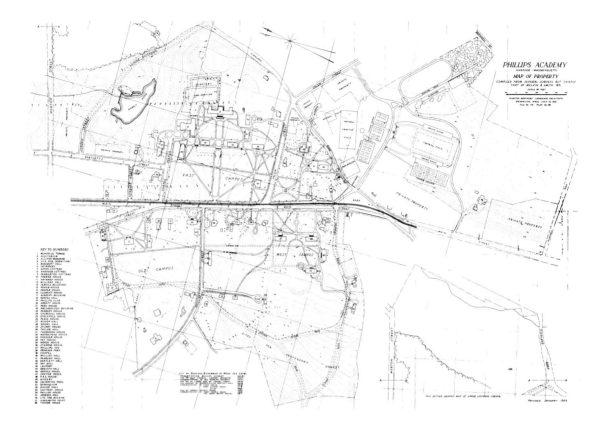

Olmsted Brothers, Phillips Academy, Map of Property, 1922, drawing. Frederick Law Olmsted NHS

reportedly reviewed the troops in 1789. The trustees, some years earlier, had designated this area as one of two locations on campus where no building could be built (the other being the Seminary Lawn); the tower that Samuel Fuller funded was considered simply a memorial and thus appropriate for the site. Sawyer's letter to Gallagher in June 1922 is indicative of the increasing power of the alumni, and the shift in reliance on consultants. "You will be interested to learn," he wrote,

> that the building committee in conjunction with Mr. Platt and Mr. Lowell, also the Trustees, decided to locate the Memorial Tower in the center of the old training field at the corner of Salem and Main Street. Some of us pointed out the advantages of a location on the west side and on the dining hall axis, but the historical and sentimental value of the old training field was quite convincing.[33]

Lowell designed a square, three-story brick and limestone shaft, supporting an octagonal wooden bell tower of three tiers ascending in a delicate, almost lacy wooden spire. It was now the highest point on Andover Hill and a beacon to approaching the school. Memorial Tower, completed in 1923, was the first structure of the new campus plan.

THOMAS COCHRAN'S INVOLVEMENT

It was 1923 and the stage was set for the next phase of development on the hill. The critical player, Thomas Cochran, joined the action that year when the board of trustees elected him to join its ranks. As loyal alumnus, benefactor, and building committee member, it was an inevitable decision. Cochran was an active member of the New York fundraising group and only three months before had offered to donate $100,000 as a challenge to nine other alumni to raise one million dollars.

The close relationship that developed between Platt, Sawyer, and Cochran drove great and speedy change on Andover Hill. Cochran had perseverance, determination, and, most important, a large bank account. A native of St. Paul, Minnesota, Cochran had graduated from the academy in 1890, and studied at Yale, where he roomed with his Andover classmate James Sawyer. After a short stint as a teacher, he rose quickly in New York banking circles.[34] At the time that he joined the building and endowment fund committee, he was a member of the New York financial firm of J. P. Morgan & Company. Early letters from Cochran are infused with strong loyalty to his alma mater, during good and bad personal times in his own life. In 1916, after several years of emotional illness and recuperation, Cochran announced himself back in the saddle.[35] It was that year he wrote an often-quoted letter to Al Stearns.

> I wish the time would come soon when I could do something more substantial for Phillips Academy. It is much in my heart and mind, and I dream about it. You and Jim are doing such fine work, that if some of us fellows could get rich, we ought to be able to give you a lift. You may rest assured that if I ever arrive, that I will remember what I owe the old school.[36]

Two years after joining the board, his fellow trustees appointed Cochran chairman of the four-member building and grounds committee, thus positioning him to influence all future development of the campus. His loyal friend and enthusiastic co-conspirator in the massive project that lay ahead was James C. Sawyer. Sawyer had joined the school administration in time to be privy to Cecil Bancroft's plans; he was the one who squired George Case and the building and endowment fund committee through the debate about the location of the new buildings; and ultimately he was the lasso that would hold the whole stampede together as it gathered storm through the mid- and late 1920s. After graduating from Yale and making a brief try at business, Sawyer returned to

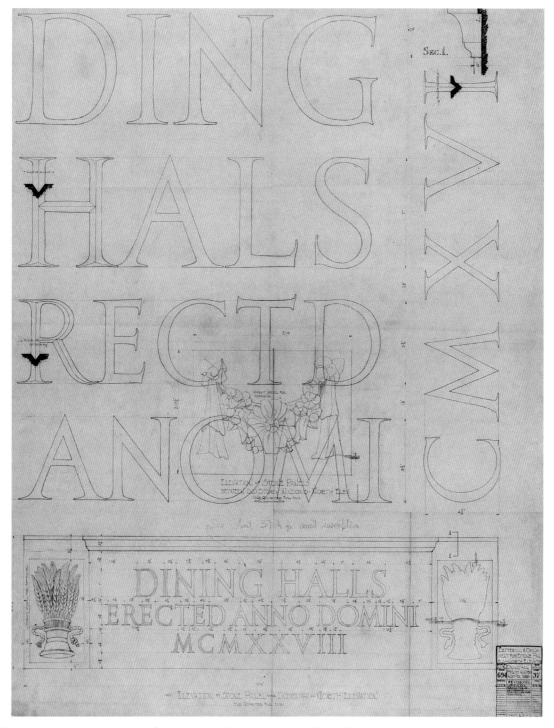

Charles A. Platt, Lettering & Ornament for Stone Panels on North Elevation, 1929, drawing. Avery Architectural & Fine Arts Library.

Andover. In 1901 he was elected to the board of trustees, and several months later appointed treasurer of Phillips Academy, a position that placed him at the critical intersection between incoming money and outgoing expenditures. Cochran trusted Sawyer's judgment about aesthetic matters and counted on him to carry out the myriad of details that made the project move forward. Sawyer was equal to the task.

Charles Platt was the third member of the triumvirate. In a letter of thanks to Sawyer written when the plans were mostly complete, Platt described the threesome,

> I feel that we have worked together with perfect sympathy &
> enjoyment & that's the only way good things can be done. I
> believe that
> > T. Cochran
> > J. Sawyer &
> > C. Platt
> make a notable triumvirate. I am proud to be of it.[37]

Cochran was entirely caught up with Platt. For James Sawyer's part, recalls his son Charles, "there was a warm personal and professional relationship between Mr. Platt and my father and Mr. Cochran, and in the latter's eyes Mr. Platt could do no wrong."[38] Elegant, nattily dressed and groomed, with a small goatee, Platt was sure of himself and his advice. As Platt's close friend, artist Barry Faulkner wrote after his death,

> The effect of his character upon his clients was almost hypnotic. .
> . . his clear vision and untroubled certainty of intention made
> unthinkable any solution other than his own. The secret of his
> power with clients lay in the remark that he made to his son
> William, that an architect had failed in his duty by his client if he
> had not educated him to desire better and finer things than he
> had been conscious of before.[39]

In the case of Phillips Academy, Platt involved himself with refinement of every architectural detail—the base of the flagpole, the lettering over the doors in Commons—and every other issue as well—the question of tablecloths in the faculty dining hall, Ropes Hall, decisions about purchases of art, the manner in which pictures were hung in the trustees room, the furnishings for the Trustees Room, the table on which the scale model of the campus was to be set. Platt had found his perfect client in Cochran, who was willing to spare no expense on behalf of a perfect product.

The year 1923 brought not only the Memorial Tower to completion, but also the Lowell-designed Case Memorial Cage, a baseball cage donated to the school by George Case and his wife in memory of their son, a Phillips Academy student who had died in the summer in 1921. In the same year, plans began in earnest for the new administration building on the east side and the

Portico of Samuel Phillips Hall, c. 1923

THE FULLER MEMORIAL TOWER AS IT WILL APPEAR WHEN COMPLETED

The Fuller Memorial Tower as it will appear when completed, THE PHILLIPS BULLETIN 17, no. 1 (October 1922)

school turned again to Lowell. The plan he developed was substantially different from his grandiose design for the west side location, mainly because it had now been decided to separate the classrooms from the auditorium. Lowell designed a symmetrical colonial revival building of brick and limestone consisting of a five-bay central block and two extended wings large enough to accommodate all the classroom needs of the school. Wide steps led up to the central pedimented porch supported by Doric columns; above the central block rose a bell tower with blue-faced clock, ending with a copper-sheathed spire. The plain expanse of brick and the boldness of the central porch were softened by the contrasting ornamentation of windows with pedimented lintels, the application of balustrades below the lower sash of each window, and the profusion of finials, corner columns, and other ornamental details on the tower.

As the school was approving Lowell's design, Platt moved to control landscape planning. In September 1923 Al Stearns wrote a revealing letter to Cochran about the grading and planting schemes that the Olmsted firm was carrying out in the new quadrangle. He reported that Mr. Platt

> was very much upset and apparently hurt to find that his original suggestions had not been fully carried out, that he had not even been consulted during the summer by the Olmstead [sic] firm, and that the plan on which work was then being done was radically at variance in important respects with his own scheme. . . . the result of Mr. Platt's visit led to a prompt conference with Olmsted's man, Mr. Gallagher. . . . Mr. Platt now writes me that the revised plans are to be submitted to him.

Stearns explained that Sawyer had allowed Olmsted to work with Platt "so that their feelings would not be hurt, inasmuch as they had formerly done this kind of work for us." However, Stearns urged that the division of authority be ended and that the "entire matter of ground planning and planting be handed over without any reservations whatever to Mr. Platt."[40]

The Olmsted firm continued to offer considerable assistance with planting, siting, and grading, but they increasingly deferred to Platt. From 1925 on, their academy work became increasingly involved with building models of the campus. Charles Platt wrote to the Olmsted firm in February 1925 that three trustees (presumably, Case, Cochran, and Walcott) had asked him about the desirability of commissioning a model of the new campus. As they expressed it to Platt, the purpose was "to show possible donors where a building should go to fill a gap." Because, as Platt explained, "The landscape part of this one would be an important element in its success,"[41] it was determined that the Olmsted office would take on this project in consultation with Lowell's office who would supply the drawings. Cochran agreed to foot the bill for a one-sixteenth-scale model to show the effect of changes already made. By the summer of 1927, another model was commissioned. This second model was important, Cochran explained to Sawyer, because it will form a basis and guide for the future physical development of Phillips Academy, and, in case anything happens to you and me, this model will stand as mute evidence, at least, of a constructive plan for the development of the Academy. . . . This model of an 'idealized Andover' will be one of our best assets because it will be a perpetual exhibit of what we are striving for."[42]

With Platt's position as the oracle secured, the Olmsted firm found itself playing an uncharacteristically subservient role, creating elaborate models of the campus.

Because Lowell's Samuel Phillips Hall was devoted exclusively to classrooms and faculty offices, a second building was needed to serve as a meeting space for the school and to house the administration. While Lowell appeared the logical choice as the designer, this time New York alumni chose Platt instead. George Case wrote to Sawyer on March 30, 1925 that the selection of the architect must proceed with tact, without slighting anyone; but, with little sympathy, he wrote again the next month, "I am glad that the architect matter has been settled. I am sorry that Mr. Lowell is disappointed but as there was no reflection intended upon him, I hope he will not allow it to rest too heavily."[43]

Olmsted Brothers, Model of Idealized Andover, 1927, showing both constructed buildings and proposals, including a chapel on site of present Addison Gallery, a Fine Arts Building between George Washington and Samuel Phillips Halls, a classroom building to the right of Samuel Phillips Hall, and a dormitory to the right of the Oliver Wendell Holmes Library, parallel to Salem Street.

The administration building, named George Washington Hall, was completed in 1926 and entirely funded by Cochran. Platt designed a refined building in the colonial revival style, three stories with hip roof.[44] Its plain brick façade, divided by horizontal stringcourses of limestone and punctuated by unornamented windows, was relieved by a slightly projecting pedimented central bay with three identical arched doorways and discreet ornamentation above. As would be the case in each of the buildings designed by Platt, this restrained version of the neocolonial by Platt stood in distinct contrast to Lowell's more elaborate interpretations of the same style.

With all but one of the buildings in the main quadrangle completed, the trustees debated about what was needed next. Sawyer leaned heavily for the construction of a new library but reluctantly conceded that the seminary's library building, Brechin Hall, could be made to adequately serve for the time being. The Samuel F. B. Morse Laboratory Building was selected to be the sixth, and completing, building of the main quadrangle. It was also to be the last building Guy Lowell would design for the academy. This time, unlike any of the architect's previous design projects for the school, the trustees reportedly allowed themselves to engage in design critique.[45] The revised design for Morse, in what *The Phillips Bulletin* was now able to characterize as "simple Colonial architecture,"[46] was sited on axis with and to the west of Bulfinch's Pearson Hall. While the trustees had been successful, with Platt's assistance, in reducing what they considered the ornate quality of the building, the use of blind arched windows on the second floor echoing the arched entrance doors and inset niches of the first reveals a more ornamented approach than Platt would adopt in his Andover buildings.

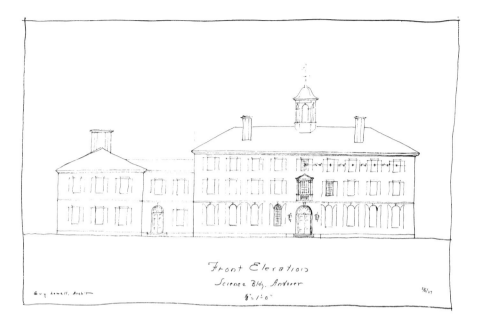

LEFT: George Washington Hall, c. 1925   ABOVE: Guy Lowell, Front Elevation, Science Bldg. Andover [Samuel F. B. Morse Hall], plan 176-431 (sheet 1), February 8, 1927, drawing. Courtesy of the Frederick Law Olmsted NHS   BELOW: Olmsted Brothers, Model of Idealized Andover, 1927, showing Lowell's original elevation for Samuel F.B. Morse Hall, a classroom building to the right of Samuel Phillips Hall, and proposed gateways connecting Morse with the classroom building and Pearson Hall

As Morse was under construction, Lowell and Platt debated whether buildings should fill in the corners of the quadrangle. Cochran reported that Platt was "very enthusiastic about the idea of a completed quadrangle with the buildings all tied in."[47] Lowell was against the idea, claiming that it would be much more successful to "keep our corners open so that the diagonals would maintain the pleasing vistas which now exist."[48] Despite George Case's report that Lowell was being uncooperative, Sawyer found Lowell entirely accommodating. Lowell developed a scheme to add a domestic-scaled colonial revival classroom building between Samuel Phillips Hall and Morse, while Platt designed an L-shaped fine arts building to fill between Samuel Phillips and George Washington Halls. The fact that these two buildings were never built suggests that others agreed with Lowell's point of view.

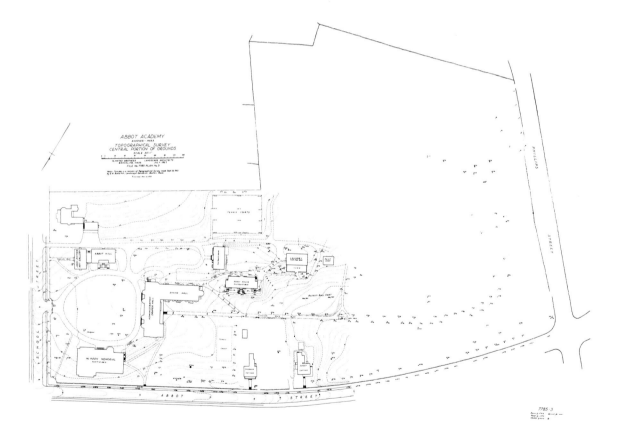

**Olmsted Brothers, Abbot Academy, Topographical Survey Central Portion of Grounds, 1927, drawing.
Frederick Law Olmsted NHS**

THE ABBOT LANDSCAPE

At the same time that Phillips Academy was carrying on this debate, Abbot Academy was taking another substantial step in campus planning. Severe wind and ice storm damage to trees in the central quadrangle caused Abbot to seek advice about plantings and repairs to the landscape.[49] E. C. Whiting of the Olmsted firm visited the Abbot campus in April 1927 to review the tree damage. While there, the academy asked Olmsted to develop "a definite planting plan for the region in the vicinity of the main buildings."[50] Whiting took with him the 1913 topographical study of the Abbot campus that E. W. Bowditch had skillfully executed. With the construction of the Hartwell, Richardson & Driver's laundry building (1911–12) and the Antoinette Hall Taylor Infirmary by Kendall, Taylor & Co. (1913–14), as well as changes in several paths and the addition of various plantings, the Bowditch plan was outdated and Whiting persuaded Abbot officials to allow the Olmsted firm to draw a new plan of current conditions.

By September Olmsted forwarded its plan for the future. "We have aimed to make the quadrangle, in front, quiet, simple and dignified: but there is also to be a certain richness of effect." Evergreen plantings were to complement red oaks and rock maples in the front, with additional hemlocks to join those already along Abbot Street. The report went on to make special note about the salient landscape features of the Abbot campus, mentioning "the fine allée of [rock maples] on the grounds," and "the largest and finest 'pure stand' of red oaks that we have ever encountered." The Olmsted report concluded, "It is remarkable. We cannot recall the like anywhere else."[51]

Abbot called on the Olmsted firm again in 1939 when the Abbey Hall dormitory was built behind Hall House. The firm designed an elaborate planting plan for the area between the two buildings, including a formal flower garden. However, the involvement of the Olmsted firm with Abbot turned out to be brief, producing only thirteen drawings in all.

PLATT TAKES CHARGE

Back up on the hill, Phillips Academy faced a pivotal moment when Guy Lowell died unexpectedly in 1927, while on a vacation trip to Europe. The alliance between Lowell, Platt, and the school had been uneasy since Platt was first brought in, yet the school's fundraising letters had been proud to boast about the grand schemes that were unfolding on Academy Hill under the care and attention of both architects. If Platt was setting the grand parameters of the campus design, Lowell was engaged in the specific debates. In spite of the overwhelming impression today that Platt was responsible for all the building on campus, Lowell actually designed more buildings for Phillips Academy than did Platt.[52] While Platt has received well-deserved credit for the final form of the academy campus, Lowell had the longest involvement with Phillips Academy of any architect in the institution's history—26 years in contrast to Platt's ten.

With Lowell's death, Platt assumed the role of the school's architect and was given nearly free rein.[53] Morse was under construction, the main quadrangle was nearing completion, and plans were moving forward for the addition of another dormitory, a dining hall, library, and

Brechin Hall under demolition, 1929

chapel. The plans drawn by Olmsted in 1927 and 1929 illustrate the extent to which the campus plan was continually being refined and altered.

This was the era of the great removal of buildings. In order to construct the new dining hall known as Commons parallel to Salem Street, the small Queen Anne building named the Sanhedrin, which was being used as a laundry and bathhouse, had to be demolished. To accommodate a proposal for a dormitory quadrangle east of Paul Revere Hall (a plan that never came to fruition), houses that stood along Salem Street—Blanchard and Berry Houses—were removed. Blanchard was relocated to Hidden Field Road; the Berry House, which had served as a boarding house for boys for many years, was torn down in 1930 after Commons opened.[54]

Although the nineteenth-century seminary buildings, Brechin Hall and the Stone Chapel, were still in use, their days were numbered. Cochran, Platt, and the school moved ahead with plans to build a new library to the south of the Seminary Row even though Brechin was still in use. When the books were eventually transferred from Brechin to the Oliver Wendell Holmes Library in 1929, the old stone building had "lost its function," *The Phillips Bulletin* offered. It was not longer beautiful. "Brechin Hall had remained beyond its time as a symbol of departed grandeur. As it vanishes, it will be regretted by an older generation, but its loss will add to the beauty of the Hill."[55]

At the other end of the great lawn, Platt planned a pendant building to balance the library. It demanded a colonial revival solution rather than the romantic Stone Chapel that was already there. Article after article in the *Bulletin* commented on the wonderful building campaign underway on the Hill and mentioned the ugliness of the extant nineteenth-century buildings. While many alumni agreed that these building were out of keeping, others remembered the Stone Chapel as a particularly precious part of their academy experience and harbored fond feelings for the Ruskinian Gothic structure. Even George Case expressed regrets about its impending demolition: "Makes me feel a bit sad, however, to think of the possible passing of the old stone chapel. First thing you know there wouldn't be many of the old landmarks of any kind left."[56] Cochran appreciated Alfred Stearns's strong sentimental attachment to the old building.[57] No matter; it did not fit into the colonial revival campus that Platt and Cochran envisioned.

THE CHAPEL AVENUE CAMPAIGN

The plans for the Chapel Avenue area went through a number of transformations before they reached the form that exists today. Returning to New York after a meeting in Andover on July 11, 1928, Cochran breathlessly summarized the sweeping changes he and Platt envisioned. "On the way down on the train yesterday afternoon," Cochran wrote, "Mr. Platt painted the following picture, which he described as a very interesting one to dream over.

> 1 - Eliminate the West wing of Phillips Inn by destroying it when the improvements on the Inn are made.
> 2 - Close Bartlet Street, as we discussed.
> 3 - Move the Headmaster's house toward Phillips Inn, occupying as part of the required space the property acquired by the closing of Bartlet Street.
> 4- Build the new chapel on a line opposite with the memorial tower and parallel with Main Street.
> 5 - Erect a stone wall along Chapel Street in front of the headmaster's house and the new Chapel, extending the wall to Main Street and down Main Street one block.
> 6 - Build a Phillips Memorial gateway on Bartlet Street between the two stone walls. Make this a significant gateway, but not an arch.
> 7 - Build an art gallery on the site where we had planned to build the new chapel.[58]

As the letter indicates, Platt's previous scheme had shown a new chapel on the site of the present location of the Addison Gallery. There had been no plan to build a separate art museum. The collection of fifty paintings that Cochran assembled and gave to the school on the occasion of the 150th anniversary of the school's founding that year were slated to be permanently displayed in an art gallery on the second floor of the library. While Cochran's letter gives credit to Platt for the idea of the art museum, correspondence suggests that others shared in the formulation of the plan. Sawyer was impressed with the art facilities he had seen on a tour of English secondary schools.

> When I returned from England and told Mr. Platt about the art buildings in connection with the schools there and what I saw in connection with them, he was much interested and pleased. I remember him saying that we should have such an opportunity here for the boys in this school. . . . I think that as a result of this conversation he has put on the plan an art building.[59]

Cochran had also been thinking about art instruction; such thoughts led him lead to think about a new building to house art classrooms. Perhaps the art gallery space slated to be in the library should be folded into one large building. Platt toyed with his previous plan to erect a classroom building for the arts in the corner between George Washington and Samuel Phillips Hall, but by May 1928, Platt was dreaming about an art museum to be located on the site due west of George Washington Hall.

Accordingly Platt and others mused about a wholly different vision for the Chapel Avenue and Bartlet Street area. With the art museum plotted at the north end of The Lawn, a new site was necessary for the chapel. Platt settled on the north side of Chapel Avenue, with the main facade of the new chapel facing across The Lawn toward Lowell's Memorial Tower, in perfect neoclassical balance. However, the principal's house, known as Samaritan House, and the Phillips Inn, which incorporated the stone Stowe House with an elaborate colonial revival wing, already stood on the north side of Chapel Avenue. Harrington House, a simple Italianate-style farmhouse dating from the days when the academy and seminary produced their own food, had been moved to a location behind the Phillips Inn on Bartlet Streets in 1925, and Woods House sat directly behind Samaritan on Wheeler Street. Bartlet Street, a town road, continued up the hill to meet Chapel Avenue.

If the new chapel was located on the site of Samaritan House on Chapel Avenue and the town was willing to close Bartlet Street at Wheeler Street, it would be possible to shift Samaritan to the west to sit between the inn and the new chapel. The plans for Phillips Inn were various, including the possibility of constructing a new inn across Main Street on the site of the old Academy Hall or enlarging the existing inn with another wing.

The Olmsted firm, which by this time was engaged in producing the second model of the idealized Andover, altered the model to show these new ideas. The model proved its worth for the first time. James Sawyer, always accommodating to the plans of Platt and Cochran, went to view the model at the Olmsted office and immediately wrote to Cochran, "I was terribly distressed to come away with an unsatisfied feeling about our whole development around Chapel Avenue."[60] He was certain the chapel was sited too close to Woods House and that the headmaster's house in its proposed location would have an unpleasant view of the new inn's service court. He even thought the facade for the art gallery was not as pleasing as in the drawing. The committee quickly convened to review the plans and dramatic alterations were made. The idea of retaining Stowe House was scrapped. Instead the wing was to be demolished and the stone house moved to the site on Bartlet Street where the Harrington House had just been placed. Woods House would need either to be demolished or moved to another location. It was agreed that Samaritan House looked awkward in its location between the inn and chapel, and plans were developed to move it across Main Street and construct a new Principal's House in its place.

TOP: **Olmsted Brothers, Model of Idealized Andover from Wheeler Street, 1928,** foreground, left to right, **the rear of the enlarged Andover Inn, Harrington House, Woods House, Samaritan House, and Cochran Chapel** BOTTOM: **Olmsted Brothers, Model of Idealized Andover from Chapel Avenue, 1928,** left to right, **Cochran Chapel, Samaritan House, Andover Inn, and Addison Gallery, designed in Italian Renaissance style**

VOICES OF CONCERN

It was now that voices of dissent were finally loud enough to be heard. The first hint had come from Al Stearns in 1925 when he had visited Cochran in New York to urge him not to move Harrington House to such an important site adjacent to Chapel Avenue.[61] The same Stearns who previously had desired to give Platt a free hand also wrote of his reservations about the architect's attention to the Andover plans. "If I only felt sure that Platt really had something definite and final to say about matters of this kind, I should rest easy. As things are, I cannot escape the feeling that Platt is more or less of a figurehead, at least in the view of those whose duty it is to handle matters of this kind here on the ground."[62]

By 1929 Stearns was the messenger of further disgruntlement on behalf of himself and his neighbors. Cochran was hardly sympathetic. "I cannot, for the life of me, see why the good people of Andover should oppose the closing of Bartlett Street. In return for the closing they receive more than they give," he wrote.[63] Sawyer warned Cochran that Stearns was unhappy about the plans to move his house to the former site of Academy Hall, which he had been led to believe was to be used for the new inn. Stearns was convinced that Woods and Samaritan Houses, set side by side on the west side of Main Street, would create another "Rotten Row," what disgruntled witnesses, in a play on the name "Faculty Row," had dubbed the final location of Blanchard and Tucker Houses along Hidden Field Road. Sawyer's warning letter mentioned that he himself had polled innkeeper John Stewart who also thought the Main Street site was preferable over Chapel Avenue. In perhaps the most strongly worded letter ever sent by the school to Cochran, Stearns himself wrote:

> I think I am not the only one who has been doing some hard thinking these last two or three weeks. . . the investment of my life and such limited talents as I possess on Andover Hill and at Phillips Academy for the last thirty-two years inevitably force me to feel pretty keenly all that is done or contemplated."

He was disturbed that the Stowe House "could apparently not be made to work into the picture," and concerned about the wholesale moving of the historic buildings off Chapel Avenue where he thought they added character and an important reference to the school's history. He was certain that a cloister connecting the chapel and a new headmaster's house was "striking a wrong note." He urged further study:

> The haste with which we are acting and disposed to act worries me more than I can express for I am convinced that the problem is too big and too complicated to justify hasty action, and that some day we or those who follow are going to regret it.

He went on to mention "two serious blunders" to fortify his position: the placement of Harrington House on a site that was considered wrong only three years after its move, and what he characterized

Andover Inn, designed by Wagner, Bottomley, & White, circa 1930

as the "jamming" of Tucker and Blanchard Houses into a corner on Hidden Field Road to create the Rotten Row. As for Samaritan, Stowe, Graves, and Berry Houses, "there is a wide-spread clamor against their departure," not limited, he added, to the normal complainers but from faculty member Charles Forbes and "others of real calibre."[64]

President of the board Alfred Ripley was distressed about these latest plans too. But when Ripley had written to Cochran the year before to gently suggest that the pace was too fast, Cochran had offered a peevish reply: "I don't know exactly what is 'involved' in the matter except improving the beauty of the School and securing a better location for the buildings that are to be moved."[65] Clarence Morgan joined the Stearns camp, expressing his annoyance that as a member of the buildings and grounds committee, "buildings were located, designed and built without my being consulted."[66] Even Cochran's most ardent supporter, George Case, was concerned about the placement of the chapel. Cochran warned that "George Case has been persuaded to agree to the new Chapel site only on the condition that it could be thoroughly isolated by a veritable grove of trees."[67]

Cochran replied to Stearns' letter with a brief and direct note saying that the letter "has hurt me so deeply."[68] Stearns was contrite, explaining that his concern for the haste of decisions was not related to all the wonderful things that had already been done but to encourage some constructive debate among friends.[69] Cochran's letters from then on pointedly suggested that no action be taken unless the headmaster approved. And the headmaster did approve.[70] Samaritan House was moved across Main Street, the compromise with Stearns being that it was sited closer to Main Street. Woods was moved to the corner of Bartlet and Judson Streets; Harrington was demolished, and Stowe took its place. Plans to refit Phelps House for the principal's residence replaced the idea of a new building. The design for the inn was assigned to the New York firm of

Addison Gallery of American Art under construction, circa 1930–31

George B. Post, whose successor firm, Bottomley, Wagner &, White, developed a two-and-a-half-story neo-Georgian building on the site formerly occupied by Stowe House.

At the same time, across the street from the inn, the new art gallery rose out of the ground. Platt had a number of museum buildings in his portfolio, including the Corcoran Gallery addition and the Freer Gallery, both in Washington, D.C., so he was well suited to take on this building. Photographs of the campus model show the evolution of Platt's ideas from a variation of the Renaissance palazzo design that he had devised for the Freer, to the final neocolonial brick structure, with a central portico supported by Doric columns and approached by a wide rise of steps and platform. Platt exercised his infinite control over every detail of the building, even serving on the art committee that chose the four hundred works of art that were the foundation of the collection.

As the plans for the art museum were going forward, the trustees continued to debate and disagree about its goals. James Ropes, now president of the trustees, was certain that the building should be designed to accommodate the teaching of art. But Cochran and Platt, in spite of their earlier expressions of interest in providing studios and art instruction, were equally determined that the visual integrity of the building should not be compromised. Ropes's impassioned arguments, his insistence that the faculty be consulted about the plans, and finally the support of his

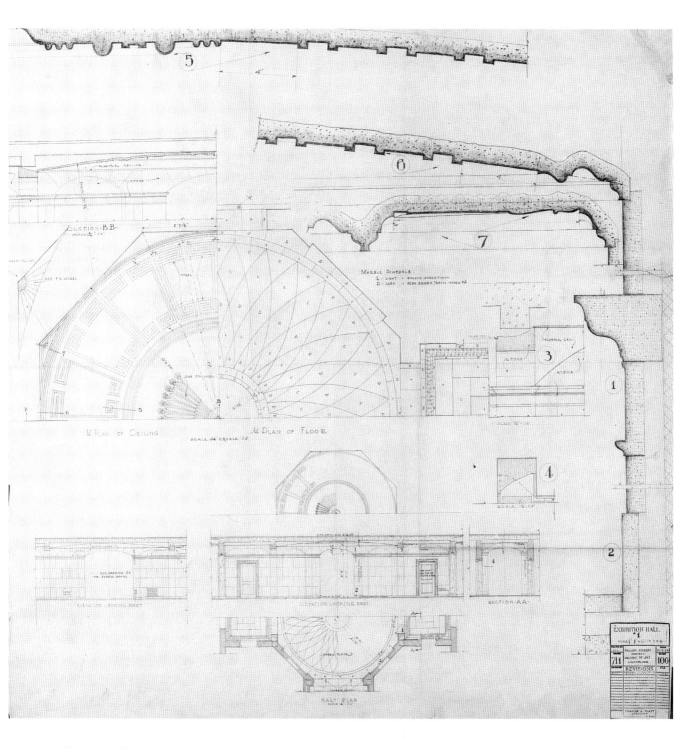

Charles A. Platt, Exhibition Hall #1 [Entrance Hall, Addison Gallery of American Art], 1929. Avery Architectural & Fine Arts Library

ideas from Professor Paul Sachs of Harvard put Cochran in an awkward position. He did not like to be thwarted and he pulled out all the stops when he wrote to Sawyer on the subject.

> The thing that now bothers me is Mr. Platt's opinion that, if we attach any substantial annex to the present Gallery, it will almost ruin it architecturally. This would make me feel very, very badly . . . . Mr. Platt wants to do what the Trustees would like to have him do, but he sincerely feels that if the Gallery is turned into a semi-recitation hall it will destroy its atmosphere and, in reality, not accomplish what we have in mind. It has always been his idea to create a thing of beauty, in the way of a small inspiring gallery.

Cochran went nose to nose with the venerable Professor Sachs.

> As you know, Mr. Platt is President of the Academy at Rome, a very cultured man, an artist, and one who has given a good deal of thought to educational problems. Since I have heard him talk and have heard your comments on what Mr. Coolidge says on the subject, I have wondered whether Professor Sachs has the only tenable point of view on this problem.[71]

By the time the vote was taken by the trustees in September, Sawyer had poured oil on the waters and could telegraph to Cochran, "Trustees unanimously approved hotel and gallery plans. No mention made of classroom requirements. Work will be under way at once."[72]

KIMBALL'S HISTORIC VILLAGE

One of the most intriguing moments for the campus came in 1930 when Francis Garvin, collector and benefactor of both Yale University and the Addison Gallery, visited with Fiske Kimball, the restoration architect and museum director from Philadelphia. Kimball was immediately taken with the fine Federal buildings that formed what was known as Faculty Row along Main Street. He recognized their rarity and proposed that the school acknowledge this group of structures by creating a "historic village" of old buildings. Garvin, whom Cochran called "an imaginative genius" and "very aggressive in his point of view about the restoration of Main Street,"[73] agreed to fund a study. Kimball wrote a detailed report, which called for the removal of the Peabody Museum (to a location behind and to the west of the Row); its replacement with Farrar House that had once stood on the site; the additional removal of the offensive Queen Anne styled Churchill House and its replacement with a "period house"; and, most ambitious, the reconstruction of the lost Mansion House to serve as a museum of decorative arts. A variant of the concept had the school purchasing the old Phillips homestead in North Andover and moving to the Mansion House site.

The Olmsted firm was asked to produce yet another model, this time of just the two sides of Main Street, to illustrate the historic restoration proposal. Stearns and Sawyer were a bit anxious about Kimball's elaborate and impractical plan. When the model was completed, much to their surprise, Sawyer reported, "our honored President [James Hardy Ropes] . . . declared it to be a real inspiration and thought it wonderful."[74] The extraordinary expense this project would have entailed, in addition to the unreality of reconstructing a major Georgian building such as the Mansion House for a use undesired by the school, meant that the idea quietly died. It is intriguing however to imagine a Colonial Williamsburg restoration of sorts as another element in the distinguished architectural campus of Phillips Academy.

THE CHAPEL: THE FINAL ELEMENT

As Garvin's and Kimball's proposal remained in model form only, the plans to complete Platt's grand scheme for the Chapel Avenue area were coming to fruition. With the moving of Samaritan, Woods, and Stowe Houses, the stage was set for the final building—the chapel. Trustee Dr. Fred Murphy had previously offered to give the building and name it in memory of three of his loved ones. Cochran, however, had already settled on the name, "America Chapel," in honor of the anthem written by Stephen Smith on the Andover campus. Cochran wrote to Sawyer suggesting that Dr. Murphy might be convinced to shift his focus to the new infirmary, which was sure to be far less expensive to build than the chapel.[75] To seal the deal, Cochran added that if that happened, he would foot the total bill for the closing of Bartlet Street, preparation of Chapel and Wheeler Streets, the moving of the various buildings, and finally, the building of the chapel. It was an offer the trustees could not refuse.[76] Ironically, in the end the trustees voted not to use the name "America" but to dedicate the new building to the memory of Cochran's mother and father. Cochran himself was very touched but a bit embarrassed, as he wrote Sawyer, "Fred's generosity seems now so unnecessary and I am sorry we stood on a false premise."[77]

Platt designed the Chapel as the last element in the grand building campaign begun in 1923. This culminated the architect's work at Andover and would be one of the last buildings he designed. It was an unusual amalgamation of styles. The facade is said to have been modeled on the Charles Bulfinch church in Lancaster, Massachusetts. However, Platt transformed the robust geometry of Benjamin's building by raising his version up on a large foundation and widening and elongating it so that the Andover building has a completely different sense of massing and scale. Rather than the restrained, circular domed tower of the Lancaster church, the steeple on the Andover chapel was stretched to four tiers topped with an octagonal spire. Inside, the conceit of the New England meetinghouse was completely dispelled by the English Christopher Wren-inspired columns, wood paneling, and elaborately ornamented choir loft and pulpit screen. In spite of the unorthodox juxtapositions of styles and materials, the Cochran Chapel is one of Andover's most significant monuments—a fitting finale to the extraordinary and unprecedented building campaign that transformed Phillips Academy forever.

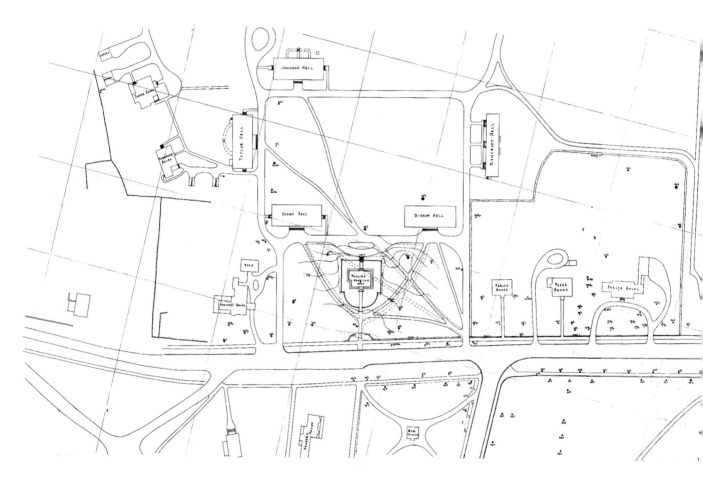

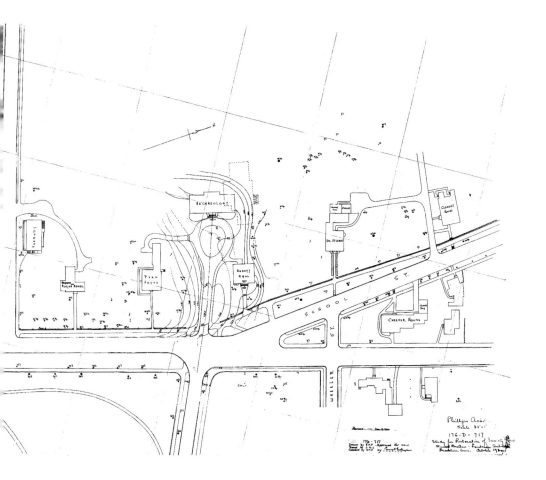

Olmsted Brothers, Phillips Academy, Study for Restoration of Faculty Row, 1930, drawing. Frederick Law Olmsted NHS

LEFT: **Charles Bulfinch, The Unitarian Church at Lancaster, Massachusetts, erected 1816, from** THE PHILLIPS BULLETIN **11, no. 1 October 1926)** RIGHT: **Cochran Chapel, circa 1932**

In 1932, as the chapel was nearing completion, Thomas Cochran, whose single-minded drive had fueled the massive undertakings on Academy Hill, was not expected to be well enough to attend the dedication. He was in the throes of what was to be his final bout with depression. First identified by Cochran in a letter to Sawyer in 1911, these periods of depression had overtaken him with increasing frequency throughout the twenties. In 1923, as the building of Samuel Phillips Hall and the development of the east side campus was occurring, Cochran had taken a long rest cure. Again, during the 1927–28 campaign for the Chapel Avenue-Bartlet Street area, he had been incapacitated for what he described as "a grievous sickness during 18 months."[78] In the busy summer months of 1929, as Cochran made his impassioned pleas for the art gallery, he had written to Sawyer, "I must now leave the whole thing for you to explore while I am gone. I am sorry I am not here to help you, but I simply must get away."[79] Now he was struck again. Amazingly these depressions, while lessening the number of daily letters sent off to his cohorts in Andover, did not keep him from being involved in the campus planning.[80] The last bout, however, did create an obsessive concern about money and his various promises to the academy. Over and over Cochran wrote to comptroller Henry Hopper, to ask about his outstanding obligations and to declare that he wanted no debt against his estate. In one bizarre request to Hopper, he asked for an account of the cost of light bulbs in use at the academy because he was "having an expert calculate exactly what it costs to burn a lamp for an hour."[81] Cochran could not control his feeling that he was being taken advantage of financially. He was sure that Platt, having an artistic character, would over-spend if unchecked.[82] Sawyer assured him that Platt was actually being very cautious and that both the art museum and the chapel were coming in under budget. As his friend and fellow trustee James Neale had written to Sawyer, "I am deeply grieved that the dear old fellow is having so much worriment. Isn't it too bad that he should have anything but the keenest happiness when he has been so wonderfully generous with his money, and best of all, with his loyalty and affection?"[83]

But his final visit surely was a moment of personal satisfaction for Cochran. When the Cochran Chapel was dedicated in May 1932, Cochran, Stearns, Sawyer, and Platt could take pride in the campus they played key roles in building. The list of projects Platt had outlined in 1928 had been achieved. In addition, an extraordinary 150-acre bird sanctuary designed by the Olmsted firm, with nesting houses, lavish plantings, two ponds, a log cabin, and a golf course, was established in 1930; Main Street was widened; a new Route 125 was created by joint efforts of the academy, Cochran, and the state to reroute traffic from this magnificent new campus; and an enclosing stone wall had been constructed to highlight the new creation. The end result was favorably received by most everyone. Sawyer had admitted to Cochran in 1931, "Some of our projects we have been obliged to explain and even defend."[84] By September 1932 he could write to Platt, "Andover is very beautiful, and it is a great satisfaction to have people say that they understand now what you have been trying to do over the years."[85]

Cochran never visited the campus again, falling into the depression that lasted until his death in 1936. Charles Platt, whose culminating work was the Andover campus, died in 1933. Alfred Stearns resigned in January 1933 while on a European sabbatical trip. James Hardy Ropes died the same month of Stearns's resignation. This was a moment of the passing of the guard and certainly the end of an era. The campus was complete. With the exception of James Sawyer, the original players were gone, and the school moved ahead to strengthen its position as one of the great private schools of the country, with a campus as perfect and immutable as if it had always been that way.

Kimberly Alexander Shilland

The Andover Campus at Mid-Twentieth Century

FOLLOWING THE ENERGETIC ERA of Guy Lowell, Charles A. Platt, and the Olmsted Brothers, the Boston firm of Perry, Shaw & Hepburn began a brief and productive tenure at Phillips Academy. Even amid the national Depression in the 1930s, the administration continued its building campaign. It was an exciting era for Andover that included the celebration of the school's 150th anniversary in May 1928, with U. S. President Calvin Coolidge as guest of honor. Perry, Shaw & Hepburn designed nine buildings for the campus between 1928 and 1937. In addition to a secret society clubhouse, a substantial addition to the infirmary, a new dormitory, and an extensive renovation of Bulfinch Hall, the firm designed five faculty houses on Hidden Field Road.[1]

After 1937 and until the mid-1950s, however, Andover commissioned a select number of secondary, out-of-the-way buildings and additions to existing structures. The school's architectural hiatus ended in 1954 when Benjamin Thompson of The Architects Collaborative (TAC) in Cambridge, developed a campus master plan and subsequently designed several Andover buildings.[2] TAC's and Thompson's era extended from 1954 through the 1960s, and brought a new face and improved organization to the campus. Despite the fact that the work of Perry, Shaw & Hepburn and TAC was separated by little more than two decades, each firm's design philosophy was dramatically different from the other.

PERRY, SHAW & HEPBURN AT ANDOVER

The Boston-based architectural firm of Perry, Shaw & Hepburn was founded in 1923 and boasts a long, distinguished record in design.[3] Recognition came early to the firm when in 1926 John D. Rockefeller commissioned it to design the restoration of Colonial Williamsburg in Virginia. It was William Graves Perry and Thomas Mott Shaw who secured the Williamsburg work, one of the most prestigious projects at that time. Perry was a 1907 graduate of the Massachusetts Institute of Technology (MIT), where he had enjoyed a particularly warm relationship with French architect

Abbot Stevens and Alfred Stearns Houses with Rabbit Pond in foreground, circa 1958

Honor Guard escorting President Calvin Coolidge, center, **Headmaster Alfred Stearns,** left, and **Grace Coolidge,** behind her husband, **past Bartlet Hall toward Samuel Phillips Hall, Phillips Academy Sesquicentennial Celebration, May 1928**

Désiré Despradelle (of the firm Codman & Despradelle), who was a highly successful alumnus of the École des Beaux-Arts.[4]

Similar to other leading Boston firms, Perry, Shaw & Hepburn was equally facile with designing in the modern and the neocolonial style.[5] The firm had designed several buildings for educational institutions, including Longfellow Hall at Radcliffe, Harvard's Houghton Library and Baker House Dormitory (with Alvar Aalto), and the Museum of Science in Cambridge. It is not surprising to find Andover attracted to this firm, which was well-equipped to carry out the needs of Phillips Academy.[6]

The first project Perry, Shaw & Hepburn built in Andover was Davison House on Old Campus Road, a clubhouse for the Phi Lamda Delta secret society. Completed in 1928 shortly after the firm's Virginia work began, Davison House was of particular interest for the strong Tudor style details—indicating the firm had yet to fully embrace the colonial revival design for which it became known—and for the excellent quality and placement of materials, including the slate-clad roof and dormers, and English bond brick with ashlar masonry trim. Indeed, the materials were integral to the total composition, exuding a certain charm. The first-floor interior with its extensive wood paneling, exposed beams, and original wall light fixtures has survived essentially intact.[7]

Perry, Shaw & Hepburn, Club House for the Davison Associates, 1928, blueprint. Frederick Law Olmsted NHS

Two years after Perry, et al, completed Davison House, noted architecture critic and art curator Fiske Kimball issued the report, *The Embodiment of American Cultural Tradition at Andover*, which urged the Andover administration to restore Faculty Row to its early Federal appearance.[8] These houses had lined Main Street since the 1810s and 1820s. Kimball's work was supported by Francis M. Garvan, a preeminent collector of American decorative arts, who would later lend pieces from his collection to the Addison Gallery of American Art. Kimball's interest in the Andover campus, he wrote, stemmed from its "position of leadership among secondary schools, both in recognition of cultural influences outside of classes and in emphasis on the value of American traditions in history and art."[9] He felt that, in addition to the opportunities Andover offered in its art museum, library, and sanctuary for "plant and animal life," an unparalleled resource lay in "the survival of many fine old houses from the early period of the Republic."[10] Kimball offered Phillips Academy specific recommendations:

1. Reconstruct the Phillips Mansion where it stood
2. Restore the Farrar House to its original site
3. Remove Churchill house elsewhere
4. Fill in the remaining gaps by the moving in other old houses

Olmsted Brothers, Model of Fiske Kimball's Plan for Faculty Row, circa 1930

Kimball concluded, "It need not be overlooked that the restoration of its colonial setting would not only give to Andover an enviable beauty of environment, but would stimulate other schools and other communities to follow its example."[11] In one of Kimball's last letters addressing his Andover work, he suggested to Percival Gallagher of Olmsted Brothers that for a model Olmsted was creating of Kimball's proposals, if there was "no old house to move in on that site, just show any colonial house. We can find one in town if necessary." The "Kimball plan" was not carried out, but it did reflect the prevailing preference on campus for historic neoclassical buildings.[12]

Seven years passed after Davison House's completion in 1928 and Perry, Shaw & Hepburn's next Andover commission. In 1935 they designed an addition to the Isham Infirmary, originally by Guy Lowell, as well as Rockwell House, the last dormitory in the West Quadrangle.[13] The Isham addition solved the long-standing need for more infirmary space. Although Charles Platt had designed a larger and freestanding infirmary in 1929–30, it was not built. Now, instead of a new building, the trustees decided to add to the existing facility. Designed to be compatible with the original colonial revival structure, the addition prominently featured such functional elements as a roof monitor and four tall chimney stacks, as well as decorative cast-iron railings, a slate roof, and six-over-six light windows.[14] Forty years later, the academy renovated Isham Infirmary for student housing, renaming it Isham Dormitory; all infirmary services were incorporated in the Perry, Shaw & Hepburn addition at this time.

Perry, et al, designed Rockwell House to fit comfortably among the other Lowell-designed dormitories, with ashlar granite door surrounds and cast stone trim. Unfortunately, later

TOP: **Addition to Isham Infirmary, circa 1935**   BOTTOM: **Rockwell Hall, circa 1935**

additions on both the west and east facades have marred the original intent, but the building remains a significant element of the West Quadrangle.[15]

By 1934, Perry Shaw & Hepburn had assumed responsibilities for the Phillips campus that superceded the role the Olmsted firm had played for years. The reason for the change was not entirely clear, yet it may have been a cost-cutting measure. In 1934 Olmsted partner Edward Whiting wrote to treasurer James Sawyer to express the firm's distress that it was not consulted about the siting of the Isham addition and Rockwell House:

> I was distinctly troubled to learn that the Academy is going ahead with two new buildings this summer with new architects and without asking our help in the related landscape problems. Of course I am disappointed personally not to have the opportunity of carrying on with a development which we have guided for so many years, but I am disturbed quite as much by the danger to the Academy development program which certainly lurks in so complete a change of horses. Is there anything we have done wrong or have left undone which has contributed to this apparent change of mind? If so, I should like to make a very special effort to "repair the damage."[16]

Mr. Sawyer responded three days later:

> I wish to assure you in regard to your relations with us. It is inconceivable that we should do anything of major importance up here without consulting with Olmsted Brothers. Personally, I feel that the reason Andover is not just another school and a group of buildings, but is an outstanding composition of beauty, is due to our relations with you. In this particular case, we are putting in a dormitory on a location which you had previously assigned, and I do not think we have yet reached the point when it seems necessary to consult you further. The addition to the Infirmary was contemplated in Mr. Lowell's design of that building, and this is being carried out. . . . I am sure that the Building Committee has no idea of eliminating you from our picture, and you must not have the idea that anything has happened to create any misunderstanding. I shall take this up with the Chairman of our Building Committee, and I am sure he will remind Perry, Shaw and Hepburn that you are now, as you always have been, our advisers in regard to the problems which you have always solved for us.[17]

The Perry firm was asked to take on the renovation of the academy's early Bulfinch Hall in 1936–37. An article by Perry for *The Phillips Bulletin*, "Bulfinch Hall Reconstructed," demonstrated the thorough historical analysis the firm completed for Bulfinch Hall, and also the reason these architects frequently surpassed their competitors with Phillips. Perry elaborated on the academic principles that guided the renovation project:

> The building has been specially adapted to the needs of the department of English; and under the guidance of Doctor Fuess and of Mr. James C. Sawyer, it has been given a character to conform to the newer conception of the manner in which English and English Literature may best be taught; namely, by fostering intimacy both between the student and his master and between the student and his course of study.[18]

Perry goes so far as to speculate on how the original architect, who was thought to be Charles Bulfinch at the time, might have responded architecturally to contemporary teaching methods. Perry contemplated:

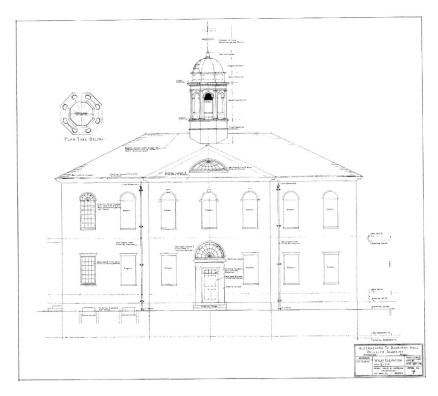

Perry, Shaw & Hepburn, Alterations to Bulfinch Hall, 1936, blueprint. Frederick Law Olmsted NHS

[Bulfinch] would have brightened at the idea of such a problem and at the architectural opportunity offered by it. "A department of English in a building apart," he might have thought, "with a series of classrooms, to be done in a quasi-domestic manner, quietly segregated and intimately adjoined to the comfortable cubicles of the masters. Splendid!" He would have lent particular attention to the reposeful character of these rooms, as has been attempted in the reconstructed building today, and also probably in their furniture.[19]

He concluded the piece by observing that the work on Bulfinch Hall did not restore the building's original design. Instead, "the new reconstruction has been guided . . . by the assumption that had the present problem arisen in Bulfinch's time, he might have solved it in a similar manner provided the outside shell were standing as it is today."[20]

Perhaps the most interesting of the Perry, Shaw & Hepburn design work for Andover, however, were the faculty houses on Hidden Field Road. The five buildings—Greenough, Lowell, Palmer, Quincy, and Weld Houses—were completed in 1937 and represented variations of the colonial revival style.[21] Standing side by side, they form a charming harmonious neighborhood within a community, suburban in nature. Replete with dormers, prominent chimneystacks, transoms and sidelights, the houses are scattered on small wooded lots. They generally have colonial revival floor plans with excellent circulation, central stairways, high-quality details, and a generous sense of space (despite their small size). Lowell House, with its square, central hall plan, is the only exception.[22]

The intriguing correspondence that dates from the Hidden Field Road project echoes elements of Fiske Kimball's report and the firm's work for Colonial Williamsburg. Perry, Shaw & Hepburn initially offered the administration three schemes: the first, Scheme A, was for thirteen houses; Schemes B and C also included thirteen homes with somewhat different siting.[23]

It should be noted that Olmsted Brothers created an elaborate plan for an 18-house development around a "village green" in June 1936, just prior to Perry Shaw & Hepburn's Hidden Field scheme.[24] None of the Olmsted plans, however appealing, were realized, primarily it seems due to financial constraints. The school had been courting Edward Harkness for a number of years. When he finally gave funds for faculty housing, Phillips could afford only five houses.

The Perry five-house design stemmed from "a definite attempt to recapture the scale and casual yet distinctive character of the old New England village residence street," stated Perry, and to avoid the stamp of a parklike subdivision or of a rigid planned housing scheme. He concluded, "The old village character—like Royalston or Fitzwilliam [Virginia] or parts of Jaffery or Peterboro [New Hampshire]—seems to us clearly the most fitting prototype."[25]

Perry, Shaw & Hepburn continued the tradition established by their predecessors of creating thoughtful, significant, and well-designed buildings. They also recognized the economic restraints brought about by the Depression. This was clear in a letter from the firm to Andover

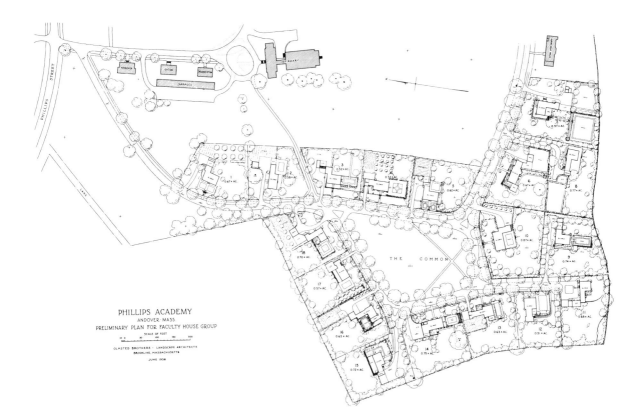

Olmsted Brothers, Preliminary Plan for Faculty House Group, 1936, drawing. Frederick Law Olmsted NHS

OM LEFT: Palmer House, circa 1937   BOTTOM RIGHT: Palmer House, interior, circa 1937

treasurer Sawyer, observing that it was not necessary to build the faculty houses on the previously envisioned large lots, as people no longer wanted the care and upkeep of front and back yards.[26]

Following Perry, Shaw & Hepburn's productive period, the architectural work in the mid-1950s was of a much different nature, designed to meet the needs of a modern campus.

THE ARCHITECTS COLLABORATIVE (TAC)

Many educational institutions in the United States experienced unprecedented growth after World War II. The return to normalcy in peacetime allowed people to once again invest time and money in education. Since the late 1930s, ideas about architecture and its role in society had changed dramatically; now, in 1945, principles of moderation, simplicity, and functionality prevailed. Important works of European modernism were going up in the Boston area, designed by architects considered "modern masters"—at Harvard University, for example, Walter Gropius designed Harkness Commons in 1947. Gropius, who formerly headed the avant-garde Bauhaus in Germany, became dean of Harvard's Graduate School of Design and a founding partner of The Architects Collaborative. At the Massachusetts Institute of Technology, the renowned Finnish architect, Alvar Aalto, assisted by Perry, Shaw & Hepburn, designed his serpentine-shaped Baker House dormitory (opened in 1949) along the banks of the Charles River.

The Architects Collaborative was founded in Cambridge, Massachusetts, in December 1945 by Sarah Pillsbury Harkness, Norman Fletcher, Benjamin Thompson, Louis McMillen, Jean Bodman Fletcher, Robert McMillan, and John Harkness. The group subsequently asked Walter Gropius to join them.[27] TAC was among the most influential firms in contemporary America. Its collaborative approach to design, its role as an exemplar of modernism, and the number and prominence of its commissions, have endowed TAC with a secure place in the history of post-World War II design.[28]

Founded as a genuinely collaborative venture, the firm made its reputation early with innovative modernist designs for private residences and educational institutions, including the Six Moon Hill houses in Lexington, the Harkness Commons (Graduate Center) at Harvard, and primary and secondary schools throughout Massachusetts. Indeed, their innovative educational work established them as the premier school designers in New England by the mid-1950s; it is therefore not surprising that Phillips Academy was interested in commissioning their work. TAC kept abreast of developments in teaching philosophy, exemplified by its architecture at Andover. It is not an overstatement to say that TAC was ultimately responsible for the postwar modernization of the Phillips campus.

During the 1950s and 1960s, the firm enjoyed a leading international practice, designing campuses, hospitals, and corporate and government facilities in the United States, Europe, and the Middle East. In 1964 the American Institute of Architects awarded TAC its Architectural Firm Award for distinguished achievement; five years later the AIA selected the firm to design its national headquarters in Washington, D.C. The firm had an especially strong influence on the architectural evolution of the Boston area, not only through built projects—as diverse in style as the JFK Federal Office Building (1967), Shawmut National Bank (1976), and Heritage on the Garden (1989)—but also through the teaching of many of the firm's designers.

At Phillips, Bartlett Hayes, then director of the Addison Gallery, reportedly summoned Walter Gropius (1883–1969) to Andover to discuss designing a new art building. TAC was greatly interested in making a contribution to campus architecture, as illustrated by Walter Gropius' 1949 *New York Times* article, "Not Gothic but Modern for Our Colleges." Gropius was emphatic about the important role of architecture in a student's education: "How can we expect our students to become bold and fearless in thought and action if we encase them timidly in sentimental shrines feigning a culture which has long since disappeared? . . . Stimulative environment is just as important to free the student's creative talent as vigorous teaching."[29] He concluded the article arguing against contextualism:

> We cannot go on indefinitely reviving revivals. Architecture must move on or die. Its new life must come from the tremendous changes in the social and technical fields during the last two generations. Neither medievalism nor colonialism can express the life of the twentieth-century man. There is no finality in architecture—only continuous change.[30]

It is not clear why Benjamin Thompson of TAC ultimately headed up the Andover work, but he was well-qualified to do so. On the selection of TAC as the firm in charge the campus work, Thompson recalled years later:

> I received the commission in the late fifties—I don't recall exactly how it happened but I suspect I was recommended by Bartlett Hayes, Director of the Andover Museum, who would have known my work. . . . I was invited for an interview, and the first thing I remember at Andover was sitting with John Kemper, the headmaster, for lunch. We were talking, and the subject of the military came up. I expressed my disdain for military training, and noticed that Kemper was tapping his ring in a very obvious way. I then saw that his ring was from Annapolis. . . . I quickly noted that I had been a member of the 90-day wonders (Naval Officers' Training) during the Second World War. Anyway, my first experience with John Kemper continued into a long-term relationship, and we became very good friends.[31]

Thompson was joined by TAC project architects J. Timothy Anderson, Thomas Greene, Joseph Maybank, Visvaldis Paukulis, Sherry Proctor, and G. W. T. Rankine, and remained involved from

the initial planning phase in 1956 through the design and construction of more than a dozen buildings. He played a vital role in the establishment of the new campus.

Thompson graduated from Harvard's Graduate School of Design to became one of TAC's founding partners. He remained there until 1965 when he established his own office, Benjamin Thompson Associates.[32] The renovation and rehabilitation of Quincy Market in Boston (1976) is perhaps Thompson's most celebrated work, innovating the "festival marketplace" design and concept as a tool of urban revitalization. Indeed, Thompson's concern in the 1950s for the heritage of the Andover campus—focusing on the integration of historic and contemporary architecture when his peer architects were concentrating almost exclusively on modernist design—became a signature of his work.

Although much current scholarship on TAC highlights certain notable buildings, the firm's approach at Andover, from extensive planning that involved individuals throughout the campus through the careful selection of building materials and the integration of technology, illustrated Benjamin Thompson's design method and the typical TAC approach.

The Architects Collaborative, model of proposed
Science Building and Rabbit Pond dormitories,
circa 1955

One surviving document from 1957, "Status Report on Phillips Academy Architectural Work," outlines TAC's recommendations for campus areas and structures that might be altered, expanded, and updated. Although this planning document was written to suggest sites for new dormitories, TAC also identified many places for potential future activity. The firm's paramount concern was to ensure respect for and preservation of the great quadrangles and the campus' historic buildings:

> Important to this work immediately was the appreciation of the existing architecture and planning to the main academic group. The Great Quadrangle is a strong design supplemented by the vista. The latter affords a visual connection between the car on Main Street and the Great Quadrangle. Andover is extremely fortunate in having the Great Lawn to provide a monumental separation between the highway and the campus.[33]

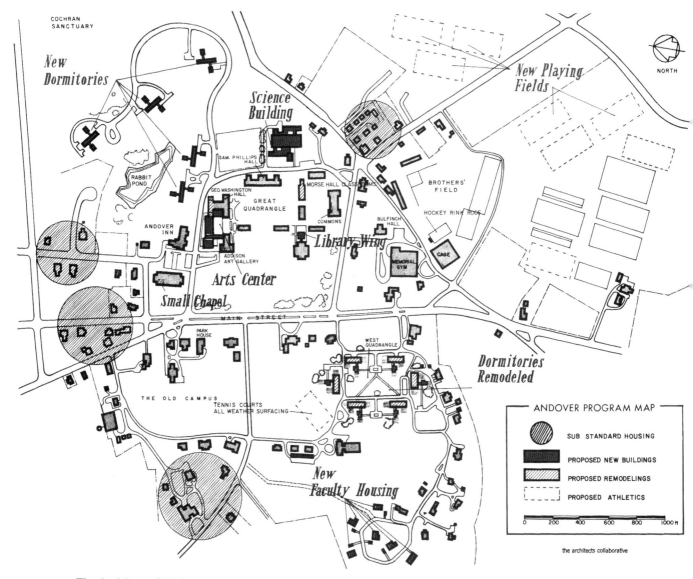

The Architects Collaborative, Andover Program Map, circa 1957

In the "Status Report," TAC mentions both the rationale and the need for completing a master plan for the campus, noting that such a document would identify short- and long-term areas for campus development. It would also present costs and cost comparisons for constructing new buildings and remodeling existing structures.[34] Among the sites singled out for discussion were George Washington Hall, the Addison Gallery, the Andover Inn, and Foxcroft, Bartlet, Samuel Phillips, and Williams Halls.

TAC also discussed potential landscaping, appropriate plantings for new buildings, the placement of flowering trees, and traffic flow around and through the campus. "The perpetuation and preservation of houses along Main Street," the report concluded, "should receive careful attention. This is, and will continue to be, one of the finest New England streets."[35] TAC was ultimately retained by Andover to develop a master plan for the campus in 1957, known as the *Andover Program*.[36]

THE ANDOVER PROGRAM OF 1958

Phillips and TAC issued the *Andover Program* of 1958. The Program stated:

> An extraordinary amount of thought has been given to the design of the new dormitories to afford the right balance of privacy and independence for both boys and housemaster, and yet to make possible a natural and friendly means of their getting together. In such buildings experienced housemasters should make their influence felt upon boys.[37]

Through descriptive text and drawings the report articulated the main points of the campus building campaign. Of particular interest were the cut-away (or, sectional) views of the dormitory, the "flexible laboratory," and the art center.

Started in 1957, the Rabbit Pond dormitories were the first buildings completed. They were designed to facilitate a casual interaction between faculty and students. Indeed, the *Andover Program* envisioned: "At the heart of the new dormitory concept is the Common Living Room, an extension of the senior housemaster's study. The aim is to provide a natural meeting ground for the housemaster and his boys."[38] Rather than featuring a typical single- or double-loaded corridor, the scheme clustered students into groups of eight, housed in single and double units. The common spaces were located on the ground floor with bedrooms on both the first and second floors.

The dorms were designed to fit into the low-rise scale of the campus and to meet the gentle topography around the pond. The clustered structures had a residential feel rather than an institutional character, exactly what the architect and the administration intended to achieve. The dormitories' pitched roofs, symmetrical facades, and simple punched windows reflected elements of modern international style design, yet nonetheless were intended to harmonize with the traditional architecture on campus. As Thompson noted:

Since all the architecture on the Andover campus was very traditional, for the first project it was necessary to prove that I could do a modern building (efficient, workable, affordable) that would fit in to a very pastoral setting. This suggested that it had to have a sloping roof and recognize the traditions of previous Andover buildings—brick walls, punched windows in a symmetrical facade. The most interesting thing about the Andover dorm program was that there would be two resident faculty members living at opposite ends of the building. Each teacher would have about 40 students living in his zone, with a common living room shared by all. This of course created certain tensions, because one teacher would usually be senior to the other teacher. We tried to make the facilities so comfortable and friendly that everyone would feel equally well accommodated and "at home." The dorm building was very successful, and eventually we built three more.[39]

TAC also created a nondenominational chapel in the basement of the existing chapel originally designed by Charles A. Platt. The new chapel was a wonderful bit of "found space." As reported in *Architectural Record* in 1963:

> Thompson found a one-way ribbed slab system left exposed in the neglected basement, had it and the supporting columns cleaned and painted white to create a handsome effect. Bartlett Hayes, director of the Addison Gallery and the visual arts program at Andover, takes special delight in the chapel and finds much that satisfies him in the fact that Thompson found rich visual qualities in a structural system which an architect of a former generation would expose only in a basement. With the exposed brick walls, slate floor and recessed lighting, the scale is intimate and the overall effect conducive to reflection.[40]

Arguably the two most significant structures for the campus and the architects were the Thomas M. Evans science building and the Art and Communications Center. Both buildings were started in 1959. The science building, referred to as the "Flexible Laboratory" in the 1958 program, was constructed to be just that, to house biology, chemistry, and physics. This project once again revealed that Thompson and the administration were thinking carefully about the requirements of the building. Indeed, design development lasted six years. Featuring wide expanses of glass, brick piers, and a heavy, projecting coffered concrete overhang, the internal structure was essentially three independent buildings, which housed each of the three hard sciences, linked by a

Thomas M. Evans Hall, Physics Wing, 1963

common lobby. While the lobby, corridors, and auditorium were permanent, the science laboratories were designed to be repartitioned according to need. The building was designed to have as few bearing walls as possible, which maximized the flexible floor space. Thompson said of the design:

> Brick, granite, slate and glass, within a stone-like bush-hammered concrete structure—would make a modern composition that would both harmonize with the traditional campus and extend its vocabulary and spirit into the century we were teaching about.[41]

The Art and Communication Center presented a substantial visual challenge, due to its location at the edge of the Great Lawn and its connection to the Addison Gallery. When viewed from the Lawn, the structure has a striking presence in its relation to the Addison Gallery and George Washington Hall. The scale, materials, and proportions are harmonious. Thompson created a complementary composition by the use of brick, which matched the neighboring buildings, and the use of bush-hammered concrete, which resembled the dressed granite. In addition, Thompson positioned the concrete cornice and piers to relate to existing stringcourses and cornices, and the large plate-glass windows echoed the fenestration of the earlier buildings. The structure's relationship to the campus was particularly clever: the building's entrance is on the northwest, leading through a spacious courtyard and into the main campus. Thompson especially enjoyed this project, because it combined:

> a direct expansion of the Addison Gallery of Art and a wholly new creative space on campus. In those days the academy had no art-making facility; art was an historical study, and whatever practice was desired in painting, sculpture, graphics, or film, it was taught in an improvised space in the basement of the Addison Gallery, which has some very fine pieces in its collection. The Art Center as we designed it became the focal point of the whole Andover campus. I wanted students to be visible at their studio art making, so others could understand the vitality and enjoyment of the processes. I wanted people to enter the Center through a portal in the courtyard—Kemper called it a "sallyport" or an arched gateway through which four men could walk without breaking rank. All the studios were on display through large glass window-walls on this courtyard side. People then walked through the art building with its open halls serving as galleries, to get to the so-called front campus. This program of

The Architects Collaborative, Fine Arts Center, circa 1960, rendering creative art studies, and its growing emphasis in the curriculum, put Andover on the leading edge among secondary schools—and indeed ahead of many fine colleges—in recognizing the important place of experiential art-making in the traditionally formal and scholarly pursuit we call education.[42]

Initially one may think that Andover's architectural commissions during the mid-twentieth century were more reflective rather than progressive. Yet the architects' and the school's sensitivity to the existing environment and the introduction of innovative technology in the campus buildings, suggested this was not the case. Of far greater importance was Andover's commitment to providing the tools for the students to succeed in an ever-changing world. The administration continued the long-standing tradition of commissioning architects who were responsive to the needs of students and faculty. The Architects Collaborative thought carefully about the users of their buildings. How would the masters and students live and interact in the dormitories? How should the science center be designed to best facilitate experimentation? Was the art center providing the space needed to explore art in many media? Was the non-denominational chapel serving the campus population?

Benjamin Thompson and TAC considered these questions and hundreds more, and in answering them, created numerous places and spaces for experiential learning, for reflection, for fostering community. Thompson summed up his Andover work in a recent interview:

> Andover was an early opportunity to press forward on solutions to the question that motivated me throughout my career: how to build for today (technically and formally) while harmonizing with the eclectic built environment of the past? How to reflect the traditional humanistic scale and quality, through selection of materials, massing, detailing, and working out of a plan, without sentimental imitation? It was harmonious continuity—carrying on the meaning of our built world by injecting new life and use into valuable usable old structures. In the 1960s my interest in creative restoration led me to projects at a larger urban scale, starting with Faneuil Hall Marketplace in Boston, followed by mixed use sites and old-new projects throughout America and abroad. The expansion of Andover makes a statement in its own terms, but in retrospect it was also a rich context and opportunity that stimulated my thinking about work I would do for the next thirty years.[43]

163

Cynthia Zaitzevsky

The Olmsted Firm:

SHAPING OF THE PHILLIPS ACADEMY LANDSCAPE

OVER A PERIOD OF MORE THAN SEVENTY YEARS, from 1891 to 1965, the Olmsted firm left an indelible mark on the landscape of Phillips Academy. The firm developed an early master plan, sited buildings, planned road systems, laid out a proposed subdivision, and prepared dozens of planting schemes, ranging in scale from tree plantings for the entire main campus to window boxes for dormitories. They worked closely with all of the academy architects, including Alexander Wadsworth Longfellow, Guy Lowell, and Charles A. Platt. They also designed a garden for the Andover Inn, gardens for Phelps House and other faculty residences, and laid out the Moncrieff Cochran Bird Sanctuary. Because of Charles Platt's prominence in the final configuration of the Phillips Academy campus, the part played by the Olmsted firm has been little appreciated.

Phillips Academy was one of the largest projects in the history of the Olmsted firm: the first plan in the Phillips file (Olmsted job number 176) is dated May 1891; the last is dated April 8, 1965. The file contains over 1,300 drawings, perhaps a record for the firm with any one client.[1] By contrast, the firm produced just over 500 drawings for Franklin Park in Boston, which remains one of the most important parks Frederick Law Olmsted Sr. designed.

When he was fifteen years old, Frederick Law Olmsted spent a year in Andover, November 1837 to November 1838, apprenticing as a civil engineer with Frederick Augustus Barton, who was studying for the ministry at the Andover Theological Seminary.[2] Olmsted was also registered at the English Academy in the same year.[3] In spite of his early connection with Andover, there is no record the senior Olmsted visited the campus between 1891 when Phillips first retained his firm and Olmsted's retirement in September 1895. Yet during this period the firm grew rapidly, with several partners, associates, and plant specialists actively engaged at the academy. As was customary, a partner was always in charge of the project. Even for engagements in which much of the responsibility was delegated to others, Olmsted always reviewed plans, was briefed thoroughly on what was being done, and approved all major decisions.

At the time the Olmsted firm began landscaping at the academy, it had designed numerous campuses. As early as 1865 Frederick Law Olmsted had developed plans and a report for the College of California in Berkeley (now the University of California, Berkeley), which were not implemented. The following year, he did the same for the Massachusetts Agricultural College in Amherst and for the Maine Agricultural College in Orono, both land grant colleges established under the Morrill Act of 1862.[4] While the trustees of these institutions rejected the schemes, the Olmsted firm designed the campus of Stanford University in Palo Alto, California, carried out between 1886 and 1914.[5] In addition to college campuses, by 1891 the firm had an established reputation for designing secondary school campuses. The first of these was the Lawrenceville School in Lawrenceville, New Jersey, begun in 1883, followed by the Groton School in Groton, Massachusetts. Like Stanford, Groton and Lawrenceville were new campuses. In keeping with the firm's later Middlesex School in Concord, Massachusetts (1901–1930), they featured an arrangement of major academic buildings around a central oval space. Groton and Lawrenceville were both designed in collaboration with Boston architects Peabody & Stearns, who also designed the gymnasium building at Phillips Academy.[6]

Over 74 years, the Olmsted firm's work at Phillips was concentrated in a number of design and construction campaigns, some of them major projects, others less significant. Exactly why the firm was engaged at the academy is not documented; perhaps their designs for Lawrenceville and Groton were recommendation enough. One personal connection might have been with Judge Robert R. Bishop, an academy trustee and an investor in the Newton Boulevard Syndicate, which hired the Olmsted firm between 1893 and 1899 to design a picturesque subdivision between Commonwealth Avenue and Beacon Street in Newton, Massachusetts.[7]

1891–1895

The Phillips Academy trustees first suggested the need for a "comprehensive plan for the grounds and buildings" in 1887.[8] Four years later they voted "that the Real Estate Committee be authorized to consult with Frederick Law Olmsted with reference to the location of the proposed new buildings, and the other buildings."[9] The Olmsted firm produced a "Preliminary Study of a plan for a comprehensive arrangement of building sites in anticipation of a large growth of the Academy." This plan set a number of parameters for future development, placing similar uses in close proximity while separating individual buildings by a system of curvilinear roads. The Olmsted firm's plan located future development of the campus in a sweep running south from Academy Hall at the juncture of Main and Salem Streets, behind Faculty Row, and curving back to Main Street to end on axis with Bulfinch Hall. Deliberately zoned by use—recitation halls, dormitories for students, and houses for faculty—it was a plan that allowed ultimate growth while imposing a careful balance of distinct yet adjacent districts. The trustees' real estate committee notes indicate that the firm presented two different plans: one described as "picturesque and irregular," which was adopted by the trustees; the other, which was rejected, called for Faculty Row to be gradually replaced by a series of imposing buildings that balanced with Seminary Row across the street.

With a master plan in hand, the initial problem the Olmsted firm faced in 1891–92 was to site a series of cottage-style dormitories on Old Campus Road. John Charles Olmsted, Olmsted's nephew and stepson and a partner in F. L. Olmsted and Co., received a letter on March 9, 1892,

166

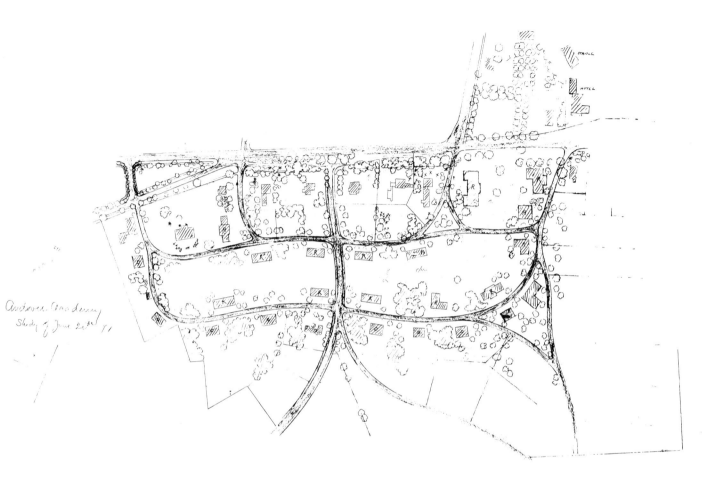

Frederick Law Olmsted & Co., Andover Academy, Study of June 20th, '91, drawing. Frederick Law
Olmsted NHS.

from architect Joseph Everett Chandler of Cole & Chandler, who were designing the second dormitory, Andover Cottage.[10] Chandler and Olmsted apparently had already met on campus, and
John Charles had given the architect some suggestions for siting.[11] Included in the Olmsted correspondence are valuable reports of visits—internal memos the firm began filing in the early 1890s
that record field inspections and client meetings. On March 29, 1892, John Charles Olmsted noted
a conference he attended with Judge Bishop, principal Cecil Bancroft, and treasurer Alpheus H.
Hardy regarding the site of Andover Cottage, money for which was being raised by subscription
from Andover citizens. John Charles offered the following opinion:

> it was desirable to group the future buildings of the Academy as
> far as possible, not only as suggested by our plan in relation to

their use, but also with regard to their architectural style, keeping, if possible, all buildings in classic style south of Phillips St., and those in the Gothic, Romanesque, or other irregular style, to the north of Phillips St.[12]

Judge Bishop took an active role in the academy's campus planning and building at this time. John Charles met again with Judge Bishop in June 1892, this time about the location of the third cottage.[13] Throughout 1892, the firm worked on site plans and road studies for the cottages and on the preliminary campus plan. By year's end the scope of the firm's work had broadened. On December 30, D. H. Coolidge, an Olmsted draftsman, reported that he had left a print of the firm's "Preliminary Plan" with architects Andrews, Jaques & Rantoul, who were making sketches for a new building for the theological seminary.[14] (They would design the John–Esther Gallery for Abbot Academy a decade later.) In 1894 the firm prepared several studies for the improvement of the grounds of the Mansion House, and on April 10, 1895, John Charles Olmsted met with Judge Bishop concerning the plantings there. Bishop wanted to discourage short cutting and Olmsted suggested an irregular mixed hedge with prickly shrubs on the outside.[15]

1900–1910

In December 1900, Olmsted Brothers began a decade of intense involvement, with both John Charles Olmsted and Frederick Law Olmsted Jr. serving as partners-in-charge. On December 15, 1900, Olmsted Jr. met with Judge Bishop and George Brown Knapp, who was a classmate of Judge Bishop and a recently appointed trustee. The board had just bought a field for athletic use, and the academy had received a legacy, which, combined with other funds, allowed them to go ahead with plans for a new athletic building. Olmsted made a couple of sketches on the spot. Although he thought it "would be stunning" to align the new building's front entrance with the axis of the Elm Walk, he drew the building closer to and at right angles to Bulfinch, where the Borden Gymnasium by Peabody & Stearns was built.[16] Throughout 1901 and 1902, Olmsteds' draftsmen worked on studies for the athletic field and a subdivision adjacent to it that was never realized.[17] Detailed planting plans were made for the grounds of the gymnasium and Bulfinch Hall.

On November 6, 1901, Frederick Law Olmsted Jr. and Guy Lowell visited Andover and together "fixed" the location for the new museum building for the department of archeology. They both agreed the building should be placed so that the axis of the museum would pass midway between the two elms in front of the site.[18] Landscaping and grading studies for the museum continued through 1902 and 1903. The firm also prepared plans for the walks between the gymnasium and Professor Graves' house (Hardy House), which had been remodeled by Boston architect William Ralph Emerson.[19] In 1903 Herbert J. Kellaway, an Olmsted firm employee, photographed existing conditions near the gymnasium, old academy building, and the site of the archaeology building.[20]

TOP: Olmsted Brothers, View taken from Rear of [Borden] Gymnasium showing the south side of the Dining Hall [Bulfinch Hall], 1902. Frederick Law Olmsted NHS   BOTTOM: Olmsted Brothers, View of the [Borden] Gymnasium before the removal of the maple in front of the building, 1902. Frederick Law Olmsted NHS

In February 1903, Frederick Law Olmsted Jr., discussed with the trustees the future growth of the academy. Olmsted's comments about the meeting indicated that the board was contemplating substantial changes to the campus:

> The tendency is to move the centre of the school life up toward the top of the hill, away from the village and the present academy building. The chief reasons for this are to concentrate the school buildings more compactly for the sake of convenience and discipline; to get the school life a little further from direct contact with the village. . . . The sentiment seemed to be decidedly in favor of a group—perhaps a quadrangle or a double L-shaped pair of quadrangles—extending west of the proposed site for the academy building and then turning north parallel with the main street but back of it.[21]

These ideas were the basis for campus plans that would continue for twenty years. The firm prepared a plan for additional buildings following these recommendations. The plan submitted to the trustees in March 1903 showed the proposed academy building, in the words of the transmittal letter, "set well back from Main Street upon the axis of the straight path leading to the dining hall, and sites are shown for two future buildings for school purposes—recitation, laboratory or otherwise." Three quadrangles of dormitories were laid out to the west of the academy building.[22] By spring 1903, the wooden English Commons buildings on the north side of Phillips Street had been removed, and the Olmsted firm had regraded the area.[23]

In 1907 the Olmsted firm prepared studies for roads near Eaton Cottage.[24] And in 1908 Olmsted Brothers prepared landscape studies for a lot at the corner of Morton and Bartlet Streets and for moving a house to a lot on Highland Road.[25] In fall 1908 the firm sent treasurer James C. Sawyer extracts from a report made by F. L. Olmsted Jr. on the care of trees in the Harvard Yard, noting that although the general condition of the trees in both places was identical, the Cambridge trees were in worse condition.[26]

Near the end of 1908 and throughout 1909 the Olmsted firm made studies for widening and developing Main Street, which still had an active streetcar line, and also School Street. Olmsted Brothers wrote to Sawyer, "The widening of Main Street is made necessary on account of the increased traffic over it, together with the lack of space for vehicles at certain points between the tracks and trees at the side of the highway."[27] Main Street would loom large in planning studies in the months ahead, largely due to the academy's purchase of the former seminary's land and buildings. A few days before Christmas 1909, Percival R. Gallagher, now Olmsted's partner-in-charge at Phillips, recorded an important meeting with treasurer Sawyer and headmaster Stearns at Olmsted Brothers' Brookline office:

Instead of the institution being practically limited to the west of Main Street it may now be considered as forming a great area with Main Street passing directly through the centre. The question seemed to be open in the minds of both Mr. Stearns and Mr. Sawyer whether either side would be considered more important than the other, although they pointed out that the natural centre of the institution seemed to be growing toward where the gymnasium and dining hall have now been located. The office of the institution will ultimately occupy the Theological Library Building, which is not far from the previously mentioned buildings.[28]

While Gallagher felt that the main lines of the firm's earlier plan were correct, Stearns believed that there were too many dormitories in the area assigned to student housing and stressed the importance of privacy. Stearns also wanted much more development to the east of the dining hall (Bulfinch Hall) and the seminary buildings. Possible sites for new academic buildings and dormitories were explored.[29] This was the opening volley in a series of proposals and discussions over the placement of academy buildings that was only resolved by the meteoric appearance of Charles A. Platt in 1922.

In early 1910 Olmsted draftsmen worked on studies that culminated in a "Revised General Plan."[30] Further studies were also made of Main Street and the lot at the corner of Bartlet and Morton Streets.[31] For the rest of the year, Olmsted partners and draftsmen studied the elm walk and other former seminary property and locations for new dormitories.[32] They also looked at a re-arrangement of Brothers Field.[33]

1911–1920

In 1911 Olmsted Brothers completed many studies for siting and planting new dormitories, beginning with Day Hall. One employee report contained one of the few references to the Great Elm, responding to Sawyer's request for advice about how to prune and care for the large elm, with its unbroken bare trunk.[34] The Olmsted firm suggested sending an assistant to campus to oversee the pruning, and also recommended that in the future, elms standing near construction sites "should be protected by fences."[35]

In 1911 Olmsted Brothers prepared site plans for the infirmary, then being designed by Guy Lowell, and in 1912 the firm worked on a study for subdividing land belonging to the academy and lying between Morton Street, Bartlet Street, and Highland Road. Olmsted partner Gallagher walked over the site with Sawyer, headmaster Stearns, and Judge Bishop, bringing with him earlier plans for a scheme of roads. The trustees felt that there was a demand for houses in this area and they wanted to dispose of the land. Stearns, however, wanted to drain Rabbit Pond; the

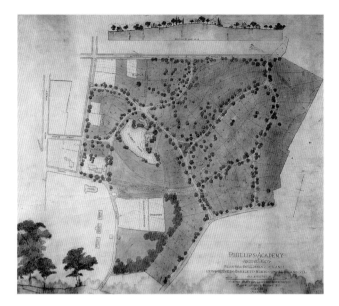

LEFT: Olmsted Brothers, Plan for Development of Lands Lying between Bartlett [sic], Morton and Highland Streets, 1912, reproduction of drawing. Office of Physical Plant, Phillips Academy   BELOW: Olmsted Brothers, General Plan of Campus, 1913, drawing. Frederick Law Olmsted NHS

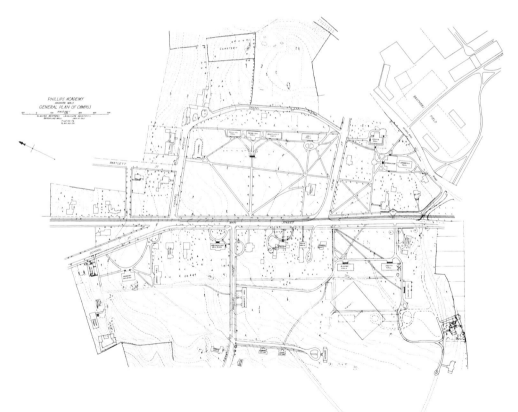

others did not agree.[36] Olmsted Brothers prepared several plans for the proposed subdivision.[37] While the trustees liked the plan, the subdivision was never developed and most of the land became part of the Moncrieff Cochran Sanctuary.[38]

In 1913 Olmsted prepared a new "Guide Map" of the campus, as well as studies for new dormitories, window boxes for South (Adams), Bishop, and Day Halls, and different plantings around treasurer Sawyer's house.[39]

Phillips and the Olmsted firm did little together during the war years, 1914–1918, save for minor studies—roads near the gymnasium; and planting schemes in 1915;[40] locations for a new flagpole; and the siting of an assembly hall and recitation building on the old Mansion House property, on the axis of the Bulfinch Hall.[41] In 1919 the Olmsted firm developed plans for locating a new auditorium and a recitation building on the west campus.[42] The firm made studies for a new elm walk west of Main Street, which was not executed.[43] The landscape architects spent a good deal of time in 1919 designing grading and planting plans for Charles Thompson on Hidden Field Road, who, while not affiliated with the academy, was building a house on school land.[44] By this time, Edward Clark Whiting had joined Percival R. Gallagher as partner-in-charge.[45]

In 1920 the Olmsted firm again prepared site plans for a new auditorium building and bell tower, this time on the west side of Main Street.[46] They also made a plan for an addition to the Chapel Cemetery.[47]

1921–1929

Olmsted partner Edward Clark Whiting arrived on campus on March 16, 1921, to visit treasurer Sawyer about plans for expanding the school enrollment to 1,000 students. Whiting reported, "I said if that were decided upon it would certainly be desirable to study the whole problem of the physical development of the Academy grounds with that in view and see just what would ultimately be needed in the way of dormitories, class room buildings, offices, athletic fields, etc., and revise the plan if necessary to meet that end."[48] Shortly after that discussion, the Olmsted firm prepared a new general plan and also studied a proposed subdivision west of the infirmary and additional tennis courts for Brothers Field.

In September 1921, the trustees' building committee retained Charles A. Platt of New York as consulting architect for new building and the memorial tower. Sawyer telephoned Olmsted Brothers on September 22 to inform them of the board's decision:

> The building committee had selected Charles A. Platt of New York as consulting architect and that Mr. Platt was going to study the problem without any knowledge of sites previously suggested for the new building and memorial tower. Mr. Sawyer was anxious for us to get off the print to Mr. Platt tonight, showing existing conditions in topography but not showing our proposed site for the new building and memorial tower.[48]

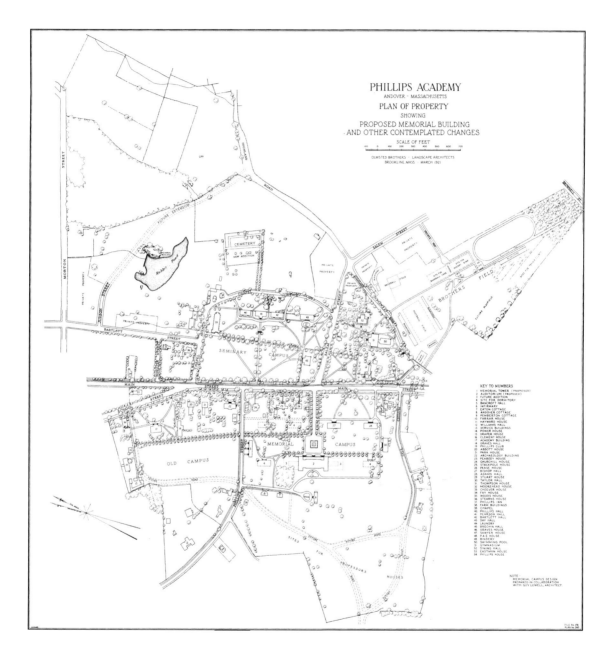

Olmsted Brothers, Plan of Property Showing Proposed Memorial Building and other Contemplated Changes, 1921, drawing. Frederick Law Olmsted NHS

The Olmsted firm complied with Sawyer's request and sent Platt its general plan of 1913. Platt came into the situation "cold," with no preconceived notions or information on existing plans, and between 1921 and 1932 he designed a radical reconfiguration of the campus. He also designed six new buildings and recommended the demolition or moving of other structures. To his credit, Platt was concerned about offending Guy Lowell and Olmsted Brothers, whose campus master plan he was in the process of scrapping. Lowell was asked to design the new classroom building, Samuel Phillips Hall, this time on the east side behind Seminary Row. [50]

In November 1921, an ice storm seriously damaged trees on the Elm Arch as well as elsewhere on campus and along Main Street. Olmsted's tree expert Hans J. Koehler came on the scene right away to report: "The work to be done consists mostly in cutting back or cutting off limbs broken by the storm. A little of this had been done, but the cuts had not been made close enough. I showed how they ought to be made."[51] Although Dutch elm disease had not yet struck Andover, Koehler wondered,

> whether the American elm is the most happy choice; I mean
> whether the conditions are good for elms. . . . Might it not be a

Devastation along the Elm Arch, November 1921

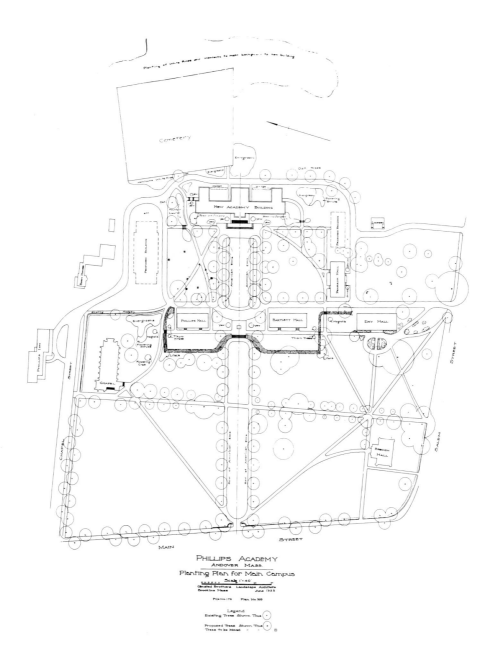

Olmsted Brothers, Planting Plan for Main Campus, 1923, drawing. Frederick Law Olmsted NHS

good scheme to retain elms for the large central areas, any replacements by young elms to follow the present design of planting. Outside of this central area, the elms to be replaced by red, scarlet, black, and white oaks; white, red and pitch pine; hemlock, English elm, European linden, European beech, and other trees. In the elm area the soil condition ought to be very much improved. Of course, the soil conditions would stand improving everywhere; especially considering the fact that the leaves have been removed for years and never has anything been added in the way of fertilizer.[52]

Shortly after Koehler's visit, the firm gave the academy a list of the tools used for tree surgery on the Boston Common; by December Phillips had enlisted a campus crew of eight men "in the trees" and two or three ground men.[53] Koehler also pointed out eighteen or so trees that could be taken out, most located where the arrangement of trees was informal and behind buildings on the northerly or northeasterly sides of the campus.[54] Koehler made site visits in January and April 1922, finding that the grounds crew's tree surgery was being done well and cost between $6 and $7 a tree for the 1,300 trees damaged by the storm.[55]

By early 1922 Platt's ideas were already making an impact. Percival Gallagher visited the campus in January with Ralph Henry of Guy Lowell's office to review grades for new dormitories. With Sawyer, he inspected the grounds near Pearson Hall, with the notion of concentrating the academic buildings there, an idea initially recommended by Platt.[56] Platt wrote to Frederick Law Olmsted Jr. for the first time in May 1922, noting his consultations with Lowell and requesting to see more of the Olmsted firm's plans. Gallagher visited Platt in his New York City office the next week. Sawyer told Gallagher in June that the trustees' building committee, in agreement with Platt and Lowell, decided to locate the memorial tower in the center of the old training field at the corner of Salem and Main Street. The tower was built the following spring in 1923.

Also in 1922, Gallagher created planting schemes for the four principal areas of the campus: Main Campus, including Academy Building (Samuel Phillips Hall); West Campus, adjacent to Adams and Bishop Halls; Memorial Commons and Tower; and Rabbit Pond. Two of these planting plans (176–338 and 176–340) were destroyed, but the planting plans for the Tower Lot (176–341) and the Main Campus (176–339) have survived. Gallagher's covering letter includes an interesting explanation of Olmsted's planting philosophy for the campus:

> In the case of the Main Campus the chief problem is the arrangement of the formal rows of American elms extending from the Main Gateway to the new Academy Building. It is Mr. Platt's recommendation that there shall be an open vista sixty feet wide between rows of trees along this main axis. Another problem is the establishment of an evergreen plantation of the native white

pine to form in time a rich green background to the Academy Building. This would be located on steep ridgy ground east of the Cemetery and would thus partially enclose it. . . . In addition, we have shown locations for groupings of spring flowering shrubs, such as forsythia, rhododendron, laurel and spiraea, together with such flowering trees as the crab, hawthorn and magnolia.

Thus it may be said that there are three types of planting: First, the avenues and rows of elms, which may be extended to include the oaks and European linden. Second, the groupings and masses of evergreens such as the white pine, the spruce and yew, intended for their winter appearance and to give strength to the general landscapes of the campus. Third, the supplementary plantings of flowering trees and shrubs sometimes in groups and sometimes disposed singly and in composition with the buildings, steps or other features of the ground.[57]

For the planting of the Memorial Commons and Tower, Gallagher tried to carry out a suggestion made by Platt—enclosing hedge of buckthorn and evergreen plantings at the entrances of the paths.[58]

LEFT: Memorial Bell Tower, circa 1923   TOP: Fairchild, Aerial Survey, taken from south, looking north along Main Street, 1928   BOTTOM: Olmsted Brothers, Model of Phillips Academy, shown from north, looking south along Main Street, 1925

A week later Gallagher met with Sawyer to discuss Olmsted Brothers' role in campus planning and Platt's employment as consulting architect. Sawyer had not attended the final meeting and thus could not argue for the continued employment of the Olmsted firm. After all, Sawyer concluded, "the particular thing for which Mr. Platt had been employed having been accomplished, it was only necessary to have O.B. make the plan." Gallagher took the news gracefully although it signaled a distinct shift in the relationship between the school and the firm.[59] For the balance of 1922, the firm developed plans for the new baseball cage being designed by Lowell, for paths and walkways, and for the moving of Pearson Hall.[60]

Pearson's relocation from the center of Seminary Row opened up a vista extending westward from Samuel Phillips Hall—a clear view from the center of campus to Mount Monadnock in New Hampshire. However, when the clearing for the vista was completed, it was found that it actually did not center on Mount Monadnock but on the foothills to the south of the mountain. The concept was identical to that of the Rainier Vista at the University of Washington in Seattle, a campus plan by Olmsted Brothers about a decade earlier.

In 1925 the trustees asked Platt, who conferred with Olmsted and Guy Lowell, about commissioning a model of the campus east of Main Street. Model maker J. W. Baston, then working for Olmsted Brothers, was assigned to make an extensive model showing the land holdings of the school. The model plotted all the buildings standing by 1925, except for the old library (Brechin Hall), and added a proposed new library, two new dormitories and a laboratory building.[61] The model was continually modified as changes occurred on campus.[62] In 1927 a second model, of the "idealized academy," showed a new chapel (on the site where Addison Gallery would eventually stand), the complete layout of Flagstaff Quadrangle, and a dormitory on Salem Street that was never built, which, with the library and Day Hall, would have formed another open court.

Olmsted Brothers prepared garden plans in summer 1928 for Tucker House, for Mrs. Claude Fuess who had moved plants there from another location. In 1929 Platt made plans for the Addison Gallery, and the Olmsted firm prepared studies for the grounds.[63] In 1929 Olmsted also began plans for the Bird Sanctuary, which Platt had suggested to Cochran half jokingly. Cochran loved the idea and the project was on.[64]

1930–1939

In 1928 the Harriet Beecher Stowe House, then the Phillips Inn, was moved from the site of the present inn to its current location, and a new inn was built from plans by W. Sydney Wagner, of Bottomley, Wagner & White. Once completed in 1930, Platt decided a large perennial garden should be planted at the back of the Andover Inn, and both he and the Olmsted firm prepared plans.[65] In addition to having its plan critiqued by Platt, the Olmsted firm incorporated suggestions "by Andover people." Ultimately, Mrs. Stewart, wife of the inn manager, was responsible for supervising the garden.[66]

The Olmsted firm's most important contribution to the campus in 1929 and the early 1930s was the Moncrieff Cochran Bird Sanctuary, for which numerous plans and photographs

Olmsted Brothers, Topographical Map of Sanctuary, 1930, drawing. Frederick Law Olmsted NHS

(but little correspondence) survive. Astonishingly, Platt and Cochran sold the trustees on the concept, and Cochran footed the bill. Was there another boys' preparatory school in the country that possessed a 150-acre naturalistic landscape devoted to the study of birds, with a log cabin and originally a bird keeper and putting greens? Most of the sanctuary was laid out on land that the school had previously intended to subdivide; the remaining land was purchased to consolidate the area between Morton, Highland, and Chestnut Streets. The extensive project involved constructing two artificial ponds, a dam, and several bridges, as well as planting trees and shrubs, primarily broad-leaved evergreens such as rhododendrons and mountain laurel. The major construction took place between spring 1929 and 1930, which was documented in a series of rare snapshots by Augustus Thompson.

In 1932 the Olmsted firm prepared a plan for Main Street, "Showing Two Travelled Ways Separated by an Isle of Safety of Turf."[67] This culminated several decades of Olmsted studies for Main Street. In 1933, Olmsted Brothers completed two relatively modest jobs on campus: one, transporting Mrs. Fuess's garden again, this time from Tucker House to the west of Phelps House, for which complete planting lists exist, together with records of new plants and design elements added by the Olmsted firm; and two, inspecting the condition of plants on campus, which Koehler systematically did twice a year. It was only in 1933 that letters between the Olmsted firm and the academy revealed any impact from the national depression, by now Phillips repeatedly telling the landscape architects that little work could be done at any one time. Work was completed incrementally, including new planting and maintenance of trees and shrubs. The academy had stockpiled a substantial inventory of trees and shrubs, and when Olmsted Brothers recommended new plants, these largely could be obtained by thinning existing plantations.

The Olmsted firm's correspondence also reveals the startling fact that the well-documented moving and demolition of buildings in the 1920s and early 1930s was accompanied by an equally dramatic moving of full-grown trees, primarily elms between 30 and 40 feet high.[68] Even before the reality of the Depression hit home, most of the trees were thriftily moved from other parts of the campus or from other locations in Andover. (The Elm Arch, a legacy of the theological seminary, remained intact, and dead trees were replaced.) In addition, the Olmsted firm purchased and planted vines—mostly 15-foot runners of Boston ivy—on new and moved buildings, at Cochran's special request to create instantaneously an ivy-covered campus. Only major architectural features, such as the Samuel Philips Hall portico and George Washington Hall's central bays were left free of vines.[69]

The Olmsted firm also planted a good deal of yew on campus in the 1920s and 1930s, which they no doubt would have done even if architect Platt, who favored the shrub, had not become the academy's advisor in 1921. To be sure, there were times when Platt specifically requested the shrub, as when he wanted to frame the distant view of the portico of Samuel Philips Hall by having a large Japanese yew to either side of the steps between the quadrangle and the Great Lawn. These were special yews, the "large, spreading type," one of which cost nearly $1,000, a large sum at the time.[70] Platt also requested yews on either side of Samuel

A. P. Thompson, Moncrieff Cochran Bird Sanctuary, May 1929 and April 1930. Frederick Law Olmsted NHS

Philips Hall's steps and yew groupings at each of the building's four corners. In addition, at Platt's request in 1931 the Olmsted firm planted yews, barberry, and spiraea in front of the Addison Gallery, even though by this time stringent economies were in effect.[71] Platt considered trees and shrubs to be important elements in the landscape; yews, in particular, formed platforms for buildings.[72]

The last major work Olmsted completed for Phillips Academy was the development of the Hidden Field faculty residences in the 1930s. The concept of faculty housing for this area had existed since the Olmsted firm first drew up its 1903 development plans for the west campus. The Olmsteds developed a plan in 1936 that laid out eighteen houses, each with gardens and garages on lots of approximately a half-acre. The houses were served by a circular street that enclosed a central green area, labeled the "Common." The elaborate plan was severely reduced for a lack of finances; two years later, with a modest donation from Edward Harkness, five houses were built to the plans of Perry, Shaw & Hepburn, served only by a winding dead-end road and a shorter-cul-de-sac. Driving by the houses on March 30, 1938, Edward Whiting bemoaned "the failure to secure the snap and individuality which we all aimed at in the beginning."[73]

TOP: A. P. Thompson, Moncrieff Cochran Bird Sanctuary, Spring 1929 and Spring 1930. Frederick Law Olmsted NHS   OPPOSITE TOP: Putting Green and Log Cabin in Moncrieff Cochran Bird Sanctuary, circa 1930   OPPOSITE BOTTOM: Stuart Travis, Entrance to Bird Sanctuary, Phillips Academy, Andover Massachusetts, 1930, drawing. Frederick Law Olmsted NHS

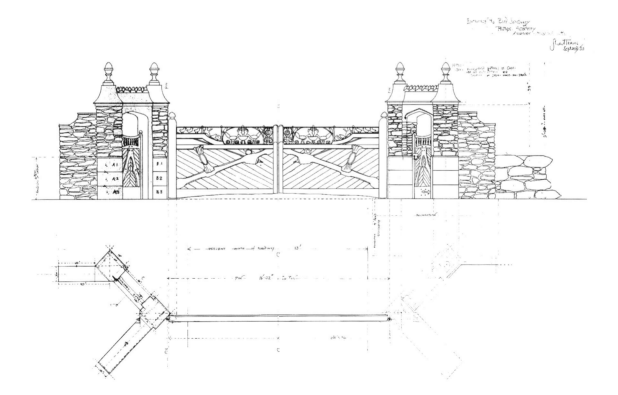

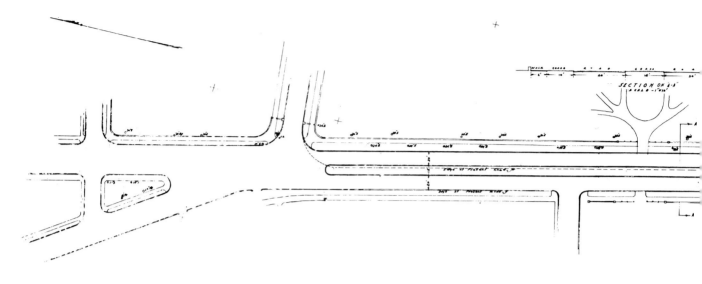

Olmsted Brothers, Study for Widening Main Street, 1932, drawing. Frederick Law Olmsted NHS

Hidden Field was not, however, the last plan the Olmsteds completed for the Phillips campus. In 1945 Olmsted Brothers prepared studies for a new Student Union that was to be located behind Samuel Philips and Morse Halls (where Evans Hall presently stands). The building by Perry, Shaw & Hepburn and the landscaping by Olmsted Brothers was never realized. In 1957, the firm was asked to do a general study of the entire campus and to make a plan for its development over the next ten years, although nothing came of the project.[74] In 1964–65, the Olmsted firm made studies for a new circulation system for the West Quadrangle, in association with the Boston architectural firm of Strickland, Brigham & Eldridge, who designed new common rooms for the six dormitories on this part of the campus. Joseph G. Hudak was Olmsted Associates' partner-in-charge for this project.[75] The firm's new circulation system was carried out, but with significant modifications.

EPILOGUE

While Charles Platt is the author of the final layout of the Phillips Academy campus, the Olmsted firm played a central role in the shaping of its landscape from their initial involvement in 1891 until their final input in 1965. This was an extraordinary range of design involvement for the Olmsted firm over an unprecedented period of time.

186

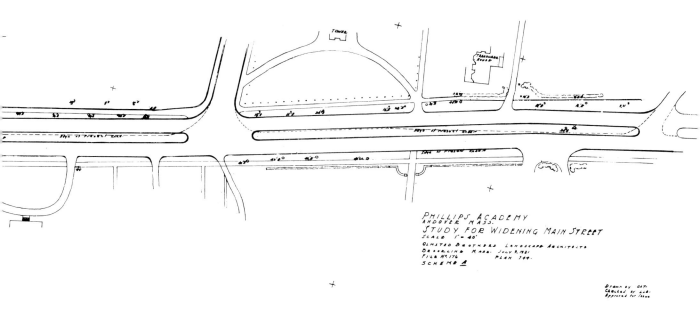

This essay is dedicated to the memory of James E. Robinson III (1933-1997), campus planner, architect and architectural historian, formerly of Sasaki Associates, Inc. Many years ago, Jack and I talked about writing a book together on the Phillips Academy campus.

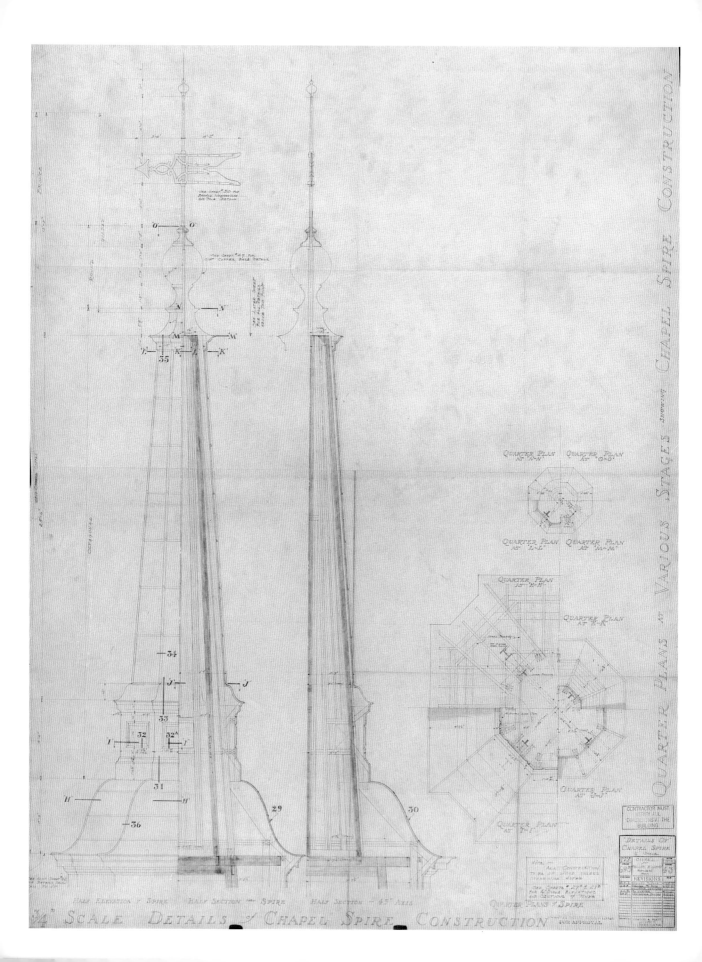

Postscript

PLANNING FOR THE FUTURE
OF THE PHILLIPS ACADEMY CAMPUS

Educational evolution is essential to a vital school and the campus must adapt to these new needs. Phillips Academy planners also hold the campus in trust for future generations, and must preserve our heritage. Successful planning for the future of the campus must strike a delicate balance between these important objectives. The school must avoid the tendency to be locked into a rigid historical configuration, and yet must also avoid the loss of significant components of the historical environment.

This balance is achieved by understanding what is important to preserve as change is considered. Not all historic elements are equally important. By making informed assessments of the effects of change and by avoiding change to the most significant components of the campus, we can introduce sensitive adaptations to the historical context without great loss. This planning process must be based on an understanding of the past. This book gives us a very valuable tool for these future planning initiatives.

MICHAEL E. WILLIAMS
Director of Facilities
Phillips Academy

Charles A. Platt, Details of Chapel Spire, 1931, drawing. Avery Architectural & Fine Arts Library

LEFT, TOP: Cochran Chapel pulpit screen and choir balcony, circa 1932

LEFT, BOTTOM: Cochran Chapel pulpit screen and choir balcony, 1999, photograph by Walter Smalling Jr.

TOP: Cochran Chapel balcony, circa 1932

BOTTOM: Cochran Chapel balcony, 1999, photograph by Walter Smalling Jr.

TURNER, "THE CAMPUS AS PALIMPSEST"

1   Sources of information on Phillips Academy and its related institutions include: Frederick S. Allis Jr., *Youth From Every Quarter: A Bicentennial History of Phillips Academy, Andover* (Andover: Phillips Academy, 1979); Susan McIntosh Lloyd, *A Singular School: Abbot Academy 1828-1973* (Andover: Phillips Academy, 1979); Robert A. Domingue, *Phillips Academy, Andover, Massachusetts: An Illustrated History of the Property* (Wilmington, MA: The Hampshire Press, 1990); and Roger Reed, Phillips Academy Historical Buildings and Landscapes Survey, unpublished, 1994, Office of Physical Plant, Phillips Academy.

2   There has been no comprehensive study of the campuses of American academies, so it is difficult to determine the exact historical relationship between Andover's campus and those of other academies. Judging from the published material that does exist (such as the histories of academies listed here in subsequent notes), it appears that Andover, as well as Phillips Exeter Academy in New Hampshire, have been unusual in their physical planning.

3   At Harvard, Samuel Phillips lived in the newly-built Hollis Hall. Allis, 21.

4   See Paul Venable Turner, *Campus, An American Planning Tradition* (Cambridge: MIT Press, 1984), 23–31, 38–51. Dartmouth's building was constructed in 1784, shortly after the founding of Andover.

5   For the history of early academies, see: Theodore R. Sizer, ed., *The Age of the Academies* (New York: Teachers College, Columbia University, 1964); Harriet Webster Marr, *The Old New England Academies* (New York: Comet Press Book, 1959); Robert Middlekauff, *Ancients and Axioms: Secondary Education in Eighteenth-Century New England* (New Haven: Yale University Press, 1963). According to a listing of academies today—covering New England, New Jersey, Pennsylvania, Maryland, Delaware, and North Carolina—seventeen were founded before Andover. *The Handbook of Private Schools*, 77th ed. (Boston: Porter Sargent Publishers, 1996). The early academies were different from contemporary prep schools in various respects, such as the age of students. Andover, for example, in its early years had students ranging in age from five to twenty-nine; the typical student, it seems, was in his early to mid-teens.

6   John W. Ragle, *Governor Dummer Academy: History, 1763–1963* (South Byfield, MA: Governor Dummer Academy, 1963). For Samuel Phillips's schooling at Dummer, see Allis, 19–21.

7   For the early history of Phillips Academy: Allis, *Youth From Every Quarter*; Sarah L. Bailey, *Historical Sketches of Andover* (Boston: Houghton, Mifflin, 1880), chapters 8 and 9; Abiel Abbot, *History of Andover* (Andover, 1829). For Phillips Exeter Academy: Laurence M. Crosbie, *The Phillips Exeter Academy, A History* (Exeter, NH: The Academy, 1923); Myron R. Williams, *The Story of Phillips Exeter* (Exeter, NH: Phillips Exeter Academy, 1957); Edward C. Echols, ed., *The Phillips Exeter Academy: A Pictorial History* (Exeter, NH: Phillips Exeter Academy Press, 1970).

8   See Allis, 35–64; Domingue, 1–2.

9   Allis, 47, 36.

10   The use of a domestic house by Governor Dummer Academy has been noted above. Leicester Academy, founded in 1783 in central Massachusetts, also used an existing house as its school building (Emory Washburn, *Brief Sketch of the History of Leicester Academy* [Boston, 1855, 6–15]). In contrast, Phillips Exeter Academy erected its first building expressly for this purpose in 1783, but it nevertheless had a domestic scale and appearance. Crosbie, 38 and illustration opposite 46; Echols, 8, 90.

11   For the complex early history of the Academy's land acquisition: Elias B. Bishop, "Report on the Real Estate Belonging to the Trustees of Phillips Academy in Andover," October 19, 1903, Treasurer's Office Real Estate, Box 2, 6.85.172, Phillips Academy Archive. A number of copies of this report are in the academy archive; tipped into one of them is the printed map entitled "Plan of Real Estate Belonging to Phillips Academy, Andover" and dated May 1891, on which are drawn in colored pencil the boundaries of the land parcels "held for benefit of Seminary," "for benefit of Academy," and "for joint benefit." While the date when these boundary lines were drawn on the map is not specified, it is likely to have coincided with the 1903 report.

12   Allis, 65, 69; Domingue, 5–6. This one-story structure is said to have measured 20 by 35 feet and held "no more than 30 or 40 scholars." (Domingue, 5), although Abbot's 1829 *History of Andover* states that it had "accommodations for sixty students" (Abbot, 115). In 1803 this building was sold and moved off the academy's grounds, and demolished in 1843 (*The Phillips Bulletin* [July 1915]:8). No contemporary representation of this structure exists, although later reconstructions of it have been attempted. Domingue, 1,6, 110–111.

13   Allis, 87, 162. According to Abbot's *History of Andover*, 115, "One room below was . . . a schoolroom . . . for 100 pupils. Two other rooms were for library, museum, recitations. The upper story was a spacious hall for speaking and exhibitions." Samuel Phillips stated the dimensions of the building in a letter to his uncle John Phillips, December 13, 1793: "Outside—64 feet, 8 inches by 33 feet, 4 inches. The length of the schoolroom inside was 36 feet. The height of the lower story was 12 feet, of the 'chamber' [second floor] 11 feet." Quoted in Allis, 710, n.8. There are no known visual representations of this building.

14   Phillips Exeter Academy followed this pattern to a large extent. Its physical nature has been described, for much of the nineteenth century, as being "merged almost imperceptibly into the surrounding town. " James McLachlan, *American Boarding Schools: A Historical Study* (New York: Scribners, 1970), 225; and according to Echols, 33, "From the beginning, the Academy has been an integral part of the town of Exeter."

15   This meeting house, on the site of the present South Church in Andover, was used by the academy until construction of the Andover Theological Seminary chapel in 1818. The academy students "occupied the three back seats in the lower front gallery" of the meeting house. Bailey, *Historical Sketches*, 433; see also Abbot, *History of Andover*, 121.

16   Phillips Exeter Academy, for example, adhered to this practice for many years. An 1832 map of the town of Exeter identifies the private houses that served as "Boarding Houses" for the academy students; reproduced in Echols, 24–25.

17   Allis, 58, 72–73, 76, 89–91, 114. In 1804 the Academy bought a house on Salem Street—the present Hardy House—to house several students; it soon was made the home of the headmaster.

18   Allis, 73, 89–90. The first student quoted is Josiah Quincy, later president of Harvard; the second is Robert H. Gardiner.

19   Allis, 76.

20   Allis, 46, 80.

21   These include Hardy House, purchased by the academy in 1804; Newman House, built in 1806-07 by preceptor Mark Newman; and Farrar House, built in 1811-12 by Samuel Farrar, treasurer of the academy. Bulfinch Hall, erected 1818–19, is the oldest surviving Academy building. Foxcroft and Pearson Halls are older, 1809 and 1817-18, but they were built for the seminary.

22   For the creation of the Andover Theological Seminary: Allis, 119–48. Allis does not address the question of how the seminary acquired its land—whether it was purchased from the Academy or whether the joint trustees simply used some of the Academy land for the Seminary. The 1903 "Report on the Real Estate Belonging to the Trustees of Phillips Academy" describes various land parcels and their original acquisitions, but does not explain clearly the relationship between academy and seminary lands, distinguishing only between lands "belonging to the Trustees for the benefit of the Academy," ". . . for benefit of the Seminary," or ". . . for joint benefit."

23   Allis, 119ff.

24   From a description of the theological seminary in *The Phillips Bulletin* 16 no. 4 (July 1922): 5.

25   There is an unsubstantiated story that the layout of the theological seminary campus was planned by Eliphalet Pearson, the first preceptor of the academy, who had left to teach at Harvard but then had returned to Andover to help found the seminary; see Allis, 127.

26   Foxcroft Hall (Phillips Hall) was the first building for the seminary. It served as a dormitory and included the chapel and library until Pearson Hall (Bartlet Chapel) was built to house the library, seminary classrooms, and chapel. Allis, 127; Domingue, 50–62. The top floors of the two dormitories were removed in the 1920s.

27   Allis, 127. This was Colonel John Phillips, the son of the founder of the academy.

28   Turner, *Campus*, 38–44.

29   The seminary students were mostly graduates of Yale and Dartmouth; see Allis, 130.

30   John Mason Kemper, *Phillips Academy at Andover, A National Public School* (New York: Newcomen Society of North America, 1957), 15.

31   Allis, 127–28, 152; Domingue, 54, 62–66, 135–38. The architects of most of these structures are not known, but Samuel Farrar supervised their construction. Stowe House was labeled "Students Workshop" in an engraving of the Andover buildings published in *Abbot's Magazine* (October 1834).

32   This land consisted of parcels that had comprised a large part of the original property of the academy, acquired by the Phillips family in 1777. "Report on the Real Estate," 1903, 111ff.

33   Turner, 47. What this space at Andover was originally called remains unknown. By the late nineteenth century it was apparently called "the common." Sarah Stuart Robbins, *Old Andover Days: Memories of a Puritan Childhood* (Boston: The Pilgrim Press,

1908), uses this term frequently, sometimes capitalized. It is called "the Campus lawn" in Claude Fuess, *An Old New England School* (Boston: Houghton Mifflin Company, 1917), 122. In April 1930, the trustees voted "that the old Seminary Lawn, west of Elm Walk, be named THE LAWN." Academy Records, Trustees of Phillips Academy, Book 3, April 20, 1930. Today it is most often called the "Great Lawn."

34   The first schoolhouse had been sold and moved off academy grounds in 1803.

35   The map accompanying the 1903 "Report on the Real Estate" designates a parcel of land at this location (the northeast corner of the intersection of Main and Salem streets) as land "held for the benefit of the Academy." By the late nineteenth century the "New Academy" building had burned and the site was occupied by the theological seminary library (Brechin Library); the fact that the site was still considered "Academy" land is an example of the fluid relationship between the properties of the two institutions.

36   The building is listed on an inventory Bulfinch made of his work. See Harold Kirker, *The Architecture of Charles Bulfinch* (Cambridge, MA: Harvard University Press, 1969), 305–06; Charles A. Place, *Charles Bulfinch, Architect and Citizen* (Boston: Houghton Mifflin, 1925), 234–37; and Charles A. Fagan IV, "Charles Bulfinch, Peter Banner, and Andover Hill," *Essex Institute Historical Collections* 20 no. 10 (April 1989): 177–95.

37   This is similar to the pattern of the façade of University Hall at Harvard, designed by Bulfinch, circa 1813.

38   Bulfinch's inventory does not list this building as one of his works. Evidence recently uncovered by David Chase indicates that Asher Benjamin was the designer for the building; the interior was completely changed in the nineteenth century and after the fire of 1896. For William Bartlet's role in this construction, see Fagan, 182–83 and David Chase. Bartlet paid for a third building at Andover, Phelps House, built 1809–11 for Professor Edward Griffin of the theological seminary; the proposed architect being Peter Banner.

39   For discussion of the history of the teachers' seminary, see Allis, 170–77 and "The Rise and Decline of the Teachers' Seminary," *The Phillips Bulletin* 10 no. 3 (April 1916): 10–15.

40   Allis, 171.

41   On page 10, the author of *The Phillips Bulletin* "Rise and Decline" article described the Stone Academy with surprisingly hyperbolic antipathy: "Bare, sombre, and unrelieved by ornamentation, the building resembled a jail or tomb, and seemed to be at once the strongest and the ugliest structure yet produced by the hand of man."

42   Allis, 152.

43   Allis, 177–79; Domingue, 18, 22–26.

44   A somewhat similar type of student-organized "boarding club" was instituted at Phillips Exeter in 1849, but it seems to have involved more administrative supervision. Echols, 31.

45   Allis, 146–48.

46   For Brechin Hall: Domingue, 66–68; for the Chapel: Domingue, 68–70.

47   Cynthia Zaitzevsky, "Cummings and Sears," *Macmillan Encyclopedia of Architects* (New York, 1982), 481–82. For Cummings, also see *The American Architect* 88 no. 4 (1905):

147–48.

48 Domingue, 57. This tower was removed in 1923 when the building was moved behind Bartlet Hall.

49 Academy Hall was designed by Charles A. Cummings, the architect of Brechin Hall and the Stone Chapel; Phillips and Graves Halls by Merrill & Cutler of Lowell, Massachusetts.

50 The reaction against the Victorian period was so strong at the academy that even when nineteenth-century architecture has long been rediscovered elsewhere, these structures continued to be described as "ugly" and even "hideous." For example: Allis, 178, 203, 236; Domingue, quotes Claude Fuess, 10, and Dr. Eaton, 12. The criticized nineteenth-century buildings include the "Stone Academy" (the English School building), the Latin and English Commons, the "Main Academy Building," and Graves Hall. The demolished buildings designed in the Victorian style included: the Academy Hall (razed 1927), Brechin Hall (razed 1929), Stone Chapel (razed 1931), and the Sanhedrin laundry and bathhouse, erected in 1881 and razed in 1929.

51 Allis, 219; see Alfred Stearns, Manuscript Reminiscences, in Headmaster Stearns' Personal Correspondence, Phillips Academy Archive, 6.37.9.P.

52 Allis, 219, 329–34.

53 James McLachlan, *American Boarding School*, 71ff, 136ff. Phillips Exeter Academy had started creating dormitories for its students in the 1850s. Echols, 32, 47–48.

54 Allis, 282–83; Domingue, 35–37, 123, 140–42.

55 Past historians have disagreed about the identity of the architects of these cottages. Allis, 283, states that all four were designed by Alexander W. Longfellow, as does the principal source of information on Longfellow's career, Margaret Henderson Floyd, *Architecture After Richardson* (Chicago: University of Chicago Press, 1994), 66, 452. However, recently discovered documentation affirms the attribution of Andover Cottage to George W. Cole and Bancroft Cottage to George C. Harding. Longfellow designed Pemberton Cottage and apparently this design was modified and used for Draper Cottage as well. (information provided to the author by Susan Montgomery, 1999).

56 Turner, 141–42, 150. Olmsted's "cottage system" proposals probably contributed to the decision of Smith College, circa 1875, to house its students in home-like structures called "cottages." The Smith cottages are described in Helen Lefkowitz Horowitz, *Alma Mater* (New York: Alfred A. Knopf, 1984), 77–78.

57 This was the first commission of what was to be a sixty-year relationship between the academy and the Olmsted firm, though Frederick Law Olmsted senior was not involved in the firm after 1895.

58 For the later uses of Bulfinch Hall: Allis, 327; Domingue, 156–59. Guy Lowell remodeled the dining hall. A dining hall had been designed by Merrill & Cutler in 1887 and another by Van Brunt & Howe; neither was executed. Both are illustrated in Domingue, 30.

59 For Bancroft Hall, see Allis, 286; Domingue, 144–45. The architect of Bancroft Hall was Alexander W. Longfellow. Reed, Phillips Academy survey.

60 Trustees minutes, June 12, 1902, 146

61 The departure of Andover Theological Seminary, the pur-

chase of its campus by the academy, and the use of its buildings, are discussed in detail in *The Phillips Bulletin* during this period—such as the issues of April 1908, September 1908, and January 1909.

62 A report entitled "Phillips Hall To Be Torn Down," in *The Phillips Bulletin* 6 no. 1 (October 1911), had to be retracted in the following issue, "Phillips Hall to be Restored," *The Phillips Bulletin* 6 no. 2 (January 1912): 6.

63 Day Hall: Domingue, 72. West Quad dorms (architect Guy Lowell): Domingue, 145–49. Regarding Taylor Hall, built 1913: "The location of the building was selected by the Olmsted Brothers"; Domingue, 147. Borden Gym and York Pool: Domingue, 160–61. Isham Infirmary: Domingue, 146–47. A design by Guy Lowell for the new Phillips Union, built adjacent to the Peabody Museum in 1915, illustrated in *The Phillips Bulletin* 9 no. 4 (April 1915).

64 Peabody Museum of Archaeology: Domingue, 124–25; Allis, 286.

65 Regarding the controversy over where the "center" of the campus was: Allis, 365.

66 Turner, 204–12

67 Lowell's plans were printed in *The Phillips Bulletin* 13 no. 3 (April 1919): 10–11. The site plan is notated "Adaptation from group-plan by Olmstead [sic] Bros., Landscape Architects. Guy Lowell Architect, 12 West St. Boston." A bird's-eye rendering of this project was illustrated in *The Phillips Bulletin* 14 no. 3 (April 1920): 25.

68 *The Phillips Bulletin* 13 no. 3 (April 1919): 4.

69 Lowell to Alfred Ripley, May 28, 1920, Treasurer's Office Correspondence, James C. Sawyer, 6.86.79; for bifurcated arrangement, see bird's-eye view of the campus in *The Phillips Bulletin* 5 no. 4 (July 1911).

70 An editorial in *The Phillips Bulletin* 14 no. 1 (October 1919): 3–4, stated, "This enterprise . . . has been conceived and carried through by graduates of the Academy and the Trustees have had little responsibility except to approve the general scheme."

71 Case to Claude M. Fuess, March 24, 1920, Treasurer's Office Correspondence, James C. Sawyer, Phillips Academy Archive, 6.85.79.

72 Alfred Stearns, "1900 to 1912," Headmaster Stearns' Personal Correspondence, 6.37.9.P

73 The decision to place the new academy building to the east of Main Street was apparently not made until late 1922. Lowell's previous plan for a new "Main Building" west of Main Street was still being described as imminent in April 1921 (*The Phillips Bulletin* 15 no. 3 [April 1921]: 3), and reports of a proposed alternative scheme for the east side of Main Street first appear in the *Bulletin* 15 no. 4 (July 21): 7–8. The January 1924 issue of the *Bulletin* described the new facilities and stated that "Now [the campus] center is abruptly shifted to the east side," 3. For the moving of Pearson Hall: Ruth Flick Quattlebaum, "Andover's Movable Campus," *Andover Bulletin* (Spring 1986): 5–8. For Samuel Phillips Hall: Domingue, 73–4.

74 Memorial Tower: Domingue, 165–67. A rendering of Lowell's design for the tower was illustrated in *The Phillips Bulletin* 17 no. 1 (October 1922): 2.

75 While hired initially only as a consultant to advise the school on the east side–west side controversy, Platt quickly became involved in all aspects of the campus planning and future development of the campus, in addition to designing six of the new buildings.

76   For Platt's work at Andover: see Morgan, 183–95; also Keith N. Morgan, ed., *Shaping an American Landscape: The Art and Architecture of Charles A. Platt* (Hanover, NH: Hood Museum, Dartmouth College, 1995), 14–16; Susan C. Faxon, "Portraits of Patronage," *Addison Gallery of American Art, 65 Years: A Selective Catalogue* (Andover: Addison Gallery of American Art, 1996), 17–22.

77   Paraphrase of Platt's words to Thomas Cochran, reported in Claude Moore Fuess, *Independent Schoolmaster* (Boston: Little, Brown, 1952), 150–51. The date of the conversation is not specified.

78   Ernest B. Chamberlain, for example, in *Our Independent Schools* (New York: American Book Co., 1944), 108–12, argued that the private secondary school should have "the appearance of harmony and beauty," should "educate the whole child," promote "culture," and cultivate "taste and standards."

79   For Cochran's role at Andover: Allis, 369–87. His benefactions to the academy were reportedly motivated in part by personal misfortune; an acquaintance recalled in 1937 that the death of Cochran's wife in childbirth in 1914 had inspired "his devotion to other people's children . . . Andover became his child." F. C. Walcott to Claude Fuess, February 26, 1937, 4. Trustees Correspondence, Cochran, Thomas, 1908–1929, Box 3, Phillips Academy Archive. In 1916 Cochran wrote to Alfred Stearns, "I wish the time would come soon when I could do something more substantial for Phillips Academy. It is much in my heart and mind, and I dream about it." Cochran to Stearns, November 21, 1916, 4. Trustee Correspondence, Cochran, Thomas, 1908–1929, Box 3. Parallels can be found elsewhere in American education, for example in the founding of Stanford University in 1886 by Leland and Jane Stanford following the death of their only child.

80   Cochran to James C. Sawyer, January 23, 1928, Treasurer's Office Correspondence, James C. Sawyer, Phillips Academy Archive, 6.85.14.79. Cochran's views are seen also in a statement in 1928 that "a true appreciation of art is something which will aid and influence [the students] for good long after their school days . . . [and] will return them large dividends as long as they live by way of culture and esthetic enjoyment" Cochran, draft letter written for Alfred Stearns, March 27, 1928, Trustees Correspondence, Cochran, Thomas, 4.

81   Also constructed during this period: Johnson Hall, 1922; Case Memorial Cage and Memorial Tower, 1923; Log Cabin, 1929; Phillips Inn (now Andover Inn), 1930.

82   Turner, Chapter 5, "The University as City Beautiful."

83   See Morgan, *Platt*, Chapter 4.

84   As the changes on campus continued into 1928–29, not everyone at Phillips Academy was as enthusiastic about the plans as Platt and Cochran. Principal Alfred Stearns expressed his own unhappiness about the plans for a new chapel, for the moving of Stowe, Harrington, and Samaritan houses, and for closing the view to Rabbit Pond. He also intimated that others among the faculty, trustees, and neighbors were distressed. (Allis, 384; Stearns to Cochran, April 30, 1929, Trustee Correspondence,

Cochran, Thomas, 4; Clarence Morgan to Stearns, January 27, 1929, Trustee Correspondence, Box 8, 4.). Moreover, in a letter Cochran wrote to Stearns, regarding the new chapel, he said, "I can understand the feeling of sentiment that you felt in your heart and soul with respect to the old structure. . . . [I]t is one that I do not happen to share." Cochran to Stearns, June 28, 1930, Trustees Correspondence, Cochran, Thomas, 4.

85   Regarding Brechin Hall, Allis (376–77) writes, "To be sure, the School had a library in Brechin Hall, but the building was ancient and Gothic, and furthermore its location in the so-called Great Lawn would destroy the balance that Cochran was trying to establish with his new buildings." See also Domingue, 67–68.

86   Domingue, 54, 62. Domingue proposes that this top-floor removal was "to reduce the fire hazard" in these two buildings. However it seems clear that the aesthetics of the buildings' proportions was the real motive, as a 1929 article in the *Bulletin* stated. "The proportions of the ancient halls are very much improved by the [removal of the top stories], and their harmony with the architecture in the immediate vicinity has been made complete. Furthermore, the removal of the fire escapes on the east side fronting on the Great Quadrangle, and the building of suitable entrances, have vastly bettered the appearance of the dormitories." *The Phillips Bulletin* 24 no. 1 (October 1929): 10.

87   Previous relocations included: 1881, Farrar House; 1887–89, Smith Hall, Abbot Hall, and Sunset Lodge, all at Abbot Academy; 1900, Churchill House; 1906, one of the English Commons buildings. Except for Abbot and Smith Halls, these were domestic buildings. See Ruth F. Quattlebaum, "Andover's Movable Campus," *Andover Bulletin* (Spring 1986): 5–8; Domingue, 177–82 (Abbot Academy buildings), 26 (English Commons building), 111–12 (Farrar House).

88   Turner, 204, 209. Schuyler's article appeared in *Architectural Record* 20 no. 10 (December 1909).

89   Relocated in 1922: Bartlet Chapel (Pearson Hall), and the Sanhedrin (razed 1929; see Domingue, 59). In 1928: Blanchard House, Tucker House, Bancroft Hall, Pemberton Cottage, Woods House. In 1929: Samaritan House, and Stowe House. (Quattlebaum, "Andover's Movable Campus.") In addition, the Phillips Memorial Gateway was moved, in 1928, from its original location on the east side of Main Street to West Quadrangle (Domingue, 149).

90   Allis, 350.

91   Also, several of the new buildings were named for prominent early Americans who had some connection with the academy, such as George Washington, Paul Revere, and Samuel F. B. Morse.

92   The Commons uses the arched recess typical of Bulfinch; Cochran Chapel is modeled partly on Bulfinch's Lancaster Meeting House. See Morgan, *Platt*, 191–94.

93   Morgan, *Platt*, 192–94.

94   Morgan, *Shaping an American Landscape*, 142.

95   Allis, 361–62; Domingue, 160. Phillips Exeter Academy had built a substantial gymnasium in 1884. Echols, 54.

96   Domingue, 161.

97   Domingue, 163.

98   Allis, 503–29. According to Allis, the Andover societies were modeled primarily on the senior societies at Yale (Allis,

303). However, "secret societies" had also existed for many years at Phillips Exeter Academy, (Echols, 21), so the phenomenon at Andover may have been inspired by that school too.

99 Allis, 205.

100 Domingue, 38–47.

101 Allis, 530. These projects included: a wing added to Isham Infirmary in 1934-35; Rockwell House (a West Quad dorm), 1934; Sumner Smith Rink, late 1950s; and War Memorial Gymnasium, 1952. There were also several faculty residences built in the 1930s.

102 The lack of building during this period, according to Allis, was not due to financial problems (465): the Academy "managed to weather the hard times [of the Depression] very well." In the early 1940s, the school considered building a student union; it never materialized, due to problems regarding "Dr. Fuess's attempt to abolish the secret societies" (Allis, 479).

103 For the Andover Program: Allis, 581–90; [Phillips Academy in association with The Architects Collaborative], *The Andover Program Workbook* [n.d.].

104 Even more "contextual" was Thompson's design for the addition to the Oliver Wendell Holmes Library, of 1959.

105 Evans Hall, 1961–63; Arts and Communications, 1962–63.

106 Turner, 260–66.

107 For the history of Abbot Academy: Susan McIntosh Lloyd, *A Singular School: Abbot Academy 1828-1973*. The original Abbot trustees included Samuel Farrar, treasurer of Phillips and Andover Theological Seminary, and Mark Newman, trustee and former headmaster of Phillips. Lloyd, 17–22.

108 For Abbot Hall: Lloyd, 26–27; Domingue, 174–78. The builder was David Hidden of Andover. It is unclear who drew the actual design, Lloyd (26) suggests that both Samuel Farrar and the first Abbot Academy principal, Charles Goddard, gave advice on the design.

109 In the early years, most Abbot students were local, but out-of-towners nevertheless constituted "over a third of every school roll through 1852." Lloyd, 37.

110 Lloyd, 75; Domingue, 181–83.

111 Lloyd, 87.

112 Turner, 133–40.

113 Lloyd, 86, 121; Domingue, 178–80.

114 Lloyd, 153–55; Loren Gary, *A Widening Circle: Abbot Academy and the Abiding Significance of Place* (Andover: Phillips Academy, 1997), 14. McKeen was designed by the same firm that had produced the 1886 master plan, now Hartwell, Richardson & Driver. Davis Hall, the old boarding house, was demolished to make way for McKeen.

115 Domingue, 186–90.

116 *Widening Circle*, 15. For example: "It was during [the] first two decades of the twentieth century that the mystique of the Circle developed. By the late teens references to the "Sacred Circle" start to appear in the school's literature . . . [T]he Circle came to stand as a symbol of Abbot's enveloping care for each student."

117 Lloyd, 182–85.

118 Turner, 212.

119 Lloyd, 283.

120 The American colleges whose campuses date from the colonial period: Harvard, William and Mary, Yale, Princeton, Brown, Dartmouth. The colonial-era academies are harder to identify, as their histories are less well documented, but they probably include: Abington Friends School, Jenkintown, PA; Moravian Academy, Bethlehem, PA; Germantown Academy, Fort Washington, PA; and Governor Dummer Academy, South Byfield, MA.

CHASE, "TO PROMOTE TRUE PIETY AND VIRTUE"

1 Jedidiah Morse, *The American Universal Geography: or, a View of the Present States of all the Empires, Kingdoms, States, and Republics in the Known World, and of the United States in Particular; Illustrated with Maps* I (Boston: Isaiah Thomas & Ebenezer T. Andrews, 1793), 370.

2 The Elm Arch promenade has never paralleled Main Street or Seminary Row. The campus at the close of the 1830s is well documented by two detailed manuscript survey maps preserved in the Phillips Academy Archive; executed by Frederick A. Barton, they are dated 1836 and 1837 and titled "Plan of the Real Estate of Phillips Academy." Frederick A. Barton (1809–1881), a civil engineer, taught mathematics and surveying on the English Academy faculty while studying for the ministry at Andover Theological Seminary. The two survey maps appear to have been created as teaching aides. He was considered an excellent teacher, and the trustees attempted to induce him to stay in Andover and continue his teaching career, but without success. Before Barton left he was paid $20 for the survey maps and they have been retained at the academy. Among Barton's pupils was fifteen-year-old Frederick Law Olmsted. Olmsted is said to have been a private student of Barton in 1837–38, but he was also enrolled in the English Academy. Olmsted boarded with the Bartons on School Street and when they left in 1838, he left with them. So far as is known, Olmsted's only formal training as a landscape architect was the work he did with Barton learning to survey. More than 50 years after he left Andover, Olmsted's firm was hired as campus planners and landscape architects, and the office continued to provide services for more than seventy years. See Cynthia Zaitzevsky, "The Olmsted Firm and the Shaping of the Phillips Academy Landscape," in this volume; Charles C. McLaughlin & Charles E. Beveridge, *The Papers of Frederick Law Olmsted* I (Baltimore: Johns Hopkins University Press, 1977), 392; Witold Rybczynski, *A Clearing in the Distance* (New York: Scribner's, 1999), 36–41; English Academy & Teachers Seminary catalogues, 1832–39, Phillips Academy Archive, Olmsted is listed in the 1838 catalogue; Cashbook, 1796–1837, September 5, 1834, January 31, and March 23, 1836, Phillips Academy Archive; *Trustee Records*, I, August 8, 1837, Phillips Academy Archive.

3 Barton survey maps, Phillips Academy Archive.

4 Oliver Wendell Holmes, who was a student in the academy in 1824–25, described the campus as an "academic village," in "Cinders from the Ashes" (1869), *Oliver Wendell Holmes: The Complete Works* VIII (New York: Sully & Kleinteich, 1911), 244, 253. At least six views of the center of the campus document it at this stage of development: Francis Alexander's "Theological Seminary, Andover," circa 1827, published as a lithograph by Pendleton; a second undated Pendleton lithograph titled "Andover Theological Seminary," marked "Pendletons Lithog'y Boston," issued in the 1830s; an engraving, "Andover Theological Seminary," undated but published in the 1830s; an unsigned engraving, "Andover Theological Seminary & Teachers Seminary," circa 1834, published with a promotional broadside by Phillips Academy's trustees in January 1839; and the "Western view of the Theological Seminary at Andover" and "Western view of Phillips Academy at Andover" printed in John W. Barber, *Historical Collections: Being a General Collection of Interesting Facts, Traditions, Biographical Sketches, Anecdotes, etc., Relating to the History and Antiquities of Every Town in Massachusetts with Geographical Descriptions* (Worcester, MA: Dorr, Howland, 1841), 161, 162.

5   The most comprehensive account of the academy's early leadership appears in the standard institutional history by Frederick S. Allis, *Youth from Every Quarter, A Bicentennial History of Phillips Academy, Andover* (Andover, MA: Phillips Academy, 1979), 9–179, passim. Also see C.C. Carpenter, *Biographical Catalogue of the Trustees, Teachers & Students of Phillips Academy, Andover, 1778–1830* (Andover, MA: Andover Press, 1903).

6   John L. Taylor, *A Memoir of His Honor Samuel Phillips, LLD* (Boston: Congregational Board of Publication, 1856); Clifford K. Skipton, ed., *Sibley's Harvard Graduates* XVII (Boston: Massachusetts Historical Society, 1975), 593–609; Allis, 17–60; *Trustee Records* I, 1–149; Samuel Phillips Jr., cited in *The Constitution of Phillips Academy, Andover, Massachusetts* (Andover, 1778; reprint, Phillips Academy, 1995), 2–3. At least one academy was a direct descendant of Phillips Academy, Andover: Phillips Exeter Academy in New Hampshire. Chartered in 1781 and opened in 1783, Dr. John Phillips of Exeter was its great patron; Samuel Phillips Jr., served on its board.

7   Allis, 31–83, 119–130; Leonard Woods, *History of the Andover Theological Seminary* (Boston: J. R. Osgood, 1885), 636, passim; Henry K. Rowe, *History of the Andover Theological Seminary* (Newton, MA, 1933), 10–50; *Trustee Records* I, 1–385; Josiah Quincy letter, September 28, 1826, Eliphalet Pearson Papers, Phillips Academy Archive; Dr. Edwards Amasa Park, in John L. Taylor, *Memorial of the Semi-Centennial Celebration of the Theological Seminary, Andover* (Andover: Warren F. Draper, 1859), 231.

8   Col. John Phillips is also frequently identified as "John Phillips Jr." He is not to be confused with his distant cousin, John Phillips of Boston, also a board member, who became that city's first mayor. Phillips and Holden started borrowing academy funds in 1804. *Trustee Records* I, 134–334; cashbooks and ledgers covering the period 1801–1820. Andover Newton Theological School, Trask Library, Archive & Special Collections [hereafter, Andover Newton Archive], Associate Foundation Journal, 1808–12, June 25, 1808. Sarah L. Bailey, *Historical Sketches of Andover* (1880; reprint, Andover, MA: Andover and North Andover Historical Societies, 1990), 156, 409, 585; Thomas B. Wyman, *The Genealogies & Estates of Charlestown* (1879; reprint, Somersworth, NH: New England History Press, 1982), 748; William Bentley, *The Diary of William Bentley* III (Salem, MA: Essex Institute, 1905), October 27, 1809.

9   John J. Currier, *A History of Newburyport* (1909; reprint, Somersworth, NH: New Hampshire Publishing Company, 1978), 234–35; Taylor, *Semi-Centennial*, 127, 132–39; Woods, 73–75, 595–635; Records of the Theological Institution, I, 157–198, Andover Newton Archive; William Bartlett letters, 1817–21, Andover Newton Archive; Samuel Farrar, "William Bartlet,

Esq.," account book, 1817–21, Andover Newton Archive.

10   William E. Park, *The Earlier Annals of Phillips Academy* (Andover, MA: Phillips Academy, 1878), 44; Claude Moore Fuess, *An Old New England School, A History of Phillips Academy, Andover* (Boston: Houghton Mifflin, 1917), 204.

11   Susan McIntosh Lloyd, *A Singular School: Abbot Academy, 1828–1973* (Andover, MA: Phillips Academy, 1979), 20–26; Allis, 149–179; Claude M. Fuess, "The Immortal Squire," *The Phillips Bulletin* (January 1917), 5–8; *Trustee Records* I, 134–485; Cashbook, 1796–1837, Phillips Academy Archive; Account Book, 1795–1841, Phillips Academy Archive; Elias B. Bishop, "Report on the Real Estate Belonging to the Trustees of Phillips Academy, Andover," typescript, 1903, passim; Phillips Academy Trustees, *Terms of Trusts & Other Documents* (Andover, MA: Andover Press, 1932), 52–53; Carpenter, 13.

12   Cashbook, 1796–1837, Phillips Academy Archive; Account Book, 1795–1841, Phillips Academy Archive; Theological Institution Account Books, 1810–17, Andover Newton Archive; Theological Institution Journal, 1808–31, Andover Newton Archive; Associate Foundation Journal, 1809–1841, account book 1810–11, entry for December 7, 1810, Andover Newton Archive; David Hidden Ledger, mss. no. 399, 10, 21, 48, Andover Historical Society.

13   William Bartlet letters, 1817–20, Andover Newton Archive; Cashbook, 1796–1837, November 14, December 16, 1817, January 3, 1818, Phillips Academy Archive; *Vital Records of Newburyport, Massachusetts: Births* I (Salem, MA: Essex Institute, 1911), 256–57.

14   Eliphalet Pearson to Jedidiah Morse, December 21, 1807, reprinted in Woods, 545; Wyman, 509–11; *Dictionary of American Biography* IX (New York: Charles Scribner's Sons, 1928–58), 138; Cashbook, 1796–1837, Phillips Academy Archive, many references to loans to Phillips and Holden, individually and separately; Associate Foundation Journal, June 25, 1808, Andover Newton Archive; "Particulars of Furniture," undated ms., circa 1809–10, concerning furnishing Phillips Foxcroft Hall and the Seminary Commons, Andover Newton Archive.

15   Account Book, 1795–1841, 269, 275–76, Phillips Academy Archive, references to Sparrell's work as architect for these two buildings, January 5, August 20, September 15, September 28, 1829; Christopher Hail, *Boston Architects and Builder 1789–1846* (Boston: Massachusetts Committee on the Preservation of Architectural Records, 1989), 270; Earle G. Shettleworth Jr., *An Index to Boston Building Contracts 1820–29* (Boston: 1995), 90–93. Bainbridge Bunting with Margaret Henderson Floyd, *Harvard, An Architectural History* (Cambridge: Harvard University Press, 1985), 50, 292, 293.

16   William Bartlet letters, 1820–21, Andover Newton Archive; Account book, 1795–1841, December 1, 1818, Phillips Academy Archive.

17   Samuel Farrar, "William Bartlet, Esq.," ledger, expenses specific to working with Bulfinch on Pearson Hall, February 28 and June 18, 1817, November 25, 1818, Andover Newton Archive; William Bartlet to Samuel Farrar, March 6, April 16, May 26, and December 24, 1817, references to Bulfinch, Andover Newton Archive; Carpenter, 4–26; Bunting, 34–35, 41–43; Harold Kirker, *The Architecture of Charles Bulfinch* (Cambridge, MA: Harvard University Press, 1969, 1998 reprint), 1–19, 216–217, 272–281,

304–306, 311–319. Carpenter, *Biographical Catalogue 1778–1830* (Andover, MA: Phillips Academy, 1903), attributed "the Old Brick Academy" to Bulfinch. William Phillips was associated with two Boston buildings designed by Charles Bulfinch: Massachusetts Bank (1809), where the Phillips Academy trustees often met, and Massachusetts General Hospital (1815–17). John Phillips was associated with two other Bulfinch buildings in Boston: the John Phillips House (circa 1805), and Manufacturers & Mechanics Bank (1814–15).

18 John F. Quinan, "The Architecture of Asher Benjamin" (Ph.D. diss., Brown University, 1973); Cashbook, 1796–1837, May 5, 1818, Phillips Academy Archive; "William Bartlet, Esq.," ledger, June 18, 1817, Andover Newton Archive. Benjamin designed at least one earlier schoolhouse, Deerfield Academy (1797), Deerfield, Massachusetts; originally a two-story, hip-roofed brick building, otherwise it was not similar to Bulfinch Hall for Andover; information on Benjamin's Deerfield Academy building, Kenneth Hafertepe, Historic Deerfield.

19 Taylor, *Phillips*, 148, 212; Bishop, 8, 40–42, 111–12; Allis, 49; Park, 18; *Trustee Records* I, April 28, 1778, April 20, 1779, April 19, 1780, August 16, 1781, Phillips Academy Archive. The 141 acres comprising the original Phillips Academy campus included the land south of Phillips Street, west of Main Street, and north of the West Quadrangle; the parcel bounded south by Phillips Street, east by Main Street, and north and west by Old Campus Road; and the land that includes most of the Great Lawn and all the Great Quadrangle, bounded north by Chapel Avenue, west by Main Street, and south approximately by an east-west line defined by the south flank of Oliver Wendell Holmes Library. The Phillips Academy trustees licensed households to board students on an annual basis. In 1778 29 houses were approved for this purpose, some more than two miles from the schoolhouse.

20 Taylor, *Phillips*, 195–196, and two mid-nineteenth-century vignettes facing 213 and 230; Allis, 87; Eliphalet Pearson Papers, March 25, 1818, box 1, mss., solicitation for funds to rebuild the academy, Phillips Academy Archive; *Trustee Records* I, April 28, 1778, April 19, 1780, August 17, 1781, July 17, 1784, and January 30, 1786. After the second academy building was completed in 1786, the original joiner's shop-schoolhouse became a singing school. It was sold in 1802, carted off campus and used as a workshop once again; *Trustee Records* I, December 22, 1802, August 23, 1803, February 7 and 20, 1804.

21 Bishop, 8–14, 13–14, 111–15, 134–37, 141–42, 167–68; *Trustee Records* I, April 28 and October 8, 1778, April 20, 1779, April 19, 1780, January 9, 1801; Barton survey map, 1836. Taylor, *Phillips*, 114–115, 230; Edwards Park to H.S. Robinson, December 8, 1899, mss. no. 764, Andover Historical Society; Bailey, *Historical Sketches of Andover*, 87, 531.

22 See Allis, 93–94; Bentley, February 21, 1789, April 1, 1791; Morse, 370.

23 Abiel Abbot, *History of Andover, Massachusetts, from its Settlement to 1829* (Andover, MA: Flagg & Gould, 1829; reprint, Newburyport, MA: Parker River Researchers, 1992), 9; *Trustee Records* I, August 19, 1806, August 23, 1808, Phillips Academy Archive. The right-of-way across campus cost the turnpike company $140.51. Bishop, 41–47, 168–170. Elias Bishop noted that the mall as surveyed in 1806 was narrowed in 1829 (to about 45 feet

wide) when the town road was moved to the east, closer to the turnpike alignment. The mall appears in that configuration on the 1836 and 1837 Barton survey maps, and later on the 1891 printed survey map by Melvin B. Smith, tipped-in to Bishop's 1903 analysis of Phillips Academy real estate holdings; Phillips Academy Archive.

24 Taylor, *Semi-Centennial*, 231–36; Woods, 64–133, 546; Allis, 119–126; *Trustee Records* I, March 20, 1806–December 31, 1807, June 21, 1809, August 20, 1811; Bishop, 21–24. That faculty houses would be provided was understood when planning for the seminary campus began in 1807. In June 1809 the trustees sold William Bartlet the lot facing the common for the first purpose-built professor's residence, Phelps House. In May 1810 Bartlet bought the lot for Moses Stuart House. In August 1811 the trustees leased a house lot to Samuel Farrar at the northeast corner of Main and Phillips Streets, at the same time agreeing to lease him additional land immediately to the north for agricultural use, with the stipulation that should it be required for faculty residences the trustees could repossess the property at any time.

25 Paul V. Turner, *Campus: An American Planning Tradition* (Cambridge, MA: The MIT Press, 1984), 38–45, 76–83; Turner, *Joseph-Jacques Ramée: International Architect of the Revolutionary Era* (Cambridge, UK: Cambridge University Press, 1996), 189–202. David Leonard's engraved view of "Rhode Island College" (Brown University), circa 1795, is reproduced in Jay Barry, *A Tale of Two Centuries, a Pictorial History of Brown University* (Providence, RI: Brown University, 1985), 17; Edwards A. Park to H.S. Robinson, December 8, 1899, mss. no. 764, Andover Historical Society; Rowe, 27; Allis, 127. There are two famous early-nineteenth-century examples of terraced campus designs, both slightly later than Andover's Seminary Row: Joseph-Jacques Ramée's Union College campus plan of 1813, and Thomas Jefferson's terraced Lawn for the University of Virginia campus in summer 1817.

26 Timothy Dwight, *Travels in New England & New York* I (New Haven: T. Dwight, 1821), 399; Account by the Rev. Newton, quoted in Taylor, *Semi-Centennial*, 212–13; Annual Report of the Theological Institution Faculty, September 23, 1811; Theological Institution Records I, November 21, 1808; Account Books, 1813–15, Andover Newton Archive. *Trustee Records* I, August 20, 1811; Cashbook, 1796–1837, 1813–1815, passim, Phillips Academy Archive.

27 William Bartlett to Samuel Farrar, 1817–18, 1820–21, Andover Newton Archive; "William Bartlet, Esq.," ledger, 1817–18, 1820–21, Andover Newton Archive; Barton survey map, 1836, Phillips Academy Archive. The Seminary Row terrace was graded down several feet in the center to only five steps up from the central walk crossing the common.

28 Although the landscape plan for the Seminary Common does not appear to be the work of a single designer, and no primary documentation exists to support such an attribution, there are two designer-candidates worth noting. The landscape plan has been attributed to Samuel F. B. Morse, a noted painter and Phillips Academy graduate of 1805, and the son of trustee Rev. Jedidiah Morse, who was a confidante of Eliphalet Pearson and much involved in launching the seminary. According to Dr. William Budington, speaking at the Andover Theological Seminary semi-centennial celebration in 1858, Samuel F. B.

Morse "proposed a plan for the embellishment of these grounds, and that eminent man . . . may yet find the sketch he furnished in his youth followed in the arrangement of these walks." There is a link to Andover at a critical point in landscaping the Seminary Common; in 1817 Samuel F.B. Morse painted Eliphalet Pearson's portrait. Despite this connection, Charles Bulfinch seems the more likely designer, if there was one. He had taken an interest in parks and public promenades since his trip to Europe in the 1780s. In the first decade of the nineteenth century he was heavily involved both as municipal official and architect for surrounding property owners in improving Boston Common, particular the elm-lined walks along Cambridge, Tremont, and Park Streets. In 1812–13 Bulfinch designed a landscaped quadrangle to surround Harvard's University Hall; more important the trustees had personally selected Bulfinch, possibly Pearson himself, to design the new seminary chapel, and he was in the employ of William Bartlet in 1817–18 when Bartlet and Farrar considered and implemented specific elements of the Seminary Commons landscaping. Nevertheless, there is no record of Bulfinch's involvement, and his influence might well have come indirectly, since the members of the board were familiar with his landscape work in Boston. See Taylor, *Semi-Centennial,* 67; Paul J. Staiti, *Samuel F.B. Morse* (New York and Cambridge: Cambridge University Press, 1989), 40–43, 254; Harold and James Kirker, *Bulfinch's Boston* (New York: Oxford University Press, 1964), 162–78; Walter Muir Whitehill, *Boston, a Topographical History,* 2nd edition (Cambridge, MA: Harvard University Press, 1968), 56–67.

29 Oliver Wendell Holmes, "The School-Boy," in *The Complete Poetical Works* (Boston: Houghton Mifflin, 1895), 347.

30 Carpenter, 7; "William Bartlet, Esq.," ledger, in which Samuel Farrar recorded expenses for building Samaritan House, Andover Newton Archive; *Constitution of the Samaritan Female Society of Andover & Vicinity* (Andover, MA: 1818), in Phillips Academy Archive; *Trustee Records* I, October 31, 1827, September 24 and 28, 1828; Bishop, 82–84; *Terms of Trusts & Other Documents,* 51–53. When Samuel Farrar established the Prize Fund in 1807 with an initial gift of $450, he reserved the right to personally designate expenditures from the fund, "consistent with the design of this Institution."

31 "Andover Theological Institution & Teachers Seminary," English Academy & Teachers Seminary brochure, January 1839, Phillips Academy Archive.

32 Phillips Academy Archive, Barton survey maps, 1836, 1837.

33 Allis, 119–128; *Trustee Records* I, February 7 and 20, 1804, March 20 and 27, July 8, September 4, November 7, 1806, June 9, 1807, August 23, 1808, August 21, 1810; Account Book, 1795–1841, 55, 61; Cashbook, 1796–1837, May 7 and August 19, 1806; July 21, 1808, July 25, 1810.

34 Woods, 537–40, 557; *Trustee Records* I, August 18, 1807; Cashbook, 1796–1837, October 20, 1808; Account Book, 1795–1841, August 21, 1809; Account Book, 1814–17, Andover Newton Archive. Farrar House (1811–12), which was part of Faculty Row until it was moved down Phillips Street in the 1880s, was not a faculty house in the early nineteenth century.

35 The designer of Phelps House is not known. It may have been builder Andrews Palmer (1766–1831), a Newburyport master carpenter who specialized in building meetinghouses. The design of Phelps House has often been attributed to Charles Bulfinch, but there is no documentation supporting the attribution, and the massing, plan and detail do not coincide with documented Bulfinch work. The most compelling attribution was made by Charles Fagan, who proposed Peter Banner as the architect, based on the similarities between the treatment of the facade of Phelps House and that of Banner's 1805 design for Elmwood, the Ebenezer Craft house on Parker Hill in Roxbury. Not only are there interesting design parallels, there is a direct link between Banner and Edward Dorr Griffin, for whom Phelps House was built. Peter Banner was architect and builder for the 1809 Park Street Church in Boston; Griffin was heavily involved in gathering the neo-Calvinist congregation the Park Street Church was built to house. With Bartlet's consent, Griffin moonlighted there as assistant minister while he taught in Andover, and Griffin took over the Park Street pulpit when he left Andover in 1811. (David Hidden Ledger, 10, Andover Historical Society. Fiske Kimball, *Domestic Architecture of the American Colonies & the Early Republic* [1921; reprint, New York: Dover, 1966], 206; Charles A. Fagan IV, "Charles Bulfinch, Peter Banner and Andover Hill," *Essex Institute Historical Collections* 75 [April 1989], 191–195; Elmer D. Keith and William L. Warren, "Peter Banner, Architect, Moves from New Haven to Boston," *Old-Time New England* 57 no.3 [January–March 1967]; Bentley, June 11, July 30, 1809, February 11, December 9, 1810; Woods, 598–634.)

36 Leonard Woods, annual report to the trustees, September 22, 1816, Andover Newton Archive.

37 Quoted in Stuart Robbins, *Old Andover Days* (Boston: Pilgrim Press, 1908), 17–18; Fuess, 154; Allis, 128; Woods, 598, 621, 634.

38 Woods, 595.

39 *Dictionary of American Biography* VII, 619–20; Taylor, 213–14; *Trustee Records* I, June 21, 1809; faculty correspondence file concerning Edward Dorr Griffin, William Bartlet to Samuel Farrar, May 27, 1809; Griffin's letter of resignation, April 22, 1811, Andover Newton Archive; David Hidden Ledger, 10, Andover Historical Society; Bentley, December 9, 1810.

40 *Trustee Records* I, March 4 and 16, June 18, August 18, 1818, August 17, 1819; William Graves Perry, "Bulfinch Hall Reconstructed," *The Phillips Bulletin* 31 no. 5 (July 1937): 5–8; Park, 33–34; Kirker, 305–306; Antoinette Forrester Downing and Vincent Scully, *The Architectural Heritage of Newport* (2nd edition, New York: Clarkson Potter, 1967), 109, pl.145; Cashbook, 1796–1837, 1818–19, Phillips Academy Archive; William Bartlet letters, June–November 1818, Andover Newton Archive. William Bartlet assisted Farrar with Bulfinch Hall by contracting for critical portions of the work on Farrar's behalf in Newburyport; documentation suggests he purchased brick and window sash, and Bartlet probably managed slating the roof. For these "sundries" he was reimbursed $1,523.66.

41 Several accounts by those who knew Bulfinch Hall in the nineteenth century are negative. For example, Oliver Wendell Holmes wrote in 1869, "The old Academy building had a dreary look, with its flat face, bare and uninteresting," in "Cinders from the Ashes," *The Complete Works* (1911), 246.

42 Abbot, 114.

43 *The Constitution of Phillips Academy* (1778; reprint, 1995), 11.

44 Abbot, 122–123; Turner, Campus, 26, 40, 48; Bunting, 34;

Trustee Records I, September 2, 1807, December 31, 1807; Woods, 545–46; miscellaneous manuscripts, mss. board meeting minutes, July 13, 1808, September 27. 1809, Andover Newton Archive. At the July 1808 board meeting, the trustees voted to open the Andover Theological Institution on September 21. Press notices announcing the opening were to state that students would be assisted finding private lodgings "till the public building be ready for their reception."

45   Board of Trustees Correspondence & Reports, Seminary Faculty Reports, September 24, 1810, September 22, 1812, September 26, 1815, September 24, 1818, Phillips Academy Archive; Woods, 141. The workshop, now Stowe House, was first proposed in the 1812 seminary faculty report; it was finally built in 1828.

46   Taylor, *Semi-Centennial,* 134–35.

47   *Trustee Records* I, February 14, 1817; William Bartlet letter, February 26, 1817, Andover Newton Archive.

48   "William Bartlet, Esquire," ledger, 1817–18; Charles Cummings to Alpheus Hardy, January 31, 1865, letter from architect Cummings proposing a scheme to alter Pearson Hall, including his sketch of the "Present Plan" and the "Present Section," Treasurer's files, Pearson Hall, Phillips Academy Archive; Kirker, 273–81, 305–06. Harvard's University Hall is much larger and more elaborately finished than Pearson Hall, but University Hall was never crowned with the handsome cupola Bulfinch had designed for it. When Pearson Hall was converted into a classroom building in 1875, the interior was gutted, Bulfinch's cupola, clock, and roof balustrade were removed, and a brick bell tower was added to the center of the building's west front. In 1922 the bell tower was demolished, the building was moved to its present site facing north into the Great Quadrangle, and Guy Lowell restored the west front, adding a roof balustrade (but no clock) and a cupola inspired by the Bulfinch originals. Bulfinch's interior is poorly documented; there are no photographs, and few written descriptions that go beyond recounting the basic layout. The *Haverhill Gazette* for September 29, 1821, described the chapel as "elegant." The fullest description, written by Sarah Stuart Robbins *Old Andover Days,* 35–36, and recalling it during the 1820s and 1830s, seems unduly negative: "In the chapel of those days there was nothing of old Solomon's magnificence. The walls were dingy blue, the pews, gallery, and desk were yellow white. Between the windows tarnished candelabra swung out, hold long, tallow dips . . . and the cold floor was without a carpet."

49   William Bartlet letters, 1817–18, Andover Newton Archive. On December 24, 1817 Bartlett wrote to Farrar to inform him that Bulfinch had been paid in full for his services; Bulfinch was about to depart Boston to become Architect of the Capitol in Washington, D.C.

50   William Bartlet letters, 1818; "William Bartlet, Esq.," ledger; Records of the Theological Institution I, September 22, 1818; Treasurer's Report, May 6, 1819; all Andover Newton Archive. Taylor, *Semi-Centennial,* 135; Pearson to Col. Revere, December 27, 1818, Pearson Papers, Phillips Academy Archive. In January 1810 Dr. Samuel Spring wrote to Professor Leonard Woods at the just-opened Andover Theological Seminary about purchasing a bell; he had received $50 as an anonymous gift for the purpose. The Rev. Spring stated that two bells were available at Revere's foundry and that they should go have a listen, and if they could not mutually

agree on which to buy, they would resort to "the awful discriminating taste of Dr. Pearson. And if one will not make him more than sick to his stomach, the bell will pass for a good sounding instrument, and answer every purpose" (Woods, 636). The grandiloquent title, "Bartlet Professor of Pulpit Eloquence," suited Edward Dorr Griffin perfectly, but not Ebenezer Porter, who chose "Bartlet Professor of Sacred Rhetoric."

51   Records of the Theological Institution I, February 14, 1817, Andover Newton Archive; Seminary Faculty Annual Report, September 21, 1819, Andover Newton Archive; *Trustee Records* I, August 18, 1817.

52   Taylor, *Semi-Centennial,* 137.

53   Faculty Reports, 1813, 1815, 1819, 1821; "William Bartlet, Esq.," ledger, 1820–21; William Bartlet to Farrar, 1820–21; Theological Institute Records I, February 14, September 24, 1817, September 25, 1821, annual meeting minutes and letter of donation from William Bartlet; all Andover Newton Archive. Theological Institute student John Todd described his Bartlet Hall room in an 1823 letter quoted in Rowe, 29: "Here you will find my chum and myself each bending over a comfortable writing-desk laid upon two marble-colored tables. You see our room ornamented with four pretty chairs, a beautiful mahogany bureau, large mirror—all furnished by the munificent Mr. Bartlet. All the rooms in this building are furnished alike. Nothing could add to our convenience . . . [save] a carpet. But this is of little consequence."

CHASE, "LIBERAL ADVANTAGES"

1   Abbot Academy promotional circular, March 13, 1829, quoted in Jane B. Carpenter, *Abbot & Miss Bailey & Abbot in the Early Years* (Andover, 1959), 160.

2   Carpenter, 155. Philena and Phebe McKeen, *A History of Abbot Academy* (Andover, 1880), 12.

3   Abbot Academy Trustee Records, March 4, 1828—May 13, 1829, passim, Phillips Academy Archive. The standard source on Abbot is the excellent institutional history written by Susan McIntosh Lloyd, *A Singular School: Abbot Academy, 1828–1973* (Andover, 1979); 6–40. See too McKeen and McKeen, 1–126; Carpenter, 155–176. For the evolution of women's education in this era see Helen Lefkowitz Horowitz, *Alma Mater: Design and Experience in the Women's College from Their Nineteenth-Century Beginnings to the 1930s* (Boston: University of Massachusetts Press, 1984, 1986 ed.), 9–18.

4   Phillips Academy Archive, Abbot Academy Trustee Records, July 24, 1828. Andover Historical Society, David Hidden Ledger, 190–94, 197, 201. Robert A. Domingue, *Phillips Academy . . . An Illustrated History of the Property* [Wilmington, MA, 1990], 176–79. The principal facade of Abbot Hall remains intact, but a variety of modifications have completely changed the way the building reads today. In 1875 a domed astrological observatory was added to the roof. In 1888 the building was moved further back from School Street, turned 90 degrees to face north into a new quadrangle, and placed upon a full basement so that it became a three-story structure approached by a new exterior staircase leading up to the original portico. In 1907–08 a large neo-Renaissance art gallery wing was added to what was then the

School Street side of the building. Nothing of the original interior survives. Abbot Hall was substantially reconfigured and updated again in a 1997 renovation.

5   William Saunders (1787–1861) was a housewright. Aside from his work on Abbot Hall and on the Phillips Academy campus, his known work, all residential, is in Cambridge. Saunders and David Hidden worked together on Abbot Hall for several months before they formed a partnership, and Saunders continued with Hidden through 1834. It is possible Saunders made the Andover connection through his wife, Sarah Flagg Saunders, whose brother, Timothy Flagg, was a partner in the Andover printing firm of Flagg & Gould (later Flagg, Gould & Newman), which did the printing for the Phillips Academy trustees and the Andover Theological Seminary faculty. Cambridge Historical Commission, Cambridge, MA, files on William Saunders; Andover Historical Society, Flagg family file; David Hidden Ledger, 193–250.

6   Abbot Academy, charter, July 4, 1828, Phillips Academy Archive.

7   Lloyd, 452–453; Carpenter, 160–61.

REED, "THE LOST VICTORIAN CAMPUS"

1   The donors were John and Peter Smith, two local mill owners. John Stevens (1824–1881) lived in Wakefield, Massachusetts. He returned to Andover to design the Punchard School for the town in 1855. He would later develop a portfolio of designs for large, elaborately ornamented Congregational churches throughout New England, including Andover and North Andover. The Steven drawings for the Punchard School are in the collections of the Andover Historical Society.

2   *The Phillips Bulletin* 9 no. 4 (April 1915): 16; *The Phillips Bulletin* 14, no. 2 (January 1930): 29-30. The interior may also have been renovated, but none of this work has survived the many subsequent renovations to this building.

3   *Andover Advertiser,* December 24, 1864, 2.

4   Report of the Committee of Exigencies, Minutes of the Trustees of Phillips Academy, July 25 1864, Phillips Academy Archive [hereafter Trustees Minutes]. Unless otherwise noted, all unpublished material is in the Phillips Academy Archive.

5   The best biographical account of Charles A. Cummings appeared in *The American Architect* after his death on August 11, 1905. See *The American Architect* 88 no. 4 (1905): 147–48. See also "Cummings, Charles Amos" in *The National Cyclopedia of American Biography* 20, 102-03; *Who Was Who* 1, 1897–1942 (Chicago: The Marquis Co., 1942).

6   *The Christian Examiner* was published in Boston. The articles by Cummings published prior to his selection as architect of Academy Hall had nothing to do with either architecture or religion, per se. See "The Later Writings of John Stuart Mill," *The Christian Examiner* 74 (January 1863): 1; "State Reform in Austria," *The Christian Examiner* 74 (May 1863): 356; "Kingslake and his Critics" *The Christian Examiner* 75 (July 1863): 81; and "Victor Hugo," *The Christian Examiner* 76 (May 1864): 301. Toward the end of his life Cummings wrote extensively on historic European architecture.

7   *The Lawrence American and Andover Advertiser,* February

10, 1866.

8   Academy Hall was drastically remodeled before it was demolished. The mansard roof and bellcote were removed in 1902 and replaced by a plain hip roof. The lancet arched windows were also altered. In 1911 the entrance pavilion and staircases were removed and new doorways built at grade. Finally, in 1927 the building was demolished.

9   *Lawrence American and Andover Advertiser,* August 6, 1866.

10   See Paul V. Turner, *Campus An American Planning Tradition* (Cambridge, MA and London, England: The MIT Press, 1984), 116–17. Turner observed that in the nineteenth century, schools with old Federal period architecture did not convey the same image of a long-established institution as did the Gothic Revival.

11   Cummings to Hardy, January 31, 1865, Alpheus Hardy papers in C. Private Papers of People Connected with the Academy, Phillips Academy Archive.

12   Ibid.

13   Philena McKeen and Phebe F. McKeen, *Annals of Fifty Years: A History of Abbot Academy, Andover, Mass., 1829–1879* (Andover: Warren F. Draper, 1880), 58–59, 62.

14   Cynthia Zaitzevsky, Evolution of the Abbot Academy Campus Landscape, draft report, February 16, 1996, Office of Physical Plant, Phillips Academy.

15   *Lawrence American and Andover Advertiser,* September 2, 1870; August 15, 1873; *Annals of Fifty Years: A History of Abbot Academy,* 60, 69–70, and frontispiece which reproduces the 1878 landscape plan. Also Philena McKeen, *Sequel to Annals of Fifty Years: A History of Abbot Academy, Andover, Mass., 1879-1892* Andover: Warren F. Draper, 1897), 17–32. Charles Gay (1848–1918) trained as a civil engineer in Boston under John B. Henck and Colonel H.W. Wilson. According to an obituary, in 1872 Gay worked in Washington, D.C. on landscape and civil engineering improvement projects. For much of his career he lived and worked in Lynn, Massachusetts as an engineer. See obituary for Charles Gay in the *Boston Daily Transcript,* February 2, 1918.

16   Cummings and Sears had shared offices at the same address as early as 1864, but did not become partners until 1867. Although he lived longer, less is known about Willard Sears. Born in New Bedford in 1837, he trained with an architect–builder named Solomon K. Eaton before moving to Boston about 1857. The firm's most important projects were the Free Hospital for Women in Roxbury in 1872, and Old South Church on Copley Square in 1874–75. Sears' most important project after Cummings retired in 1889 was the Gardner Museum in the Fenway for Isabella Stewart Gardner in 1899. His obituary appeared in *The Boston Globe* on May 20, 1920. See also, *Who Was Who* 1, 1897–1942, *op. cit.*

17   According to one source the chapel was actually begun as early as 1864, but this assumes that the chapel discussed in correspondence with Cummings was actually begun at that time. Claude M. Fuess, *An Old New England School: A History of Phillips Academy, Andover* (Boston and New York: Houghton Mifflin Company, 1917), 360–61.

18   The rear bell tower was removed when the nave was extended in 1919 to increase the chapel's capacity.

19   *Lawrence American and Andover Advertiser,* October 6, 1876.

20 *The Phillipian,* October 19, 1878. No information has come to light regarding the identity of the architect.

21 *Lawrence American and Andover Advertiser,* March 17, 1880. Originally the trustees planned to move an existing building to this site, but this proved impractical.

22 *Lawrence American and Andover Advertiser,* April 15, 1881. The building contained bathrooms, a laundry, and "other conveniences" and cost $10,000.

23 *American Architect and Building News,* January 28, 1882; *Lawrence American and Andover Advertiser,* September 24, 1880 (Tucker House); April 21, 1882 (Jewett House). Dominque incorrectly states that the Tucker House was built in 1881 and designed by the Lowell architects Merrill & Cutler; in fact, it was designed by Merrill and his previous partner. Robert A. Domingue, *Phillips Academy, Andover, Massachusetts* (Wilmington, Massachusetts: The Hampshire Press, 1990), p. 139. For information on Newcomb, see the author's, "Levi and Edgar Allen Poe Newcomb", unpublished manuscript prepared for *A Biographical Dictionary of Architects in Maine,* vol. 8, Earle G. Shettleworth, Jr., ed.

24 The Phillips Academy Archive contains Emerson's original specifications, as well as bid proposals from contractors. Emerson's wing, which had already been extensively altered in the inside, was recently demolished and replaced.

25 For an extensive description of the plan and its goals, see Annie Sawyer Downs, "Abbot Academy, Andover. A Sketch of its History, and of the Plan for Erecting a Group of New Buildings." This pamphlet was an off print of an article that appeared in *The New England Magazine* in February 1886. Down's account mentions that a free competition was held but the other architects who competed were not mentioned. The Hartwell & Richardson plan was exhibited by Draper in his business establishment to generate public interest and support. See *Lawrence American and Andover Advertiser,* May 29, 1885. Henry W. Hartwell (1833–1919) trained in the office of Hammatt and Joseph Billings before establishing his own practice in Boston in 1856. He worked alone or in partnership with Alfred Swazey and George Tilden until 1882. In that year he went into partnership with William C. Richardson (1854–1935), who had trained in the architectural program at M. I. T. and at the École des Beaux Arts in Paris. Richardson is considered to have been the principal designer of the firm. The domestic character of their plan for Abbot Academy buildings is especially evident in comparison to the house they designed for Moses Stevens in North Andover in 1884. Prior to the construction of Draper Hall, Hartwell & Richardson was hired to design Christ Church in Andover in 1886. See Susan Maycock Vogel, "Hartwell and Richardson: An Introduction to Their Work," *Journal of the Society of Architectural Historians* 32 (May 1973): 132–46. In 1888 Brookline civil engineer and landscape architect Ernest W. Bowditch also prepared a plan for the Abbot campus. It is not clear if Bowditch developed this scheme independently or in conjunction with Hartwell & Richardson, a firm he worked with on his own development in Brookline. The Bowditch plan is in the archive of the Office of Physical Plant, Phillips Academy.

26 Warren F. Draper owned a local publishing company in Andover. In 1869 he constructed a very fashionable mansard style dwelling on School Street opposite Abbot Academy. A trustee since 1868, Draper was appointed treasurer of Abbot Academy in 1876.

27 *The Phillipian,* October 8, 1887; September 28, 1888; October 25, 1889; January 23, 1891; September 21, 1892; *Andover Advertiser,* February 24, 1888; June 24, 1888; July 13,1888. Completed in 1890, Draper was enlarged in 1941 with a Colonial Revival wing to the north and a one story dining hall to the west that created an enclosed square with central courtyard. The two later additions plus the south portion of the original L–shaped structure were demolished in 1994 and Draper was renovated to provide faculty apartments and schools offices.

28 *Abbot Courant,* (June 1903): 27–28; (February 1904): 31; (June 1904): 28–29.

29 *Abbot Courant,* (June 1906): 20; (January 1907): 25–26. Esther Smith Byers had attended Abbot Academy in 1853–54 and married John Byers of New York in 1865. After the death of her husband she built a summer home in Andover in 1891. When she left her art collection she wanted it named in honor of both her and her husband. Robert D. Andrews (1857–1928) and Herbert Jaques (1857–1916) both attended the architectural school at M. I. T. The firm of Andrews & Jaques was formed in 1885, and they were later joined by Augustus N. Rantoul (1864–1934). The firm worked on major projects throughout New England and Denver, Colorado, where they established a second office. The firm was known for its work in large country homes and summer houses. The building for Abbot Academy is the only known art gallery by Andrews, Jaques & Rantoul.

30 *Trustees Minutes,* June 21, 1880; June 19, 1882. Otis A. Merrill (1844–?) trained as a carpenter in Haverhill before becoming an architect in Lowell in 1873. He first practiced alone, then with Charles S. Eaton. In 1882 he formed a partnership with Arthur S. Cutler (1854–1903), who trained as a draftsman in his office. The firm designed a large number of major buildings in Lowell, including the city hall. Cutler attended public school in Lawrence and art school in Boston. Merrill hired him as a draftsman in 1876. The firm of Merrill & Cutler lasted until about 1896.

31 *Andover Advertiser,* March 23, 1883; *The Phillipian,* June 3, 1891.

32 *Trustees Minutes,* June 23, 1885; *Philo Mirror,* 1887; Cecil F. B. Bancroft, Report to the Trustees, 1887,. Headmaster Bancroft Papers, 6.37.8., P. *The Andover Advertiser* commented on the problem faced by Phillips Academy. Its shared location with the theological seminary hindered its own efforts to construct new buildings. *Andover Advertiser,* September 14, 1888.

33 *The Phillipian,* September 26, 1885; *Andover Advertiser,* July 31, 1888.

34 The building that had served as the old treasurer's office, which was located along Faculty Row, was moved to the rear of Academy Hall for use as both a reading room and a clubhouse for the athletic association. Andover Advertiser, September 4, 1885.

35 *The Phillipian,* October 4, 1886; September 28, 1887.

36 Dominque, 38–47.

37 *American Architect and Building News,* November 7, 1891.

38 Today all of the fraternity houses belong to Phillips Academy and serve a variety of uses for the school, from dormitories, to faculty houses, to meeting spaces, and art studios.

39 *Trustees Minutes,* June 24, 1889.

40 *Trustees Minutes,* June 9, 1891

41 These 1891 plans for expanding the campus and siting the cottages exist in the archive of the National Park Service, Frederick Law Olmsted National Historic Site, Brookline, Massachusetts. Despite the mention of plural "institutions" in the trustees minutes, the plan that Olmsted developed was solely for Phillips Academy. On the preliminary plan, #176–5, the seminary buildings were omitted.

42 Memorandum from the Committee of the Trustees, Treasurer's Correspondence, S. Fletcher, J.L. & E. Taylor & A. Hardy, 85.36.

43 Pemberton Cottage, originally known as Taylor Cottage, was ultimately renamed in 1914 and moved to Old Campus Road to align with Andover and Eaton cottages. See *Andover Townsman,* June 16, 1891; October 21, 1891; January 1, 1892; *The Phillipian,* September 26, 1891; October 22, 1892. Alexander W. Longfellow (1854–1934) attended Harvard and the École des Beaux Arts in Paris. He was a draftsman in the office of famed Boston architect H.H. Richardson. In 1887 he formed a partnership with Frank Alden and Alfred Harlow. The firm had offices in Pittsburgh and Boston, where Longfellow preferred to remain. Although Taylor Cottage is credited in contemporary accounts solely to Longfellow, the Cambridge City Hall which was built at the same time was by the Longfellow, Alden & Harlow firm. See Margaret Henderson Floyd, *Architecture After Richardson Regionalism before Modernism—Longfellow, Alden and Harlow in Boston and Pittsburgh* (Chicago and London: University of Chicago Press, 1994).

44 *Andover Townsman,* May 22, 1891; January 1, 1892; May 6, 1892; January 6, 1893; *The Phillipian,* May 23, 1891; April 16, 1892; May 7, 1892; October 22, 1892; January 11, 1893.

45 *Andover Townsman,* October 28, 1892; *The Phillipian,* May 10, 1893.

46 *The Phillipian,* October 22, 1892, reported "The Draper Cottage, now being built on the site of the old second house, English Commons, will be exactly like the one mentioned above [Pemberton Cottage]."

47 *Andover Townsman,* January 1, 1892; July 29, 1892; October 20, 1892; *The Phillipian,* October 2, 1892; May 6, 1893. George C. Harding (1867–1921) attended the School of Architecture at M.I.T. in 1888. He later formed a partnership with Henry M. Seaver.

48 *The Phillipian,* October 22, 1892; J.E. Chandler to J.C. Olmsted, March 9, 1892, Olmsted Associates Records, Series B, Job 176, Manuscript Division, Library of Congress, Washington, D.C. [hereafter Olmsted Associates Records]. Chandler much preferred "old Colonial" as a style for the school. He felt that the English inspiration for Andover Cottage was "hardly recognizable as such because of our forced economy in architectural detail." In this letter Chandler essentially rejected the design for Andover Cottage and called for all the buildings to be stylistically harmonious.

49 *The Phillips Bulletin* 23 no. 1 (October 1928): 91; Bancroft House, Treasurer's Office Correspondence, James C. Sawyer, Buildings, 6.85.10.

50 Olmsted Brothers to A.W.Longfellow, August 21, 1899; Olmsted Brothers to Robert R. Bishop, August 24, 1899, Olmsted Associates Records.

FAXON, "FORCES OF CHANGE"

1 Cecil F. B. Bancroft, Report to the Trustees, June 1879, Headmaster Bancroft Papers, Phillips Academy Archive, 6.37.8.P. [Unless indicated otherwise, all unpublished material is in the Phillips Academy Archive].

2 James Hardy Ropes to the Board of Trustees, March 10, 1902, Academy Records, Trustees of Phillips Academy, Book 2 [hereafter Trustees Minutes], 138–39.

3 *The Phillips Bulletin* 22 no. 2 (January 1928): 5.

4 When Melville Day, who had already financed the building of the Eaton, Pemberton, and Bancroft Cottages, offered to fund yet another dormitory in early 1902, James Sawyer had replied, "You know that the Seminary has fallen off in numbers very rapidly in past few years until now there are ten students enrolled. It is quite material to ask how is this to end. If anything happens to the Seminary, a removal or whatever, the Academy will have the care of two dormitories and a recitation hall sufficient for its present needs." James C. Sawyer to Melville C. Day, January 31, 1902, Correspondence of the Treasurer, Letterbook of Alpheus H. Hardy and James C. Sawyer, vol. 7 (November 1898–March 1904), 138. Two months later, the Board voted, "The period has arrived when the prosperity of the Theological Seminary will be promoted by its removal from Andover, if satisfactory arrangements can be made for its establishment elsewhere." (Trustees Minutes, March 31, 1902, 141) However, in June 1902, after painful consultation with seminary faculty, alumni, and Congregational leaders, and with no feasible plan for the move, further action was postponed.

5 Trustees Minutes, June 12, 1902, 146.

6 The buildings were to include: Peabody Museum, 1901–03; Moorehead House, 1904; Cooley House (Pi Alpha Epsilon), 1908; Day Hall, 1911; Bishop Hall, 1911; Adams Hall, 1912; Taylor Hall, 1913; Phillips Gate, 1914; Phillips Union, 1915; Newton-Hinman House (Phi Beta Chi), 1921–22; Johnson Hall, 1922; Case Memorial Cage, 1922–23; Memorial Bell Tower, 1923; Samuel Phillips Hall, 1924; and Samuel F.B. Morse, 1927–28.

7 Benjamin F. W. Russell, "The Works of Guy Lowell," *The Architectural Review* 13 no. 2 (February 1906): 33.

8 The reason for the siting of the archaeology building at the corner of Main and Phillips Street remains unknown. This corner had been the site of the carpenter shop used by Phillips Academy in the first years of its founding in 1778. In 1812 the three-story Federal house known as Farrar House had taken its place on the site. Then in 1888 Farrar House was moved down the hill to sit beside the eighteenth-century Phillips family farmhouse, then known as the Shawsheen Club, on Phillips Street.

9 See Annie Sawyer Downs, "Abbot Academy, Andover. A Sketch of its History, and of the Plan for Erecting a Group of New Buildings," reprint from *The New England Magazine* (February 1886), Phillips Academy Archive, for a full description of the Abbot Academy master plan by Hartwell & Richardson.

10 It is noteworthy that the female academy on Andover Hill had added art history and art appreciation to its academic experience some 25 years before a similar effort would be made at Phillips Academy.

11 Alfred E. Stearns, "Academy Building Unsafe,"

Headmaster Stearns' Personal Correspondence, Box 7, 6.37.9.P.

12   F. L. Olmsted Jr., memorandum to the files, February 10, 1903, Olmsted Associates Records, Series B, Job 176, Manuscript Division, Library of Congress, Washington, D.C. [hereafter Olmsted Associates Records].

13   Plans #79 and #80, Olmsted Brothers Landscape Architects, Job 176, National Park Service, Frederick Law Omsted National Historic Site, Brookline, Massachusetts.

14   Frederick S. Allis Jr., *Youth from Every Quarter: A Bicentennial History of Phillips Academy, Andover* (Andover: Phillips Academy, 1979), 355–57; Alfred Stearns, "1900 to 1912," Headmaster Stearns' Personal Correspondence, 6.37.9.P.

15   The Trustees faced two difficult problems: how to define, and then assess, the seminary land, and how to divide the governing board so the schools could stand independently of each other. Trustee Henry Stimson, with the assistance of Harvard Law School professor John Chipman Gray, worked out the mechanics for creating two separate boards for the two institutions. In 1903 trustee Elias Bishop prepared a meticulously detailed report of the deeded lands of each institution, which served as the basis for assessment of the seminary property. Elias B. Bishop, "Report on the Real Estate Belonging to the Trustees of Phillips Academy in Andover," typescript, Oct 19, 1903, Treasurer's Office Real Estate, Box 2, 6.85.172.

16   Stearns, "1900 to 1912," Headmaster Stearns' Personal Correspondence, 6.37.9.P.

17   Trustees Minutes, Oct 11, 1913, 388. In 1913 the committee consisted of Francis Appleton, '71, Tracy Harris, '82, Oliver Jennings, '83, D. Mark Cummings, '85, William D. Sawyer, '85, Thomas Cochran, '90, John Crosby, '86, Robert Speer, '86, Fred C. Walcott, '87, George Case, '90, and Harold S. Wallace, '97.

18   As the *Bulletin* noted in April 1918, "Nobody on Andover Hill in these days is talking much about new buildings or school expansion. . . .We are now debating, not expenditure, but retrenchment; we are interested deeply in saving food and coal; and it is evident that the attractive plans of landscape architects must perforce be locked up until our war is won." *The Phillips Bulletin* 12 no. 3 (April 1918): 4.

19   Trustees Minutes, January 21, 1919, 478.

20   Trustees Minutes, April 15, 1919, 481.

21   Stearns, "1900 to 1912," Headmaster Stearns' Personal Correspondence, 6.37.9.P.

22   I am grateful to Michael Foss, Class of 1998, whose independent project paper, "The Fulfillment of a Remarkable Vision 1923–1933," December 7, 1998, pointed out the pivotal role played by George Case in the development of the campus.

23   George B. Case to James C. Sawyer, May 27, 1919, Treasurer's Office Correspondence, James C. Sawyer, 6.85.79.

24   Sawyer to Case, June 4, 1919, Treasurer's Office Correspondence, James C. Sawyer, 6.85.79.

25   Guy Lowell to Alfred Ripley, May 28, 1920, Treasurer's Office Correspondence, James C. Sawyer, 6.85.14.79.

26   Case to Fuess, March 24, 1920, Treasurer's Office Correspondence, James C. Sawyer, 6.85.79; Stearns, "1900 to 1912," Headmaster Stearns' Personal Correspondence, 6.37.9.P. Alfred Stearns described an undated visit by Case to the campus: one early morning before a meeting with fellow trustees, Case walked along the east side of the Seminary Row. He returned to spell out his concept of blasting the rocky ledge on the east side to create "ample room for buildings and an attractive quadrangle." According to Stearns, Charles Platt attended the meeting and heartily endorsed the plan. Since Platt was not involved with the campus planning until after 1922, this event could not have occurred until after Platt had already made his recommendations for the east side development.

27   Case to Sawyer, March 26, 1920, Treasurer's Office Correspondence, James C. Sawyer, 6.85.79.

28   Clerk of the Board of Trustees to Cochran, February 2, 1921, Trustee Correspondence, Cochran, Thomas, 4.

29   Alternate explanations to the question of how Platt was chosen have been proposed over the years. One story reported by Claude Fuess, in *Independent Schoolmaster* (Boston: Little, Brown, 1952), 150–51, claimed that it was Alfred Stearns's housekeeper, Miss Clemens, who mentioned Platt's name to Cochran over dinner at the principal's house one evening. However, this story is entirely refuted by James Sawyer's son, Charles, who grew up on the campus and who served as the director of the Addison Gallery of American Art from its opening in 1931 until 1940. In a letter to the author dated November 30, 1995, Addison Gallery Archive, he offered the belief that the two men met through their mutual acquaintance, New Yorker Dwight Morrow, who was Cochran's closest personal friend and a fellow partner at J.P. Morgan. In addition, Platt had both Boston and Andover connections through his wife, Eleanor Hardy, the daughter of former Phillips Academy Treasurer and Boston businessman, Alpheus H. Hardy, who had served on the Board of Trustees from 1885 to 1902. The file notes of Olmsted partner Percival Gallagher offer yet another link. "I understood he [Platt] was Lowell's selection but urged by New York Alumni," he wrote. Percival Gallagher, memorandum to the files, January 17, 1922, Olmsted Associates Records.

30   Guy Lowell, ed., *American Gardens* (Boston: Bates & Guild, 1901), included Platt's garden designs for "Glen Elsinore," Pomfret, CT; "Hilltop," Peterborough NH; "Villa Narcault," Montclair, NJ; and his own house and garden, Cornish, NH.

31   In December 1921 Platt was also hired as consulting architect to the University of Illinois as they developed a new south campus. His involvement, lasting from 1921 to 1929 through the same period that he designed buildings for Phillips Academy, resulting on the Illinois campus in a comprehensive master plan consisting of a formal axial system of enclosed quadrangles organized in a regularized geometric arrangement. Platt designed nine impressive colonial revival buildings for Illinois, including the library, designed in 1926 in a style similar to that of the academy's George Washington Hall of the same date. Another link between the two projects was formed when Platt asked Barry Faulkner to design murals for the Illinois library and, four years later, to complete murals for the walls of Ropes Room, the faculty dining room in the Phillips Academy dining hall.

32   Gallagher, memorandum to the files, January 17, 1922, Olmsted Associates Records.

33   Sawyer to Gallagher, June 9, 1922, Olmsted Associates Records.

34   Manuscript biography supplied by Cochran's assistant,

George Jordan, to James Sawyer, December 11, 1934, Treasurer's Office Correspondence, James C. Sawyer, 6.85.14.79.

35 In the first of what were to be recurring bouts of depression over the next twenty or so years, Cochran wrote to Sawyer in the summer of 1910, "Nervous break down. Can't tell about the outcome yet." In September of that year, he announced that he was ordered by his doctor to take a year off because of "an extreme case of neurasthenia" and added that he and his secretary, Martha Griffin, were to be married. This marked a period of silence that lasted until 1915. During that time, Cochran and his new wife recuperated in California. Upon their return to Englewood, New Jersey, in 1914, his wife died in childbirth, as did the newborn child. A year later, in 1915, Sawyer responded to a letter from his friend, "I am glad to receive your letter to find you improved." Treasurer's Office Correspondence, James C. Sawyer, 6.85.14.79.

36 Cochran to Stearns, November 21, 1916, Trustee Correspondence, Cochran, Thomas, 4.

37 Platt to Sawyer, January 6, 1930, Treasurer's Office Correspondence, James C. Sawyer, Buildings, 6.85.10.

38 Charles H. Sawyer to Henry Hope Reed, January 31, 1958, Collection of the Platt Family.

39 Barry Faulkner, "C.A.P. A Narrative Written for His Family," n.d. [c. 1933], typescript, Collection of the Platt Family.

40 Stearns to Cochran, September 14, 1923, Trustee Correspondence, Cochran, Thomas, 4.

41 Platt to Olmsted Brothers, February 10, 1925, Olmsted Associates Records.

42 Cochran to Sawyer, July 15, 1927, Treasurer's Office Correspondence, James C. Sawyer, 6.85.79.

43 Case to Sawyer, April 14, 1925, Treasurer's Office Correspondence, James C. Sawyer, 6.85.79.

44 Cochran was a prime mover in the naming of this and most of the other buildings in the building campaign. While Cochran's desire to reflect the relationships between the school and important figures of American history in the naming of the new buildings was shared by many, lively debate ensued about such matters as whether it should be George Washington Hall or George Washington Building. The latter, Cochran claimed, would "hurt my sense of good taste enormously." It resolved in favor of the former. Cochran's choice of names was sentimental as well as astute, as he revealed in a letter to Sawyer: "You and I are cranks about capitalizing the historical names connected with our School because we both believe it is good business policy as well as School policy. If we can take advantage of these fine names we have, it will inure to the benefit of the school in a financial way." Cochran to Sawyer, November 11, 1925, Treasurer's Office Correspondence, James C. Sawyer, 6.85.79.

45 On January 15, 1927, the trustees asked Lowell to redraw his elevation for Morse Hall because, as their minutes noted, "the plans were perhaps too elaborate in their outer detail to fit in properly with the general scheme of the quadrangle in which the building is to be located." Academy Records, Trustees of Phillips Academy, Book 3, 83–84.

46 "Samuel F. B. Morse Hall Nearing Completion," *The Phillips Bulletin* 22 no. 1 (January 1928): 38.

47 Cochran to Stearns, June 23, 1926, Treasurer's Office Correspondence, James C. Sawyer, 6.85.79.

48 Sawyer to Cochran, January 22, 1927, Treasurer's Office Correspondence, James C. Sawyer, 6.85.79.

49 Burton S. Flagg to Olmsted Brothers, March 24, 1927, Job 7785, Olmsted Associates Records, Series B, Manuscript Division, Library of Congress, Washington, D. C.

50 E. C. Whiting, memorandum to the files, April 26, 1927, Job 7785, Olmsted Associates Records.

51 Olmsted Brothers to Burton S. Flagg, September 17, 1927, Job 7785, Olmsted Associates Records.

52 Lowell completed fourteen building projects on the campus, while Platt was responsible for the design of six: George Washington Hall, 1925–26; Paul Revere Hall, 1928–29; Oliver Wendell Holmes Library 1928–29; Commons, 1928–30; Addison Gallery of American Art, 1929–31; and Cochran Chapel, 1930–32.

53 While there is no specific vote recorded to this effect, there are several references in the Trustees Minutes to Platt as the school's architect, among them, Trustees Minutes, October 6, 1927, 101 and January 21, 1928, 105.

54 Robert A. Domingue, *Phillips Academy Andover, Massachusetts: An Illustrated History of the Property (Including Abbot Academy)* (Wilmington, MA: Hampshire Press, 1990), 48.

55 Claude M. Fuess, "And the Place Therof Shall Know it No More," *The Phillips Bulletin* 24, no. 1 (October 1929): 8.

56 Case to Sawyer, June 18, 1928, Treasurer's Office Correspondence, James C. Sawyer, 6.85.79.

57 Cochran to Stearns, June 28, 1930. Trustee Correspondence, Cochran, Thomas, 4.

58 Cochran to Sawyer, July 11, 1928, Treasurer's Office Correspondence, James C. Sawyer, 6.85.79.

59 Sawyer to Cochran, December 10, 1927, Treasurer's Office Correspondence, James C. Sawyer, 6.85.79.

60 Sawyer to Cochran, February 27, 1929, Treasurer's Office Correspondence, James C. Sawyer, 6.85.14.79.

61 Recounted in Stearns to Clarence Morgan, April 30, 1929, Trustee Correspondence, Box 8,4.

62 Stearns to Cochran, November 13, 1925, Trustee Correspondence, Cochran, Thomas, 4.

63 Cochran to Henry S. Hopper, February 18, 1929, Treasurer's Office Correspondence, largely H. Hopper & Mr. Gould in the 1930s–1940s, 6.85.39.

64 Stearns to Cochran, April 30, 1929, Trustee Correspondence, Cochran, Thomas, 4.

65 Cochran to Stearns, April 20, 1928, Trustee Correspondence, Cochran, Thomas, 4.

66 Clarence Morgan to Stearns, January 27, 1929, Trustee Correspondence, Box 8, 4. The correspondence between Morgan and Stearns outlined in great detail the latter's concerns about the changes on campus.

67 Cochran to Sawyer, March 21, 1929, Treasurer's Office Correspondence, James C. Sawyer, 6.85.14.79.

68 Cochran to Stearns, May 6, 1929, Treasurer's Office Correspondence, James C. Sawyer, 6.85.14.79.

69 Stearns to Cochran, May 7, 1929, Trustee Correspondence, Cochran, Thomas, 4.

70 The relationship between Cochran and Stearns repaired itself sufficiently so that Cochran and Sawyer could conspire to tweak Stearns with a series of letters that claimed that there was a "humiliating lack of progress." Correspondence between Cochran, Stearns, and Sawyer, September 1929, Trustee Correspondence, Cochran, Thomas, 4; and Treasurer's Office Correspondence, James C. Sawyer, 6.85.14.79.

71 Cochran to Sawyer, July 30, 1929, Treasurer's Office Correspondence, James C. Sawyer, 6.85.14.79.

72 Sawyer to Cochran, September 22, 1929, Treasurer's Office Correspondence, James C. Sawyer, 6.85.14.79.

73 Cochran to Sawyer, March 14, 1931, Trustee Correspondence, Cochran, Thomas, 4; Cochran to Sawyer, July 29, 1930, Treasurer's Office Correspondence, James C. Sawyer, 6.85.14.79.

74 Sawyer to Cochran, April 23, 1931, Treasurer's Office Correspondence, James C. Sawyer, 6.85.14.79.

75 The issue of a larger and more modern infirmary would be debated for several more years. The school had quickly outgrown the Guy Lowell-designed Isham Infirmary of 1913 that stood at the end of Old Campus Road beyond the cottages. Platt was asked to design a new building and numerous locations for the building were proposed by the Olmsted firm and others, among them, a location beyond Samuel Phillips and Morse Halls, a site within the dormitory quadrangle on the west side, and even in the place of Hardy House on Salem Street. The resolution of the infirmary's location and its cost did not occur until 1934–35, when plans for a separate building were abandoned and Perry, Shaw & Hepburn designed a large addition for the rear of Isham. The original Isham eventually became a dormitory with the new wing serving as the infirmary of the same name.

76 Cochran to Sawyer, March 22, 1929, Treasurer's Office Correspondence, James C. Sawyer, 6.85.14.79.

77 Cochran to Sawyer, June 15, 1930, Treasurer's Office Correspondence, James C. Sawyer, 6.85.14.79.

78 Cochran to Stearns, January 31, 1929, Trustee Correspondence, Cochran, Thomas, 4.

79 Cochran to Sawyer, July 30, 1929, Treasurer's Office Correspondence, James C. Sawyer, 6.85.14.79.

80 At this same time Cochran raised both the idea of moving Double Brick onto the site of Phillips Hall to create a vista at the end of Chapel Avenue and the idea of a natural history museum. Without his debilitating illness, it is intriguing to contemplate what more Cochran might have been proposed for Phillips Academy.

81 Cochran to Hopper, August 3, 1931, Treasurer's Office Correspondence, James C. Sawyer, 6.85.39.

82 Cochran's fears were not entirely unfounded. For the dining hall project, even Platt admitted, "We have spent money-to a certain extent-like drunken sailors on this building in the work which was authorized before we saw any particular reason for retrenchment, as Mr. Cochran urged me to do what I thought best irrespective of cost." Platt to Sawyer, December 19, 1929, Treasurer's Office Correspondence, James C. Sawyer, Buildings, 6.85.10.

83 James B. Neale to Sawyer, January 16, 1928, Treasurer's Office Correspondence, James C. Sawyer, 6.85.79.

84 Sawyer to Cochran, June 18, 1931, Treasurer's Office Correspondence, James C. Sawyer, Buildings, 6.85.10.

85 Sawyer to Platt, September 28, 1932, Treasurer's Office Correspondence, James C. Sawyer, Buildings, 6.85.10.

SHILLAND, "THE ANDOVER CAMPUS AT MID-TWENTIETH CENTURY"

1 Olmsted Associates Records, Series B, Job 176, Manuscript Division, Library of Congress [hereafter, Olmsted Associates Records], includes correspondence between Andover officials and the various campus architects: Charles Platt, Olmsted Brothers, Perry Shaw & Hepburn, Fiske Kimball and many others. The author is indebted to Susan Faxon, Susan Montgomery, and Karen Haas for not only providing information and access to materials but, above all, for giving so freely of their time and sharing their extensive knowledge of the campus.

2 Included among the projects TAC completed for the Andover campus between 1957–1962 are: Art and Communication Center, Copley Addition to the Oliver Wendell Holmes Library, Chapel Remodeling, Rabbit Pond Dormitories, and the Evans Science Building, as well as several other remodelings. In addition, Ben Thompson completed a master plan for the Andover campus in 1957 and for Abbot Academy in 1965.

3 For information on the partners, see the archives of Perry Dean Rogers & Partners: Architects and the MIT Museum Historical Collections, Biographical files and Architecture & Design Collection. The author is grateful for the assistance of David Fixler, Director of Historic Preservation, at Perry Dean Rogers & Partners for his assistance.

4 For information on Codman & Despradelle, see the author's Master's Thesis, "On the Work of Désiré Despradelle" Art History Department, Boston University, January 1989.

5 For information on the early years of the Perry firm, consult audiocassette oral history interview conducted by the author, at the home of Robert C. Dean, 13 April 1993. MIT Museum Architecture & Design Collection. Robert Dean joined the firm in 1927 after graduating from MIT. A skilled draughtsman, Dean was anxious to cut his teeth on "modern" work rather than colonial revival, but he recognized the economic necessity of working in this idiom due to its enduring local popularity.

6 Among their New England educational and institutional work one may mention Longfellow Hall, Radcliffe, 1929–1930; Houghton Library, Harvard University, 1937–1941; Baker House Dormitory (associated architects with Alvar Aalto), 1947–1949; Museum of Science, Cambridge, 1951; and Wellesley College Science Center, 1978.

7 An invaluable resource for studying Phillips Andover's architectural history is Roger Reed, Phillips Academy Historical the Buildings and Landscape, Survey, unpublished, 1994, Office of Physical Plant, Phillips Academy.

8 "The Embodiment of American Cultural Tradition at Andover" report prepared by Fiske Kimball for Mr. Frank Garvan, 1930, 1–2, Manuscript Division, Library of Congress.

9 Ibid., 2

10 Ibid., 3

11 Ibid., 6

12 Fiske Kimball to Percival Gallagher, Olmsted Brothers, August 11, 1930, Olmsted Associates Records.

13 See campus survey forms by Roger Reed for Isham Infirmary and Rockwell Dormitory.

14 Ibid.

15 Ibid.

16 Mr. Edward Whiting, Olmsted Brothers, to Mr. James C. Sawyer, treasurer, June 26, 1934. Olmsted Associates Records.

17 Mr. James Sawyer, treasurer, to Mr. Edward Whiting, Olmsted Brothers, June 29, 1934. Olmsted Associates Records.

18 *The Phillips Bulletin*, 31 no. 5, July 1937, 5.

19 Ibid., 5

20 Ibid,, 7

21 See Roger G. Reed's survey forms for the Hidden Field Houses, 1994.

22 See Roger G. Reed's floor plan for Lowell House, 1994.

23 Perry Shaw & Hepburn, to Mr. James C. Sawyer, treasurer May 8, 1936. Olmsted Associates Records.

24 Olmsted Brothers, Preliminary Plan for Faculty House Group, 1936, plan 176–881.

25 Letter to Mr. James C. Sawyer, Treasurer from Perry Shaw & Hepburn, May 8, 1936. Olmsted Associates Records.

26 Ibid.

27 The author extends thanks to Tracy Myers, Assistant Curator for Architecture, Heinz Architecture Center, Carnegie Museum of Art, for generously sharing her research, particularly the valuable information surrounding the founding of The Architects Collaborative from her forthcoming dissertation entitled, "Yankee Modern: Designs for Education by The Architects Collaborative (TAC), 1945–1960."

28 For information on The Architects Collaborative, see "TAC: The Heritage of Walter Gropius," *Process: Architecture*, no. 19, (1980)(the entire issue is devoted to the firm); TAC, 1950–1970.

29 *New York Times*, October 23, 1949

30 Ibid.

31 "Benjamin C. Thompson at Andover," October 1999 interview with Benjamin C. Thompson, FAIA. The author is indebted to Mr. Benjamin C. Thompson for so willingly providing the information needed to understand TAC's Andover work, to Ms. Jane Thompson for her invaluable assistance, and to Ms. Bobbie Coogan for her time and effort.

32 Today the firm is known as Thompson Design Group.

33 *Status Report on Phillips Academy Architectural Work*, April 26, 1957, 1.

34 Ibid.

35 *Status Report*, 4.

36 The architectural drawings for Andover's master plan and several other buildings are located at the MIT Museum in the Architecture & Design Collection. When TAC closed its doors in 1995, the future of its vast archive was uncertain. MIT's School of Architecture & Planning and the MIT Museum assumed care of the drawings, while MIT's Rotch Library houses the firm's microfilm and Harvard's Loeb Library maintains the firm's extensive slide collection. The firm continued its founders' tradition of close ties to architectural education at both Harvard and MIT, with a steady exchange of architects/professors with both schools. In fact, there was a veritable resource triangle between Harvard, MIT and TAC. Among the names associated with this "triangle" of students, architects and professors are Stanley Tigerman, I.M.Pei, Eduardo Catalano, Carl Koch, Richard Filipowski, John Hayes, H. Morse Payne. One of the firm's founding partners, Norman Fletcher, taught at MIT. Institute Professor Pietro Belluschi collaborated with TAC on several projects including the Pan Am Building and an MIT undergraduate dormitory. In 1963, eight of thirty associates, three of twelve senior associates and two of five managing partners were MIT educated.

37 Andover Program, 1958, Phillips Academy Archive, not paginated.

38 Andover Program, 1958

39 "Benjamin C. Thompson at Andover" October 1999 interview with Benjamin C. Thompson, FAIA. Typescript, 2.

40 *Architectural Record*, September 1963.

41 "Benjamin C. Thompson at Andover" October 1999 interview with Benjamin C. Thompson, FAIA. In 1999 the trustees deemed that Evans Hall had reached the end of its useful life and voted to erect a new, state-of-the-art science center to serve new teaching needs of the faculty. At the time of this publication, Evans Hall was slated for demolition, to occur when the new center is completed in 2003.

42 "Benjamin C. Thompson at Andover" October 1999 interview with Benjamin C. Thompson, FAIA.

43 "Benjamin C. Thompson at Andover" October 1999 interview with Benjamin C. Thompson, FAIA.

ZAITZEVSKY, "THE OLMSTED FIRM AND THE SHAPING OF THE PHILLIPS ACADEMY LANDSCAPE"

1 In the holdings of the National Park Service, Frederick Law Olmsted National Historic Site, for job number 176, there are 1,321 drawings dated 1891 to 1965; nine file folders of planting lists dated 1901 to 1938, and five photograph albums from 1902 to 1949 that include 296 prints. See Plan Index Cards for Phillips Academy, Job Number 176, Frederick Law Olmsted National Historic Site, Brookline, Massachusetts; Linda C. Genovese, Supervisory Archivist, to Susan Faxon, September 30, 1997, Addison Gallery Archive.

2 Charles Capen McLaughlin, Editor-in-Chief, *The Formative Years, 1822–1852*, volume 1 of *The Papers of Frederick Law Olmsted* (Baltimore: Johns Hopkins University Press, 1977), 5, 47 (n. 12), 117, and 120 (n. 10).

3 David Chase, "To Promote True Piety and Virtue: Development of the Phillips Academy Campus, 1778–1838," herein, above.

4 Laura Wood Roper, *FLO: A Biography of Frederick Law Olmsted* (Baltimore: Johns Hopkins University Press, 1973), 305–15. A complete listing of the Olmsted firms projects for college and school campuses, with job numbers and dates, is found in Charles E. Beveridge and Carolyn F. Hoffman, comps., *The Master List of Design Projects of the Olmsted Firm, 1857–1950* (Boston: National Association for Olmsted Parks and Massachusetts Association for Olmsted Parks, 1987), 51–61.

5 Mr. and Mrs. Leland Stanford made numerous changes that compromised Olmsted's original design objectives. Paul V. Turner, Marcia E. Vetrocq, and Karen Weitze, *The Founders & The Architects: The Design of Stanford University* (Stanford, CA: Department of Art, Stanford University, 1976).

6 For further information about the firm, see Wheaton A. Holden, "The Peabody Touch: Peabody and Stearns of Boston,

1870–1917," *Journal of the Society of Architectural Historians* 32 no. 2 (May 1973): 114–31.

7   Beveridge and Hoffman, *Master List* , 42, 100.

8   Phillips Academy, Minutes of the Board of Trustees, Book 2, June 20, 1887, 52, [hereafter Trustees Minutes].

9   Trustees Minutes, June 9, 1891.

10   Unfortunately many of the early letters in the voluminous correspondence at the Library of Congress for this project have faded and are unreadable. J. E. Chandler to J. C. Olmsted, March 9, 1892, Phillips Academy, Job no. 176, Olmsted Associates Records, Series B, Manuscript Division, Library of Congress, Washington, D.C.; [hereafter Olmsted Associates Records].

11   For John Charles Olmsted, see "John Charles Olmsted: A Minute on His Life and Service," *Transactions of the American Society of Landscape Architects* 2 (1909–1921); Emanuel Tillman Mische, "In Memoriam: John Charles Olmsted," *Parks and Recreation* 3 (April 1920): 52–54; and Cynthia Zaitzevsky, *Frederick Law Olmsted and the Boston Park System* (Cambridge, MA: Harvard University Press, 1992), 130–31.

12   J. C. Olmsted, Report of Visit, March 29, 1892, E-Files, Olmsted Associates Records.

13   J. C. Olmsted, Report of Visit, June 6, 1892, E-Files, Olmsted Associates Records.

14   D. H. Coolidge, Jr., Report of Visit, December 30, 1892, E-Files, Olmsted Associates Records.

15   J. C. Olmsted, Report of Visit, April 10, 1895, E-Files, Olmsted Associates Records.

16   F. L. Olmsted Jr., Report of Visit, December 15, 1900, Olmsted Associates Records. For Frederick Law Olmsted Jr., see Edward Clark Whiting and William Lyman Phillips, "Frederick Law Olmsted Jr., 1870–1957: An Appreciation of the Man and His Achievements," *Landscape Architecture* 48 no. 3 (April 1958): 144–57.

17   Reports of visits relating to the athletic field and proposed subdivision are as follows: F. L. Olmsted Jr. and J. B. H[erbst], Report of Visit, April 13, 1901, Olmsted Associates Records; John C. Olmsted, Report of Visit, July 1, 1901, Olmsted Associates Records; and F. L. Olmsted Jr., Report of Visit, October 15, 1901, Olmsted Associates Records. These meetings concerned various types of athletic facilities to be planned and also a problem of drainage.

18   Olmsted Brothers to Bishop, November 9, 1901, Olmsted Associates Records.

19   H. J. Kellaway, Report of Visit, May 14, 1902; H. J. Kellaway, Report of Visit, July 11, 1902; Olmsted Brothers to Arthur E. Hill, 12 July 1902; H. J. Kellaway, Report of Visit, July 31, 1902; and Mr. Mische, Report of Visit, September 1902, Olmsted Associates Records. For William Ralph Emerson, see Cynthia Zaitzevsky, *The Architecture of William Ralph Emerson, 1833–1917* (Cambridge, MA: Fogg Art Museum, Harvard University, 1969) and Roger Reed, "The Lost Victorian Campus, 1838–1908," herein, above.

20   Olmsted Brothers to James C. Sawyer, August 7, 1902; H. J. Kellaway, Report of Visit, September 2, 1902; and Olmsted Brothers to R. D. Kimball, September 3, 1902, Olmsted Associates Records. Kellaway also talked with Judge Bishop about the additions to the school, in Herbert J. Kellaway, Report

of Visit, April 27, 1903, Olmsted Associates Records.

21   F. L. Olmsted Jr., Report of Visit, February 10, 1903, Olmsted Associates Records.

22   Olmsted Brothers to Trustees of Phillips Academy, March 27, 1903, Olmsted Associates Records.

23   Herbert J. Kellaway, Report of Visit, April 28, 1903; Olmsted Brothers to Sawyer, June 1903, Olmsted Associates Records.

24   George Gibbs Jr., Report of Visit, May 22, 1907; Olmsted Brothers to Sawyer, May 24, 1907, Olmsted Associates Records.

25   Sawyer to Olmsted Brothers, April 24, 1908; J. Harold Melledge to Olmsted Brothers, May 14, 1908; Olmsted Brothers to Sawyer, June 8, 1908, Olmsted Associates Records.

26   Olmsted Brothers to Sawyer, October 7, 1908, Olmsted Associates Records.

27   Olmsted Brothers to Sawyer, January 12, 1909; see also Olmsted Brothers to Sawyer, October 5, 1909, Olmsted Associates Records.

28   Percival R. Gallagher, Report of Visit, December 23, 1909, Olmsted Associates Records. For Gallagher, see Frederick Law Olmsted, "Percival Gallagher," *Landscape Architecture* 24 no. 3 (April 1934): 166–68; newspaper clippings about Gallagher, dated January 8, 1934 and filed under Brookline Biography, Brookline Public Library; and Cynthia Zaitzevsky, Entry on the Olmsted firm on Long Island, in Robert B. MacKay, Anthony K. Baker, and Carol A. Traynor, eds., *Long Island Country Houses and Their Architects, 1860–1940* (New York: Society for the Preservation of Long Island Antiquities in Association with W. W. Norton & Company, 1997), 316, 321–24, 328–30.

29   Gallagher, Report of Visit, December 23, 1909, Olmsted Associates Records.

30   Olmsted Brothers to Sawyer, February 6, 1910, Olmsted Associates Records.

31   Sawyer to Olmsted Brothers, February 26, 1910; Olmsted Brothers to Sawyer, March 4, 1910; Olmsted to Sawyer, May 20, 1910; and H. H. Blossom, Report of Visit, October 10, 1910, Olmsted Associates Records.

32   Olmsted Brothers to Sawyer, November 16 1910; Percival Gallagher, Report of Visit, November 19, 1910; and Percival Gallagher, Report of Visit, November 22, 1910, Olmsted Associates Records.

33   Olmsted Brothers to Sawyer, December 22, 1910; Olmsted Brothers to Sawyer, January 19, 1911, Olmsted Associates Records.

34   Report of Visit, February 20, 1911, Olmsted Associates Records.

35   Olmsted Brothers to J. C. Sawyer, Treasurer, February 24, 1911, Olmsted Associates Records.

36   Gallagher, Report of Visit, January 2, 1912, Olmsted Associates Records.

37   Olmsted Brothers to Sawyer, March 23, 1912, Olmsted Associates Records.

38   Sawyer to Olmsted Brothers, April 1, 1912, Olmsted Associates Records.

39   Olmsted Brothers to Sawyer, April 3, 1912; Sawyer to Olmsted Brothers, May 22, 1913, Olmsted Associates Records.

40   Phillips Academy to Mr. L. S. Adams, Olmsted Brothers,

April 15, 1915, Olmsted Associates Records.

41   Gallagher, Report of Visit, April 4, 1917, Olmsted Associates Records.

42   Olmsted Brothers to Sawyer, January 20, 1919; Olmsted Brothers to Sawyer, January 21, 1919; and Olmsted Brothers to Sawyer, February 7, 1919, Olmsted Associates Records.

43   Olmsted Brothers to Sawyer, April 7, 1919; Sawyer to Olmsted Brothers, April 15, 1919, Olmsted Associates Records.

44   Whiting, Report of Visit, July 11, 1919; Sawyer to Whiting, Telephone Message, July 15, 1919, Sawyer to Olmsted Brothers, October 16, 1919; Whiting, Report of Visit, 11 November 1919, Olmsted Associates Records.

45   For Edward Clark Whiting see W. B. Marquis, A. P. Richardson, and J. G. Hudak, "Memorial Minute. Edward Clark Whiting," *ASLA Bulletin*, no. 105 (August 1962), 10; and Zaitzevsky, the Olmsted firm on Long Island in MacKay, et. al., eds., *Long Island Country Houses and Their Architects*, 316, 321–23.

46   Olmsted Brothers to Sawyer, March 24, 1920; Olmsted Brothers to Guy Lowell, March 24, 1920, Olmsted Associates Records.

47   Sawyer to Olmsted Brothers, November 2, 1920; Olmsted Brothers to Sawyer, December 17, 1920, Olmsted Associates Records.

48   Whiting, Report of Visit, March 16, 1921, Olmsted Associates Records.

49   Sawyer to C. R. P. [Carl Parker], telephone message, September 22, 1921, Olmsted Associates Records.

50   Susan C. Faxon, "Forces of Change: The Transformation of the Campus, 1900–1932," herein, above; Keith N. Morgan, *Charles A. Platt: The Artist as Architect* (Cambridge, MA: Architectural History Foundation and M.I.T. Press, 1985), 183–94; and Ruth Flick Quattlebaum, "Andover's Movable Campus," *Andover Bulletin* (Spring 1980): 5–8.

51   H. J. Koehler, Report of Visit, December 21, 1921, Olmsted Associates Records. For Koehler, see "Hans Koehler Landscaping Artist Dies," *Marlboro Daily Enterprise* (July 16, 1951), 1. Koehler was born in Hoboken, New Jersey, of German-born parents. His father was a curator at the Museum of Fine Arts.

52   Kohler, Report of Visit, December 12, 1921, Olmsted Associates Records.

53   Olmsted Brothers to Sawyer, December 14, 1921, Olmsted Associates Records.

54   H. J. K., Report of Visit, December 20, 1921, Olmsted Associates Records.

55   Koehler, Report of Visit, January 19, 1922; Koehler, Report of Visit, April 25, 1922, Olmsted Associates Records.

56   Sawyer to Gallagher, June 9, 1922, Olmsted Associates Records.

57   Olmsted Brothers [Gallagher] to Sawyer, June 14, 1922, Olmsted Associates Records.

58   Ibid.

59   Gallagher, Report of Visit, June 21, 1922, Olmsted Associates Records.

60   Ibid.; Olmsted Brothers [Gallagher] to Sawyer, June 22, 1922; Olmsted Brothers [Gallagher] to Platt, September 14, 1922; and Platt to Gallagher, September 15, 1922, Olmsted Associates

Records.

61   Platt to Olmsted Brothers [Gallagher], February 10, 1925; Platt to Olmsted Brothers [Gallagher], February 18, 1925; Platt to Olmsted Brothers, February 25, 1925; Olmsted Brothers to Sawyer, June 9, 1925; and Platt to Olmsted Brothers [Whiting], October 8, 1925, Olmsted Associates Records.

62   As late as 1927 and 1928, Baston was adding buildings (Morse Hall) and tinkering with the model, which by then was kept at the academy. J. W. Baston, Report of Visit, August 21, 22, 24, 1927; J. W. Baston, Report of Visit, August 28, 1928, Olmsted Associates Records.

63   Platt to Olmsted Brothers [Gallagher], September 19, 1929, Olmsted Associates Records.

64   Frederick S. Allis Jr., *Youth from Every Quarter: A Bicentennial History of Phillips Academy, Andover* (Hanover, NH: University Press of New England, 1979), 372–73.

65   Olmsted Brothers [Gallagher] to Sawyer, January 4, 1930; Olmsted Brothers [Gallagher] to Platt, August 2, 1930; Olmsted Brothers to Platt, August 8, 1930; and Olmsted Brothers to Platt, October 6, 1930, Olmsted Associates Records.

66   This was the "Mrs. Stewart" mentioned in the letter from the Olmsted firm to Platt on October 6, 1930. Mr. Stewart was the manager of Andover Inn.

67   Olmsted Brothers to Sawyer, February 25, 1932; Henry S. Hopper to Gallagher, March 4, 1932, Olmsted Associates Records.

68   Olmsted Brothers to Sawyer, February 28, 1923; Olmsted Brothers to Edward J. Halloran, Feburary 29, 1923; and Olmsted Brothers to Sawyer, December 23, 1923, Olmsted Associates Records.

69   Olmsted Brothers, "A Scheme for the Planting of Vines on the Academy Buildings," March 16, 1931, Olmsted Associates Records.

70   Olmsted Brothers to Sawyer, August 14, 1928, Platt to Olmsted Brothers, August 23, 1928, Olmsted Brothers to Hopper, December 27, 1929, Olmsted Associates Records.

71   Platt to Olmsted Brothers, October 1, 1911, Olmsted Brothers to Sawyer, quoting Platt's letter, October 6, 1931, Olmsted Brothers to Platt, October 7, 1931, Olmsted Associates Records.

72   Ibid.

73   Whiting, Report of Visit, March 30, 1938, Olmsted Associates Records.

74   Henry W. Schereschewsky to Whiting, telephone message, January 4, 1957; Whiting and A. P. Richardson, Report of Visit, January 23, 1957; Olmsted Brothers [Whiting] to Schereschewsky, January 28, 1957; Schereschewsky to Whiting, February 4, 1957; Olmsted Brothers [Whiting] to Schereschewsky, February 8, 1957; all post-1949 correspondence at Olmsted National Historic Site, Job number 176.

75   Olmsted Associates [Joseph Hudak] to Mr. Frederic A. Stott, April 22, 1964; Olmsted Associates [Hudak] to Stott, January 26, 1965, Olmsted National Historic Site, Job number 176. Joseph Hudak practices landscape architecture in Westwood, Massachusetts.

Major Architects and Buildings

PHILLIPS ACADEMY

JOHN RADFORD ABBOT *Andover, Massachusetts*
Office of Physical Plant, 1955–1956

ANDREWS, JAQUES & RANTOUL *Boston, Massachusetts*
John-Esther Gallery, 1906–1907

PETER BANNER *Boston, Massachusetts*
Phelps House, 1809–1810 [attributed]

PIETRO BELLUSCHI & JUNG/BRANNEN *Boston, Massachusetts*
Elbridge H. Stuart House, 1970

ASHER BENJAMIN *Boston, Massachusetts*
Bulfinch Hall, 1818–1819

BOGNER & BILLINGS *Boston, Massachusetts*
Benner House, 1928–1929

BOTTOMLEY, WAGNER & WHITE *New York, New York*
Andover Inn, 1929–1930

WILLIAM C. BROCKLESBY *Hartford, Connecticut*
Alumni Hall, 1901

CHARLES BULFINCH *Boston, Massachusetts*
Pearson Hall, 1817–1818

EDWIN R. CLARK *Chelmsford, Massachusetts*
Thompson House, 1919

CODMAN & DESPRADELLE *Boston, Massachusetts*
Graham House, 1915

Samuel Phillips Hall, showing Foxcroft and Bartlet Halls, circa 1926

COLE & CHANDLER *New London, Connecticut*
Andover Cottage, 1892

CUMMINGS & SEARS *Boston, Massachusetts*
* Brechin Hall, 1866 (Cummings)
* Academy Hall, 1865–1866 (Cummings)
* Stone Chapel, 1875–1876 (Cummings & Sears)

GEORGE C. HARDING *Pittsfield, Massachusetts*
Eaton Cottage, 1892–1893

HARTWELL & RICHARDSON *Boston, Massachusetts*
Draper Hall, 1888–1890
McKeen Memorial Hall, 1903–1904 (Hartwell, Richardson & Driver)
Abbot Laundry, 1913–1914 (Hartwell, Richardson & Driver)

HENRY & RICHMOND *Boston, Massachusetts*
Tilton House, 1930

KENDALL, TAYLOR & COMPANY *Boston, Massachusetts*
* Hall House, 1913–1914

JENS FREDERICK LARSON *Hanover, New Hampshire*
* Abbey House, 1939

LONGFELLOW, ALDEN & HARLOW *Boston, Massachusetts and Pittsburgh, Pennsylvania*
Pemberton Cottage, 1891–1892
Draper Cottage, 1892–1893 [attributed]
Bancroft Hall, 1899–1900

GUY LOWELL *Boston, Massachusetts*
Robert S. Peabody Museum of Archaeology, 1901–1903
Moorehead House, 1904
Cooley House, 1908
Day Hall, 1910–1911
Bishop Hall, 1911
Adams Hall, 1912
Taylor Hall, 1913
Isham Dormitory, 1913
Phillips Gate, Main Street, 1914
* Peabody Union, 1915
Newton-Hinman House, 1921–1922

Johnson Hall, 1922
Case Memorial Cage, 1922-23
Memorial Bell Tower, 1922-23
Samuel Phillips Hall, 1924
Samuel F. B. Morse Hall, 1927-28

MCKIM, MEAD & WHITE *New York, New York*
Merrill Memorial Gate, 1921

MERRILL & CUTLER *Lowell, Massachusetts*
Jewett-Tucker House, 1880 (Merrill & Eaton)
Graves Hall, 1882–1883; addition 1891
Phillips Hall, 1884–1885

EDGAR ALLEN POE NEWCOMB *Boston, Massachusetts*
* The Sanhedrin, 1881
Churchill House, 1882

PEABODY & STEARNS *Boston, Massachusetts*
Borden Gymnasium, 1901–1902

PERRY, SHAW & HEPBURN *Boston, Massachusetts*
Davison House, 1928
Rockwell House, 1934–1935
Isham Infirmary, 1934
Greenough House, 1937
Lowell House, 1937
Palmer House, 1937
Quincy House, 1937
Weld House, 1937

CHARLES A. PLATT *New York, New York*
George Washington Hall, 1925–1926
Paul Revere Hall, 1928–1929
Oliver Wendell Holmes Library, 1928–1929
Commons, 1928–1930
Addison Gallery of American Art, 1929–1931
Cochran Chapel, 1930–1932

WILLIAM SPARRELL *Boston, Massachusetts*
* Stone Academy, 1828–1830
Double Brick House, 1829

Blasting for construction of Thomas M. Evans Hall, circa 1961, showing Samuel Phillips Hall in background

JOHN STEVENS   *Boston, Massachusetts*
   *Smith Hall, 1854

TECHBUILT, INCORPORATED   *Cambridge, Massachusetts*
   Wisconsin House, 1961
   Wooley House, 1961

THE ARCHITECTS COLLABORATIVE   *Cambridge, Massachusetts*
   Alfred E. Stearns House, 1957
   Abbott Stevens House, 1958
   Henry L. Stimson House, 1960–1961
   Claude M. Fuess House, 1961–1962
   Thomas M. Evans Hall, 1961–1963
   Elson Art Center, 1962–1963

BENJAMIN THOMPSON ASSOCIATES   *Cambridge, Massachusetts*
   Nathan Hale House, 1966

*demolished

Contributors' Biographies

PAUL V. TURNER

Dr. Turner has been Professor of Architectural History since 1972 and Wattis Professor of Art since 1992 at Stanford University, and in 1994 received the Excellence in Education Award from the American Institute of Architects. His 1984 publication, *Campus, An American Planning Tradition*, was recognized as the best book on architecture that year with the Alice Davis Hitchcock Award from the Society of Architectural Historians. He earned his B.A. from Union College, M. Architecture from the Harvard University Graduate School of Design, and M.A. and PH.D. in Fine Arts from Harvard University.

DAVID CHASE

Mr. Chase is the Director of Stewardship at Phillips Academy. Trained in architectural history at Brown University, he has served as Architectural Historian for the Rhode Island Historic Preservation Commission and Curator at the National Building Museum in Washington, D.C. More recently, Mr. Chase was Director of the Society for the Preservation of Maryland Antiquities (Preservation Maryland).

ROGER G. REED

Mr. Reed is an architectural historian and preservation planner. He received a B.A. in History from Windham College, an M.A. in American History from Northern Illinois University, and an M.A. in Historic Preservation Planning from Cornell University. In 1994 he completed an Historic Building and Landscape Survey of the Phillips Academy Campus. For the past six years he has been a Preservation Planner for the Brookline Preservation Commission.

SUSAN C. FAXON

Ms. Faxon has been Associate Director and Robert M. Walker Curator of Paintings, Prints and Drawings at the Addison Gallery of American Art since 1986. She has been responsible for numerous exhibitions, including the recent *Addison Gallery of American Art: 65 Years*, for which she was co-curator. Ms. Faxon holds a B.A. in art from Smith College and an M.S. in Architectural

Preservation and Restoration from the Columbia University School of Architecture. She has been a member of the Phillips Academy Design Review Committee since 1990.

KIMBERLY ALEXANDER SHILLAND
Dr. Shilland has been the Curator of Architectural Collections at the Massachusetts Institute of Technology Museum since 1990. Her specialty is nineteenth- and twentieth- century American architecture and urban design. She received a B.A. with Distinction in History from Colby College, and an M.A. and PH.D. in Art History from Boston University.

CYNTHIA ZAITZEVSKY
Dr. Zaitzevsky teaches in the Graduate Program in Landscape Design and Landscape Design History of the Radcliffe Seminars, and frequently serves as a consultant to architecural firms and institutions. She has been a member of the Phillips Academy Design Review Committee since 1990 and consulted with Child Associates on the academy's Campus Master Plan of 1995–1996. She earned her A.B. from Harvard College, and her A.M. and PH.D. in Fine Arts from Harvard University. She received the Laurence L. Winship Award of the *Boston Globe* and the Distinguished Publication Award of the National Association for Olmsted Parks for her 1982 publication, *Frederick Law Olmsted and the Boston Park System.*

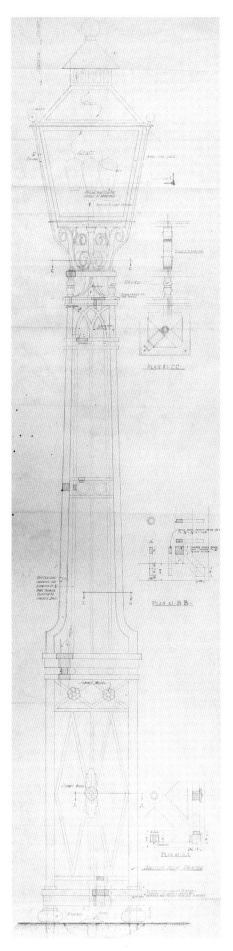

Index

Charles A. Platt, Lamp Standard for Campus, 1928, drawing.

Avery Architectural & Fine Arts Library